EPUB from the Ground Up

About the Author

Jarret W. Buse (Huntingburg, Indiana) is a Microsoft Certified Trainer and a Microsoft Certified Systems Engineer. Jarret has been the coauthor of or a contributor to several books on certification topics. He has years of experience working with e-books, including EPUB. He can be contacted at JarretBuse@hotmail.com.

About the Technical Reviewer

Devyn Collier Johnson graduated high school at age 16 and has earned four computer certifications: NCLA, Linux+, LPIC-1, and DCTS. He has also created his own chatbot and markup language called Xaiml. Devyn hosts his chatbot, Neo, and the new Xaiml language at https://launchpad.net/neobot. Devyn can be contacted at DevynCJohnson@gmail.com.

EPUB from the Ground Up

A Hands-on Guide to EPUB 2 and EPUB 3

Jarret W. Buse

New York Chicago San Francisco
Athens London Madrid Mexico City
Milan New Delhi Singapore Sydney Toronto

Cataloging-in-Publication Data is on file with the Library of Congress

McGraw-Hill Education books are available at special quantity discounts to use as premiums and sales promotions, or for use in corporate training programs. To contact a representative, please visit the Contact Us pages at www.mhprofessional.com.

EPUB from the Ground Up: A Hands-on Guide to EPUB 2 and EPUB 3

1 2 3 4 5 6 7 8 9 0 DOC DOC 1 0 9 8 7 6 5 4 3

ISBN 978-0-07-183052-2
MHID 0-07-183052-9

Sponsoring Editor Roger Stewart
Editorial Supervisor Janet Walden
Project Manager Raghavi Khullar, Cenveo® Publisher Services
Acquisitions Coordinator Amanda Russell
Technical Editor Devyn Collier Johnson
Copy Editor Lisa McCoy
Proofreader Madhu Prasher
Indexer Jack Lewis
Production Supervisor Jean Bodeaux
Composition Cenveo Publisher Services
Illustration Cenveo Publisher Services
Art Director, Cover Jeff Weeks

I dedicate this book to my beautiful wife, Cassandra. With her, my life is full and would be empty without. God has put us together and kept us together while our love has only grown. Nearly 20 years ago we met, and it seemed that we were the only two souls in the world because it felt as if I'd known you forever. The world did not exist, and we knew we would be together always.

Along with my wife I also dedicate this book to our children, all fourteen: the seven we have and the seven lost before birth. To Devyn, Logan, Caleb, Eilly, Alyse, Morgan, and Grant: you were all loved, even before you were born, and with love you endure to face this world. Never give in to the world, for you are always loved. All of you are in my heart, never to leave it.

Contents at a Glance

Contents

Acknowledgments

I acknowledge my family, who worked with me to get this book completed. Without their support, this project would not have been finished; my wife Cassandra, who helped with editing, and my son, Devyn, for his research and technical editing. Their help made the content better than it was originally.

I also need to give a very special thanks to Roger Stewart at McGraw-Hill for believing in my proposal, and a thanks to Amanda Russell for answering my never-ending list of questions. Also, the others at McGraw-Hill who edited my content even more and placed everything together. Thanks to Melinda Lytle for the figures I needed enhanced.

Special thanks to everyone at "Ron's Place": Ron, Bobby, Jan, Tanya, Chad, Jen, James, Jim, Big John, Sylvia, Darlene, Stacia, and the rest of the crew. They were there when I needed a break to go play billiards with my wife and eat the world's best pizza, the Strom Pizza. Thanks again to all our friends at Ron's!

And last, but greatest of all, I thank God for all He has given me, my wife and children, my only loved ones. Through Him all things are possible. I would not have been able to write this book without Him.

Acknowledgments

Introduction

The market has seen an explosion of reading devices. The devices use two main file formats: EPUB or AZW (Kindle). Would you like to create and manipulate these files? If so, this book is for you.

This book takes you through the processes of creating and manipulating the EPUB files with embedded fonts, images, audio, and video. EPUB files can be used to create not only books, but magazines, pamphlets, brochures, and whatever else you may need to make. This book also covers the details of converting the EPUB to a Kindle format so you can cover all devices by creating only one e-book.

Why This Book?

I attempted to not only show the basics to someone who has no prior knowledge of HTML, CSS, etc., but to allow the book to be used as a reference for those who do know the subjects. I also wanted to give examples and allow a reader to create their own files without requiring expensive applications. I found all the free software listed here to accomplish everything covered in the book:

- **Sigil** One of the main applications used is Sigil. It can be found at http://code.google.com/p/sigil/ along with the source code. This program allows you to edit and create EPUB files. You can get a version for Windows, Linux, or Mac. It supports EPUB Standard 2 (covered in Chapter 1). This application is used extensively in this book, so please be sure to download and install Sigil.
- **Calibre** Calibre is another useful program, found at http://code.google.com/p/calibre-ebook/ as well as the source code. More information can be found at http://calibre-ebook.com/. This program is also available for use on Windows, Linux, or Mac. Calibre is not an EPUB editor, but it allows for the management of EPUB libraries. It also creates EPUB files by converting files from one format to EPUB (covered in Chapter 6). The conversion ability is what makes Calibre extremely useful.
- **Type light free** Type light free is a font program that can be downloaded from www.cr8software.net/typelight.html. It is useful for opening and viewing font files or even creating your own.
- **Libre Office** Libre Office is a productivity suite of tools similar to Microsoft Office (for this book, you only need the Writer tool). Libre Office is available for Windows, Mac, or Linux. It is a free, open-source application located at www.libreoffice.org/download/. An extension called Writer2EPUB.oxt or Writer2HTML.oxt can be used to convert your documents to EPUB.
- **Google Chrome** and **Readium** To emulate an EPUB 3 e-reader, you can use the International Digital Publishing Forum (IDPF) Readium extension on Google Chrome or Chromium. Chrome can be downloaded from www.google.com/chrome. Once Chrome is installed, go to www.readium.org. Select the Install From Chrome Web Store button. Even though the extension is for EPUB 3 files, you can use it for EPUB 2 files as well.
- **Audacity** and its libraries To create Synchronized Multimedia Integration Language (SMIL) files, which are narrated, you need Audacity. The Audacity files can be downloaded from http://audacity.sourceforge.net/download/. Once installed, you'll need to add two libraries: the LAME MP3 encoding library and the FFmpeg import/export library found at http://audacity.sourceforge.net/download/plugins. You may also need a microphone, or you can use Balabolka to create the narration files.

- **Balabolka** Balabolka is a useful EPUB reader that can also use speech to read an EPUB book to you. Options are available to save the speech as an MP3 file or other audio format. It is available at www.cross-plus-a.com/balabolka.htm for Windows only.
- **Inkscape** An image program to create and modify SVG files that can be downloaded from www.inkscape.org.
- **PIXResizer** A utility to change image sizes and convert to various formats from http://bluefive.pair.com.
- **Nook e-reader emulator** To emulate an e-reader, you can use the Barnes & Noble Nook emulator. It can be used on a Windows, Mac, iPad, Android Tablet, iPhone, iPod touch, and a smartphone running Android. The main download page is located at www.barnesandnoble.com/u/free-nook-apps/379003593. From this page you select the device you want to install the emulator on and install it.
- **Kindle e-reader emulator** You can also use the Amazon Kindle emulator. It is available for smartphones such as the iPhone, Android, Windows Phone 7, and the Blackberry, as well as the iPod touch. It can be downloaded for a PC running Windows or a Mac. It can be installed on an iPad or an Android Tablet. These free apps can be downloaded at www.amazon.com/gp/feature.html/ref=sv_kstore_1?ie=UTF8&docId=1000493771. The Kindle Emulator will be used in Chapter 6 to view EPUB files in the Kindle AZW format.
- **7-Zip** EPUB files are packaged within a ZIP file and then renamed to EPUB. You will need a ZIP program to extract or compress the files when needed. 7-Zip is a free, open-source application found at http://7-zip.org/, with various Windows and processor versions available. For Linux and Mac, a version of 7-Zip called p7zip is also available on the download page.
- **SHA-1 Checksum Utility** Go to www.cnet.com and in the search box, type **MD5 SHA-1 Utility**. Download the MD5 & SHA Checksum Utility. The utility allows you to create SHA-1 hashes for files.
- **NotePad++** A file editor that has numerous uses. It can be found at www.notepad-plus-plus.org.
- **Clipyard** Flash creator for Windows found at www.goldshell.com/clipyard.
- **QFlash** Flash creator for Linux that can be downloaded from www.sourceforge.net/projects/qflash.

- **Websites** Two websites that will be necessary to obtain e-books to use for examples are http://manybooks.net/ and http://www.gutenberg.org/. Both of these sites have numerous free e-books in EPUB and other formats. Any example used in the book will give the web address and the book title.
- **www.ComicBookPlus.com** Has numerous public-domain comic books to download for free.
- **www.DaFont.com** A website to download free font files.

NOTE

I would ask anyone who finds these applications and websites useful to please make a donation for their improvements.

What to Do Next?

Some people may ask what can be done with the knowledge they learn from this book. One thing you can do is create EPUB books and sell them. Sites such as www.NookPress.com will sell your EPUB books for you. If you convert your EPUB books to Kindle format (covered in Chapter 6), the books can be sold at Amazon's site: kdp.amazon.com. Many other websites can sell EPUB files, and this can be profitable for some people.

Who Should Read This Book

This book is for anyone who wants to be able to create or edit EPUB files. No prior knowledge of EPUB is necessary other than some ability to learn basic HTML, XHTML, XML, CSS, and JavaScript.

This book is for you if

- You are a newcomer to EPUB. You must be able to download and install files from the Internet. These files include applications and free EPUB files to use as samples.
- You have some knowledge of EPUB or even advanced experience. This book can extend your knowledge using more tools and techniques.
- You have experience with HTML and wish to learn XML or CSS.
- You wish to learn the basics of JavaScript to enhance EPUB functionality.

What This Book Covers

This book covers the following:

- Chapter 1 introduces you to EPUB standards and the contents of the EPUB file, with some important background information. The chapter sets the groundwork for the remaining chapters.
- Chapter 2 covers the basics of HTML and XHTML that are supported by EPUB standards.You will learn how to code the main book parts displayed on any device. The chapter gets you started on creating the body of your EPUB.
- Chapter 3 shows how CSS is used to manipulate the style of the XHTML files and enhance the visual quality of the EPUB. It continues the work of Chapter 2 by showing you how to use CSS to enhance the format of your book body. This is more than bold, underline, italics and the like.
- Chapter 4 goes into fonts, images, and colors. Learn how to further enhance an EPUB by changing fonts and colors, as well as adding images. Chapter 4 includes sample files that can be downloaded from McGraw-Hill (all remaining chapters contain samples).

NOTE

All sample files referred to in the book can be downloaded from www.mhprofessional.com/EPUB.

- Chapter 5 details the structure and use of the Navigation Center eXtended (NCX) and Open Packaging Format (OPF) files. These are used to set up reading order and create the table of contents.
- Chapter 6 explains how to convert many e-book and file formats to EPUB. It also shows how to take an EPUB file and convert it to other formats, including the Kindle format and others.
- Chapter 7 has information about the use of digital rights management (DRM), signatures, and font obfuscation to protect an EPUB and prevent it from being shared freely.
- Chapter 8 provides details about the enhancements of EPUB 3. It explains how to add audio and video files, how to use Mathematics Markup Language (MathML), how to set up the new navigational file, how to make fixed layouts, how to create SMIL, and how to add Flash files to your EPUB.
- Chapter 9 details the use of JavaScript to enhance EPUB 3 files and create interactive e-books, which can provide added functionality.

You can read this book all the way through, or you can look over just the chapters that interest you. Examples in each chapter do not rely completely on material created in other chapters.

Chapters 4 through 9 include working examples to help you understand the concepts that are being covered in that chapter. Each chapter has a list of key points at the beginning to summarize these concepts.

Many chapters contain Notes, Tips, and Cautions. Keep these sections in mind as you read.

Chapter 1

EPUB Defined

- Learn EPUB 2 standards for text and text e-readers
- See how to form files within the EPUB
- Learn some basic XML
- Understand what files are necessary for EPUB
- Discover what usable HTML tags to use in an EPUB
- Be able to view the contents of an EPUB

The world of reading has forever changed. Paper books, magazines, and other such items have been evolving to a digital format. This affects not only readers, but writers as well. Electronic reading devices are popular, and with them, so are *electronic books* (e-books).

As a reader, you want to be able to enjoy a book visually. Little enhancements can make an e-book more pleasing. Changing fonts, adding images, and adjusting the text layout can be a few tricks you can use to "fix" an e-book. As a writer, you want to make the reader's experience more enjoyable. To be able to keep the reader entertained and want to read more of your material is a definite plus.

In this chapter, you will learn about the EPUB version 2 standard, referred to as EPUB 2. You will understand where the standard is, as well as where it is going. Some standards are mainly for the black-and-white e-readers, while others are for the color e-readers. For example, some standards are compliant for the color e-readers, which allows for the use of video, text, and audio. Other e-readers may only allow for text. EPUB 2 is mainly for the black-and-white e-readers, but can be viewed on color devices as well.

EPUB Version 2 (EPUB 2)

Three basic parts comprise the EPUB 2 standard, as shown in Figure 1-1.

The three parts are as follows:

- **OEBPS Container Format (OCF)** Container holding all the files making up the publication. Collection of the individual files within a ZIP file, renamed to EPUB.

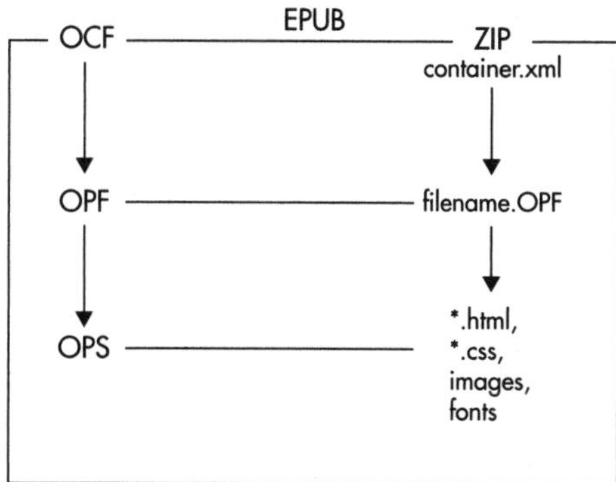

Figure 1-1 Three parts of EPUB

- **Open Packaging Format (OPF)** Describes and references the components within the publication. Includes content information, content list, content order, and the document parts.
- **Open Publication Structure (OPS)** Contents of the publication. Made up of XHTML/HTML, CSS, fonts, and images.

NOTE

Files within the EPUB can have an extension of HTML or XHTML. From now on, I will refer to both as XHTML unless otherwise needed.

Each part has specific requirements that you should be aware of when dealing with EPUB files. Be sure you understand the fundamentals for each section. Details follow for each section, with some discussed in greater depth in later chapters.

Open Container Format

From what you've seen in Figure 1-1, you may be wondering how all of this information is put into one file. It is actually very simple, but, of course, with many details and requirements. Don't worry; most of the information is not used in most EPUB files.

The answer to this question is a ZIP file. A ZIP file is a single file that contains one or more files that are either stored or compressed. Stored files within the ZIP are "as-is" with no file size change, while the compressed files are written in such a way that they have a smaller file size.

The International Digital Publishing Forum (IDPF) states that the OCF is an abstract collection of files—the abstract container, which is the collection of various files and folders. This abstract container is inside a ZIP file, which is the physical container.

The abstract container has the following requirements:

- The file system within the archive must have a single root directory.
- All embedded files other than those required must be in a directory off the root.
- Special files required by the OCF must be in the \META-INF directory (discussed later in this chapter).

NOTE

An EPUB file without a META-INF directory is corrupted. Each EPUB must have a META-INF directory to hold specific files required for the e-reader device. The only necessary file is container.xml, which specifies the OPF file location.

Key Word Usage

Many of the standards used by the IDPF and other organizations use words like "required," "must," "should," etc. Sometimes these meanings can be a bit overwhelming when seeing them over and over. The following table designates their meanings:

Key Word	Meaning
Must, Required, Shall	Absolute requirement
Must Not	Absolutely prohibited
Should, Recommend	Should be followed, but can be ignored only with consideration
Should Not, Not Recommended	Should not be followed, but can be implemented with consideration
May, Optional	Can or cannot be implemented with discretion

The physical container has the following requirement:

- The file system structure must be a one-to-one mapping just like on a hard disk or other storage media.

ZIP Requirements

Imagine that a ZIP file is a physical hard disk. When we copy files to it and view those files in a directory structure, we see the root directory and the files and folders. This listing is our abstract container. The ZIP file on the storage media is then our physical container.

Since our ZIP file is similar to a hard disk, it has one single root directory. There is a mandatory directory in the root called META-INF. Other files in the EPUB needed for display are in another directory from the root. Just like a hard disk, all files and directories are mapped one-to-one. This means there is only one META-INF directory. Each filename is used by only one file within the same folder.

Programs that produce ZIP files allow for the ZIP file to be split over various media. For instance, if you want to save a ZIP file to a DVD and the total file size requires more than one DVD, you can split the ZIP into multiple parts that would fill a DVD, with the rest on the next disk. EPUB files cannot be split in this manner and must be one complete ZIP file renamed with an EPUB extension.

EPUB files must be Flate compressed or Stored. Flate compression is the same as Deflate and is a lossless compression method. Lossless compression means that no information is lost from the original file and all data still exists. The Flate/Deflate method works best for text files and black-and-white/grayscale images. Stored data is when the files cannot or will not be compressed and are therefore only placed within the ZIP file in their original state. Stored files are not reduced in size, even though other files within the ZIP may be compressed. Other compression methods should generate an error by the reading device.

If the reading device or system supports ZIP64 extensions, you can use the ZIP64 compression format. The extension removes the limits of regular ZIP files on file sizes and the number of files within the archive, as shown in Table 1-1. This can drastically increase the number of files in a ZIP, as well as the sizes of the files being compressed.

	Standard Format	Zip64 Format
Number of files inside an archive	65,535	$2^{64} - 1$ (18,446,744,073,709,551,615)
Size of a file inside an archive (bytes)	4,294,967,295 (4GB)	18,446,744,073,709,551,615 (18EB*)
Size of an archive (bytes)	4,294,967,295 (4GB)	18,446,744,073,709,551,615 (18EB)
Central directory size (bytes)	4,294,967,295 (4GB)	18,446,744,073,709,551,615 (18EB)

*EB = Exabyte

Table 1-1 Differences in Standard and ZIP64 Formats

Version Needed	Hex Value	Version	Feature Version
10	0A	1.0	Default
20	14	2.0	Deflate
45	2D	4.5	ZIP64

Table 1-2 Version Needed Field

ZIP files can be encrypted from the archive program, requiring a password to access the contents. EPUB does not allow for encryption to be managed by the ZIP file. To use encryption, see a later section entitled "Encryption.XML."

A ZIP file must encode filenames in the archive using UTF-8. UTF (Unicode Transformation Format) is a way of using 1 to 4 bytes to represent Unicode characters. The set of Unicode characters designates different text and script characters. Unicode not only supports text and script, but also punctuation, mathematical symbols, numbers, and so on. Each UTF character represents a value that corresponds to a Unicode value. The Unicode values represent a character from the world's written languages. Unicode values can represent English letters, Greek letters, Hebrew script, and many more. For a more comprehensive list of languages, go to www.unicode.org/charts/.

The EPUB standard requires the Version Needed To Extract field in the ZIP header be 10, 20, or 45. The location of the 2-byte field is in the local header at offset 04 in the ZIP header. The values are shown with the version feature in Table 1-2. The EPUB file example shown in Figure 1-2 is a Deflate file.

The compression method must be either 0 or 8. Any other value causes the EPUB to be in error. As you can see in Figure 1-3, the sample EPUB file shown has compression method 08 at offset 8. Value 0 means the files have been Stored in the archive, while 8 means the files have been "Deflated." For reference purposes, other compression values are shown in Table 1-3. Remember that only the values 00 and 08 are valid.

```
Offset(h) 00 01 02 03 04 05 06 07 08 09 0A 0B 0C 0D 0E 0F

00000000  50 4B 03 04 14 00 00 00 08 00 23 8C 50 3B 41 86  PK..▯.....#ŒP;A†
00000010  5D 90 00 03 00 00 5B 0C 00 00 0B 00 00 00 63 6F  ].....[.......co
00000020  6E 74 65 6E 74 2E 6F 70 66 B5 97 CB 72 9B 30 14  ntent.opfµ—Ër›0.
00000030  86 F7 79 0A 86 8D 17 1D 10 32 60 30 63 3B 33 E9  †÷y.†....2`0c;3é
```

Figure 1-2 ZIP header value from hex editor

Value	Meaning
00	Stored (no compression)
01	Shrunk
02	Reduced with compression factor 1
03	Reduced with compression factor 2
04	Reduced with compression factor 3
05	Reduced with compression factor 4
06	Imploded
07	Reserved
08	Deflated

Table 1-3 Compression Methods and Their Values

An EPUB with an archive decryption header or archive extra data record is invalid. As previously stated, the ZIP file must not control encryption. When a ZIP manages its encryption, the archive decryption header and archive extra data record contain the information about the encryption.

The first file placed in the ZIP root must be the mimetype file, with no extra spacing or changes made to the contents. The mimetype file must not be compressed or encrypted, and there should not be an extra field in the ZIP header. The extra field is used to store extra information for special application or platform requirements. If these items are not present, then the information from Table 1-4 will appear at the specified location of the EPUB, as shown in Figure 1-4. When this occurs, it is the "magic number" defined in RFC 2048. Of course, this may not always be the case, since not all EPUB files produce the "magic number," as you can see looking back at Figures 1-2 and 1-3. All ZIP files should start with "PK" no matter what other settings have been changed.

```
Offset(h) 00 01 02 03 04 05 06 07 08 09 0A 0B 0C 0D 0E 0F

00000000  50 4B 03 04 14 00 00 00 08 00 23 8C 50 3B 41 86  PK........#ŒP;A†
00000010  5D 90 00 03 00 00 5B 0C 00 00 0B 00 00 00 63 6F  ].....[.......co
00000020  6E 74 65 6E 74 2E 6F 70 66 B5 97 CB 72 9B 30 14  ntent.opfµ—Ër›0.
```

Figure 1-3 EPUB hex editor showing a deflated compression method

Offset (hex)	Offset (decimal)	Value
00	00	PK
30	48	Mimetype
38	56	application/epub+zip

Table 1-4 "Magic Number" Values and Placement

Now that we've covered the ZIP file as a whole, let's look at the rules for inside the archive—namely, the directories and files. Directories are like folders, and files can be thought of as the papers within them. Of course, the ZIP file is the container in which the folders and papers are placed.

The root starts with a backslash (\), and all folders are separated with backslashes as well. Filenames also are separated from the directory names with a backslash. For example, if we were to note the path starting at the ROOT to the container.xml file, we would write it like this:

```
\META-INF\container.xml
```

All files in the archive must be UTF-8 encoded and not exceed 255 bytes or characters. Paths must not exceed 65,535 bytes or characters.

Directory and filenames must not include any of the following:

```
/, ", *, :, <, >, ?, \
```

Also, the filename cannot end with a period.

Some ZIP programs may support case sensitivity on filenames. This means the file container.xml is a different file from Container.xml. All files within a single folder must

```
Offset(h) 00 01 02 03 04 05 06 07 08 09 0A 0B 0C 0D 0E 0F
00000000  50 4B 03 04 14 00 00 00 00 00 10 5F 5C 41 6F 61  PK........._\Aoa
00000010  AB 2C 14 00 00 00 14 00 00 00 08 00 00 00 6D 69  «,............mi
00000020  6D 65 74 79 70 65 61 70 70 6C 69 63 61 74 69 6F  metypeapplicatio
00000030  6E 2F 65 70 75 62 2B 7A 69 70 50 4B 03 04 14 00  n/epub+zipPK....
00000040  00 00 08 00 E6 5D 5C 41 9E 77 47 26 B4 00 00 00  ....æ]\AžwG&´...
```

Figure 1-4 "Magic number" in EPUB

not have the same name after the filenames have all been lowercased or uppercased (this includes directory names as well).

NOTE

E-reader devices that support external memory cards, usually Secure Digital cards, support FAT-16 or FAT-32. SD cards are typically preformatted as FAT-32. The name limitations are based on this file system.

Depending on the language used (other than English), accent marks may be used. These must also be removed so no two files have the same name in the same directory. For example, it would see "Résumé" as "Resume."

In most cases, it may be best to stick with ASCII codes for filenames and directory names. Otherwise, names may not be retained after they are uncompressed from the archive.

NOTE

The ASCII characters are those represented on a keyboard.

META-INF Requirements

We previously discussed the META-INF directory, which must be included in the EPUB file. Without it, the file is considered corrupted.

Within the META-INF directory, there are five optional files and one required file. We'll cover the purpose of these files now, but the contents of the files will be explained later in this chapter and some other chapters.

manifest.xml The manifest.xml file is an optional file only needed for backwards compatibility with OpenDocument Format (ODF).

The ODF is an open XML-based document format that is nonproprietary, allowing for easier sharing and conversion of data. An example application suite is LibreOffice.

If the manifest.xml file exists, it lists the contents of the EPUB file. The file must not be encrypted.

The manifest list is part of the OPF file and will be covered in the "Open Packaging Format (OPF)" section.

metadata.xml The metadata.xml file is an optional file that contains the metadata about the publication. The XML file uses Dublin Core extensions to describe the title, author, publisher, etc. The data specified is for the container level, since it is part of the OCF. Metadata in the OPF is publication level.

NOTE

Dublin Core extensions will be covered a little later in this chapter.

If the metadata.xml file exists, it cannot be encrypted.

The metadata.xml file is part of the OPF file and will be covered in the "Open Packaging Format (OPF)" section.

signatures.xml The signatures.xml file contains a list of files signed using Secure Hash Algorithm 1 (SHA-1). The algorithm is a fancy way to perform a calculation to generate a string of data called a hash. The value produced will be identically created each time the file is put through the algorithm. This allows a user to verify the files have not been changed or been corrupted.

If each file within the EPUB is signed individually, then each hash must be in signatures .xml. By having so many different hash values, the file will be larger. Multiple files may be signed together making the signatures.xml file smaller.

To add, remove, or change files in an EPUB without causing the file to appear corrupted, do not sign the signatures.xml file. If no files are to be added, removed, or changed, the signatures.xml file should be signed. If the signatures.xml file exists, it may not be encrypted.

Signatures.xml refers to EPUB security and will be covered more in Chapter 8.

encryption.xml Some EPUB files are purchased on the Internet from various vendors, usually the vendor of your reading device. The books you buy are not supposed to be readily shared with others. To prevent this, the contents of the EPUB file are encrypted. As you have seen so far, no files within the META-INF directory can be encrypted, including encryption .xml. If any publications are encrypted, then the encryption.xml file specifies how to decrypt those files. If the file is deleted from an encrypted EPUB, the EPUB is corrupted.

Files are encrypted individually, but the whole container, excluding the META-INF folder, can be encrypted. When a file is encrypted, the whole file must be encrypted, not just a portion. If the files within the ZIP are compressed before they are encrypted, they must be Stored, not Flated.

Care needs to be taken when including fonts within an EPUB, as discussed in Chapter 4. If the font is to be protected from being freely shared, the font file should be encrypted as well. The procedure of encrypting the font is called font mangling.

Signatures.xml will be present when rights.xml exists and may not be encrypted.

rights.xml The rights.xml file is an optional file that is used to specify licensing rights by encrypting the data. This procedure refers to Digital Rights Management (DRM), covered in Chapter 8. If the EPUB is DRM protected and the rights.xml file is removed, the EPUB is corrupted. The rights.xml file cannot be encrypted.

container.xml The container.xml file is a required file. If the file is missing or encrypted, the EPUB is considered corrupted. The contents of the container.xml file point to the OPF file location that will be discussed in the next section.

Open Packaging Format (OPF)

The OPF is made up of two files. The first file is the .OPF file, which contains the description and references to the files within the OPS portion of the publication. It also fixes the order of the viewable files to ensure that everything is displayed in the proper order. The second file, the global navigation structure (NCX), provides a structure similar to a table of contents. It gives quick access to pages without requiring you to go through a publication page by page.

The OPF file is covered in detail in Chapter 6, while the NCX file is explained in Chapter 5.

Open Publication Structure (OPS)

Before we go on too far, let us discuss the devices. Available e-readers include the Barnes and Noble Nook, Kobo, the Apple iPad, etc. There are also PC apps for Barnes and Noble Nook, Kobo, etc. So an e-reader is any device that allows a reader to read an electronic book (e-book).

What About the Kindle?

The Amazon Kindle is a popular e-reader that, unfortunately, does not support the EPUB standard. Do not worry about this, though. There are easy ways to convert an EPUB to the Kindle format, known as AZW, covered in Chapter 7. For most people, it is easier to create and manipulate an EPUB file and then convert it to AZW.

The OPS is made up of files containing the viewable content of the publication. Basically, it is what you will see on the e-reader's screen. With EPUB files, this content comes from Extensible Hypertext Markup Language (XHTML) files. The content can be visually manipulated with one or more Cascading Style Sheets (CSS). Finally, the last part of the OPS is image files and fonts. The images can be in PNG, JPG (JPEG), GIF, and SVG formats. Fonts may be in TTF, OTF, or SVG formats (some reading systems may support other formats, such as WOFF or EOT).

What Is SVG?

Scalable Vector Graphics (SVG) is a standard created by the World Wide Web Consortium (W3C). SVG can be fonts, images, and animation. Fonts can be smoother since they are made up of shapes rather than points. Animation can be controlled by JavaScript in EPUB 3 only.

All SVG files are based on XML and can, therefore, be viewed in a text editor. Since they are text-based files, they can be compressed a lot in the ZIP file. By compressing SVG files, the EPUB files are smaller than when using other fonts or image types (examples are given in Chapter 4).

EPUB 2 supports SVG fonts and images. SVG images that have embedded text can be searched with the publication text. SVG images can be also be used to contain links for navigation purposes.

Be aware that some e-readers may not support SVG even though it is part of the EPUB standard.

All the OPS files work together to create the viewable material comprising the publication or e-book. By using XHTML, even though not all elements and attributes are supported, most have CSS values to replace them. The main thing to remember is the text is supposed to flow and will be viewable on various devices. Having the text and images flow is similar to a webpage, which can be viewed in various screen sizes and resolutions.

NOTE

Device screen size may vary from a larger device such as a Nook or iPad to a smartphone, but the screen resolution is a minimum of 600 × 800 pixels.

There are various requirements for OPS and XHTML documents:

- It is a well-formed XML document.
- Encoded in UTF-8 or UTF-16.
- It is a valid XML document according to the Namespace-based Validation Dispatching Language (NVDL) schema.
- MIMETYPE of application/xhtml+xml or text/x-oebl-document (deprecated).
- XHTML elements and attributes not contained in the inline XML island are drawn from the XHTML subset

Requirements for the DTBook are as follows:

- It is a well-formed XML document.
- Encoded in UTF-8 or UTF-16.
- It is a valid XML document.
- MIMETYPE of application/x-dtbook+xml.

The out-of-line XML document requirements are as follows:

- It is a well-formed XML document.
- Encoded in UTF-8 or UTF-16.
- MIMETYPE of:
  - application/xhtml+xml (not an extended module)
  - text/x-oebl-document
  - application/x-dtbook+xml

CSS requirements for the OPS are as follows:

- The external CSS style sheet must be referenced by the OPS document.
- Encoded in UTF-8 or UTF-16.
- UTF-16 requires a byte order mark (BOM).
- UTF-8 has an optional BOM.

The reading system requirements are as follows:

- Correctly process XML as required by XML 1.0 specifications, including handling errors
- Recognize permitted markups and process them consistently
- Must not render img or object elements of unsupported media types in the absence of fallbacks
- Verify existence of appropriate namespace specifications
- Correctly process CSS style sheets

What Is Namespace-based Validation Dispatching Language (NVDL)?

NVDL is a set of rules used to allow an XML file to be validated to assure that the XML tags are correct according to the namespace being used.

What Is DAISY or DTBook?

Before EPUB, there was the DAISY Consortium. Digital Accessible Information SYstem (DAISY) created the DTBook, or DAISY Digital Talking Book, for people with accessibility issues. The Open eBook (OEB), formerly the Open eBook Publication Structure (OEBPS) 1.2, became EPUB 2.0, and now the DAISY Consortium has joined EPUB to create EPUB 3.

The OPS standard requires the use of XHTML processing of the elements listed in Table 1-5. The items in the table will be detailed in Chapter 2.

NOTE

If you do not know XHTML, then Chapter 2 will cover those details and get you up to speed. For now, just realize that these are the elements used to create the text body of the book as well as to manipulate images.

Since the OPS was taken from OEB (later OEBPS), there is a resemblance to DAISY DTBooks. Navigation to chapters and individual pages can allow a reader to move around in the book easily. DTBook content must be validated to the DTBook XML vocabulary. Any elements dealing with Synchronized Multimedia Integration Language (SMIL) are not allowed in EPUB 2. SMIL is the multimedia component of DAISY, but EPUB 2 does not handle multimedia, and therefore is not allowed. For more information on multimedia support, see Chapters 8 and 9.

Some basic changes from OEBPS 1.2 to OPS 2.0 meant that XML namespace processing is now required. The support for SVG has been added, as well as embedded fonts. In addition, some MIME types were changed.

NOTE

Any MIME types that were dropped from DTBooks are not mentioned in this book. If the element was deprecated, then there is no need to learn it for EPUB.

XHTML 1.1 Module Name	Elements (non-normative)
Structure	body, head, html, title
Text	abbr, acronym, address, blockquote, br, cite, code, dfn, div, em, h1, h2, h3, h4, h5, h6, kbd, p, pre, q, samp, span, strong, var
Hypertext	a
List	dl, dt, dd, ol, ul, li
Object	object, param
Presentation	b, big, hr, i, small, sub, sup, tt
Edit	del, ins
Bidirectional Text	bdo
Table	caption, col, colgroup, table, tbody, td, tfoot, th, thead, tr
Image	img
Client-Side Image Map	area, map
Meta-Information	meta
Style Sheet	style
Link	link
Base	base

Table 1-5 OPS XHTML Elements

OPS supports Cascading Style Sheets (CSS), an external file to store styles for XHTML code, but not all CSS items are supported on all reading systems. For example, devices that do not have color screens cannot support color elements. The color elements can be rendered in shades of gray, however, to emulate color differences.

OPS supports various MIME types. MIME, or Multipurpose Internet Mail Extensions, was originally used to designate file formats over the Internet. It was specifically used by SMTP (Simple Mail Transport Protocol) for e-mail attachments. After being used with protocols such as HTTP and others, it has expanded to other protocols.

MIMETYPE is usually referred to as Media Type now and exists for different types (see Table 1-6).

Type	Description
Application	For files of various purposes
Audio	Audio files
Example	Examples
Image	Image files
Message	Message types
Model	3-D models
Multipart	For objects with more than one part
Text	Text and source code
Video	Video files

Table 1-6 MIME Types

There is a whole list of subtypes, some of which are supported within an EPUB. Table 1-6 lists types and subtypes that are supported in EPUB 2. The items in Table 1-7 give you an idea of what file types can be used to create EPUB, which are covered in detail in Chapter 6.

MIMETYPE	USE
image/gif	Raster Graphics (GIF)
image/jpeg	Raster Graphics (JPG, JPEG)
image/png	Raster Graphics (PNG)
image/svg+xml	Vector Graphics (SVG)
application/x-dtbook+xml	DAISY DTBook
application/xhtml+xml	XHTML File
text/css	CSS 2.0
application/xml	Out-of-Line XML Islands
application/x-dtbncx+xml	NCX file

Table 1-7 OPS MIMETYPE and Usage

I know you are probably thinking that this is a lot of information to throw out all at once. Believe me, it isn't as bad as it seems. Through the rest of this chapter and those that follow, we will cover these standards in greater detail. Be patient with it, and go over each chapter and learn the subjects. As you go through various EPUB files, these things will become second nature to you.

What Is an EPUB?

An EPUB file is a collection of files within a ZIP file renamed to EPUB. This means that any EPUB file can be opened with a ZIP archival application. Depending on the program, you may need to rename the file's extension from EPUB to ZIP. I will give a shortcut momentarily for Windows XP systems that allows you to open an EPUB file without renaming it.

Various chapters of this book cover the different files within the EPUB. Some you may need to edit at times, and others you may never need to change at all. It is best to understand what these files do so you can be sure not to modify or delete them, which can cause problems.

Preparing to View the Contents of an EPUB File

Before we get too far into the standards, let's look at the contents of an EPUB file. This will help illustrate what we are covering as we go along.

At this point, you need to make sure you have a ZIP compression utility. I suggest 7-Zip since it is freeware. I will cover some basics to set things up in the Windows context menu, which is what appears when you right-click an EPUB file. As noted in the introduction, you can download 7-Zip from www.7-zip.org. Download and install the application, and then perform the following steps to create the context menu on a Windows system.

NOTE

Be sure you have installed Sigil as well. You can find it at http://code.google.com/p/sigil/. For Linux, go to the address for your specific distribution of Linux:

Debian-Based Linux https://launchpad.net/~rgibert/+archive/ebook/+packages/
Fedora http://rpms.limbasan.ro/fedora/
ArchLinux https://www.archlinux.org/packages/?q=sigil
Slackware http://connie.slackware.com/~alien/slackbuilds/sigil/
OpenSuse https://build.opensuse.org/package/repositories?package=sigil&project=home%3Axwaver
Gentoo http://gentoo-portage.com/app-text/sigil

Windows 7

1. Open Control Panel, select Programs, and then select Default Programs.
2. Select Associate A File Type Or Protocol With A Program.
3. Select EPUB (if EPUB is not in the list, close the open windows, install SIGIL, and then restart from step 1).
4. Select Change Program.
5. Browse for 7-Zip and then click OK (unless you use a different archive program).
6. Click Close.
7. Find an EPUB file and right-click it.
8. From the menu that opened, select Open With.
9. You can choose Sigil to edit the file or 7-Zip to open the archive (or your archive program instead of 7-Zip).

Windows XP

1. Open My Computer.
2. Click Tools and select Folder Options.
3. Once the Registered File Types list is populated, scroll down to find ZIP.
4. Highlight ZIP and select the Advanced button.
5. Highlight Open under Actions and then click the Edit button.
6. Under Application To Perform Action, you should see C:\Program files\7-Zip\7zFM .exe%1. Make a note of the exact line (the drive letter may be different depending on where you installed it).
7. Select Cancel twice to get back to the Folder Options screen.
8. Scroll and select EPUB and then click the Advanced button (if EPUB is not in the list, close the open windows, install SIGIL, and then restart from step 1).
9. In the Actions section, you should see an entry for Open. Select the New button.
10. Under Actions, type **View Contents**.
11. Under Application To Perform Action, enter the information you noted in step 6.
12. Check the option to use DDE, and the box should expand.
13. Under Application, type in the 7-Zip filename: **7zFM.exe**.

NOTE

If you use a different ZIP program, make sure that in step 13 you use the correct filename for your application.

14. Under Topic, type **System**.
15. Select OK and close all windows you have opened for these steps.

Linux

For Linux systems, you want to use either Ark or Xarchiver as your ZIP viewer. Follow the instructions next for your specific file manager.

Nautilus

1. First, right-click the EPUB and select Properties.
2. Next, click the Open With tab.
3. Finally, choose an EPUB-compatible archiving program.

Dolphin and Konqueror

1. First, right-click the EPUB and select Properties.
2. Then, click the only icon by the Type property.
3. Next, set the application preference order for opening files with the EPUB extension.

Thunar

1. First, right-click the EPUB file and select Properties.
2. Finally, choose the default program to use when opening EPUB files.

X File Explorer (XFE)

1. Before beginning, open a command line and type **which** ***name of preferred archive manager***. This will return the file path of the executable. Write this down, or copy it to the clipboard. For example:
   - User input: which ark
   - System output: /usr/bin/ark
2. After that, right-click the EPUB and click Properties.
3. Then, click the File Associations tab.
4. Last, paste or type the system output file path into the Open line, and finish by clicking Accept.

Viewing the Contents of an EPUB File

Now, you need to download an EPUB file to test this new feature. Use your browser and go to www.ManyBooks.net. On the first page, type **Household Tales** in the Search box. Download the EPUB file when you have the option and save it to an accessible folder. For Windows, right-click the file and you should see an option toward the top of the list—View Contents. Select View Contents and 7-Zip should open. This context menu should now work on all EPUB files. If it doesn't work, go back through the steps and try again. For Linux systems, right-click, select Open With, and choose the archiver you installed.

The archiver program you installed should display a folder and 21 objects (unless it is an updated file); these are the contents of the EPUB file.

You should see something similar to Figure 1-5, depending on your archiver program. As you can see, most of the files are .html; in some cases, .xhtml. These are the heart of the text displayed on the e-reader. Image files make up the cover image, book illustrations, pictures, etc. The .css file is the Cascading Style Sheet, which enhances the XHTML pages.

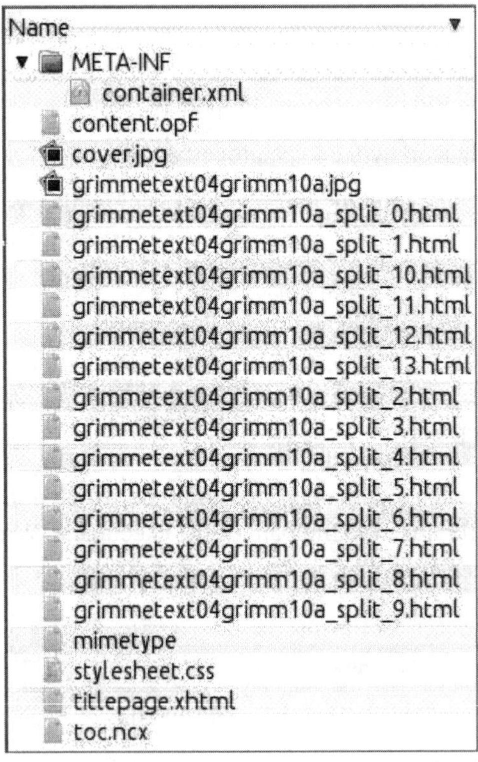

Figure 1-5 Contents of Household Tales EPUB

Everything else is used to create the EPUB file and determine the reading order of the files, table of contents, and much more.

XML Basics

Most of these items are covered in later chapters. Here I will discuss the container.xml, manifest.xml, metadata.xml, and mimetype files. In Chapter 7 we will cover the other XML files: signatures.xml, rights.xml, and encryption.xml. First, we need to cover some basics of XML.

EPUB uses a few XML files, and a basic knowledge of XML is required to manipulate some of the files. Sigil and other programs can do this for you, but sometimes it is easier to manage the files yourself, or at least is better to understand them.

Extensible Markup Language (XML) is used to describe data. XML is used in various places within the EPUB file. Tags are placed within chevrons (< >), and most tags have a beginning tag to designate the beginning of a section. Each section ends with a closing tag, which starts with a forward slash before the tag name (</ >). XML tags are case-sensitive, can contain no spaces, and typically are lowercase.

For example, let's suppose we had a database we wanted to create for a book catalog. Of course, there would be more information, but this is just a basic example.

```
<catalog>
      <book>
            <title>King Solomon's Mines</title>
            <author>H.R. Haggard</author>
            <isbn>0486447820</isbn>
      </book>
      <book>
            <title>Journey to the Center of the Earth</title>
            <author>Jules Verne</author>
            <isbn>1402773137</isbn>
      </book>
</catalog>
```

As you can see, there is an overall tag for <catalog> and a matching end tag. This designates the catalog as a whole, and everything between the two tags are within the <catalog>. Within the main tag are nested tags—tags that are inside other tags. In this case, the <book> tags are nested within <catalog>. Each <book> has nested information about a single book. Here the first book is *King Solomon's Mines* and the second is *Journey to the Center of the Earth.* Each of these books includes <title>, <author>, and <isbn>. Notice the information within the tag itself (< >) is all lowercased. Tag names are case-sensitive, so the start tag and end tag must be identical in case. Data included between the tags can be in any required case needed, as shown in the example.

Nested tags are called children. <book> is a child tag while <catalog> is a parent. <title>, <author>, and <isbn> are siblings of one another and children of <book>.

Now to access this XML file from an application, the application must understand what the tags mean. To specify the tag meanings, or XML vocabulary, we use an XML namespace (xmlns).

Now that you should have a basic understanding of XML, we can look at the container .xml file that is part of the OCF.

container.xml

The container.xml file is required to show the OPF file location—in this case, content.opf. Chapter 6 covers the OPF file.

When using Sigil to create or edit EPUB files, the program manages the container.xml file. If you should change something manually, you need to know how it all works.

The container.xml file *must* be contained in a directory named META-INF. If this directory or file does not exist, the EPUB is considered corrupted and cannot be viewed on any device or edited in Sigil. To fix the problem, you will need to re-create the file manually.

The content of the container.xml for Household Tales is as follows:

```
<?xml version="1.0" encoding="UTF-8"?>
<container version="1.0" xmlns="urn:oasis:names:tc:opendocument:xmlns:container">
    <rootfiles>
        <rootfile full-path="OEBPS/content.opf" media-type="application/oebps-package+xml"/>
   </rootfiles>
</container>
```

The file can be the same from any EPUB, except for the fourth line. The full-path points to the OPF file location, which can have any valid filename, but must have the OPF extension.

The beginning of the first line, `<?xml version="1.0"`, is standard for all XML files. The first line declares to any program using it that it is XML and version 1.

The second part of the first line, `encoding="UTF-8"?>`, shows the file uses UTF-8.

EPUB requires UTF-8 or UTF-16, but some e-reader devices may not support UTF-16. It is best to stick with UTF-8 as often as you can. If you need to use special characters, then you will want to include the suitable font file. Chapter 4 covers adding font files.

The second line shows the container version is "1.0," which is mandatory. Then the next part, xmlns="urn:oasis:names:tc:opendocument:xmlns:container", shows the namespace used by XML, which will never need to be changed for the container.xml file. The only thing that may ever change in the file is the line `<rootfile full-path="OEBPS/content.opf" media-type="application/oebps-package+xml"/>`, which shows the OPF file location.

The <rootfiles> section must contain one <rootfile> element that specifies the OPF location for the publication. It is possible to include more than one <rootfile> element, but this is for fallback purposes only. For example:

```
<?xml version="1.0" encoding="UTF-8"?>
<container version="1.0" xmlns="urn:oasis:names:tc:opendocument:xmlns:container">
    <rootfiles>
        <rootfile full-path="OEBPS/content.opf" media-type="application/oebps-package+xml"/>
        <rootfile full-path="PDF/example.pdf" media-type="application/pdf"/>
   </rootfiles>
</container>
```

If, for some reason, the reading system cannot manage the OPF correctly, it should display the PDF, if possible, as a fallback. Be aware that in this case, the reading device must be able to handle EPUB to be able to get this far into the container.xml.

manifest.xml

The manifest.xml file is optional, as most of its content has been moved to the OPF. Following is a sample manifest.xml file using basic information for the manifest list:

```
<manifest>
<item href="Images/grimmetext04grimm10a.jpg" id="added" media-type="image/jpeg"/>
<item href="Text/grimmetext04grimm10a_split_7.html" id="html7" media-type="application/xhtml+xml"/>
<item href="Images/cover.jpg" id="cover" media-type="image/jpeg"/>
<item href="Text/grimmetext04grimm10a_split_4.html" id="html10" media-type="application/xhtml+xml"/>
<item href="Text/grimmetext04grimm10a_split_9.html" id="html5" media-type="application/xhtml+xml"/>
<item href="Text/grimmetext04grimm10a_split_5.html" id="html9" media-type="application/xhtml+xml"/>
<item href="Text/grimmetext04grimm10a_split_10.html" id="html4" media-type="application/xhtml+xml"/>
<item href="Text/titlepage.xhtml" id="titlepage" media-type="application/xhtml+xml"/>
<item href="Text/grimmetext04grimm10a_split_3.html" id="html11" media-type="application/xhtml+xml"/>
<item href="Text/grimmetext04grimm10a_split_12.html" id="html2" media-type="application/xhtml+xml"/>
<item href="Text/grimmetext04grimm10a_split_2.html" id="html12" media-type="application/xhtml+xml"/>
<item href="Text/grimmetext04grimm10a_split_11.html" id="html3" media-type="application/xhtml+xml"/>
<item href="Styles/stylesheet.css" id="css" media-type="text/css"/>
<item href="Text/grimmetext04grimm10a_split_8.html" id="html6" media-type="application/xhtml+xml"/>
<item href="Text/grimmetext04grimm10a_split_6.html" id="html8" media-type="application/xhtml+xml"/>
<item href="Text/grimmetext04grimm10a_split_0.html" id="html14" media-type="application/xhtml+xml"/>
<item href="Text/grimmetext04grimm10a_split_1.html" id="html13" media-type="application/xhtml+xml"/>
<item href="Text/grimmetext04grimm10a_split_13.html" id="html1" media-type="application/xhtml+xml"/>
<item href="toc.ncx" id="ncx" media-type="application/x-dtbncx+xml"/>
</manifest>
```

As we noted before about a fallback, we can include this in the manifest.xml file as well. If, for some reason, we have a nonviewable file—say it is missing or corrupted—we can specify a fallback. Say we have each section of XHTML files saved as a PDF file; we can then call the PDF in case the XHTML fails. The following example has two sections for the first XHTML file. The first has an ID of "section1," which is for the HTML file. The section also shows the file's media type as application/xhtml+xml. Also included is a fallback attribute for a section ID called "section1pdf." The second section, the fallback, has an ID of “section1pdf” as noted from the fallback of the previous section. Here is a reference to the PDF file with the appropriate mimetype. Since there is no fallback for this section, that attribute is missing. Of course, we should have a section for each file listed in the previous sample of the manifest.xml with a fallback for each. I hope you can see how this works. Remember that if a fallback is listed for the PDF file, it cannot point back to the first section. The fallbacks may not be circular in nature. If all sections fail, then the reading device must be able to gracefully handle this without failure.

```
<manifest>
<item id="section1" href="Text/grimmetext04grimm10a_split_0.html"
media-type="application/xhtml+xml" fallback="section1pdf"/>
<item id="section1pdf" href="Text/grimmetext04grimm10a_split_0.pdf"
media-type="application/pdf"/>
</manifest>
```

Keep in mind that the manifest.xml file is for backwards compatibility; this information will be repeated in Chapter 6 for the OPF file.

Any files within the EPUB not listed in the manifest.xml (or the manifest of the OPF) cannot be displayed as part of the publication.

metadata.xml

Like the manifest.xml file, this is also an optional file that is for backwards compatibility since it is now contained in the OPF file.

Metadata is data about the publication. It is a set of 15 properties created by the Dublin Core Metadata Initiative (DCMI). It was named Dublin since it met at an invitational workshop in Dublin, Ohio. The “Core” is based on the fact the references are for a broad variety of resources. So Dublin Core is abbreviated as DC, as you will see in the examples.

Table 1-8 shows the 15 properties.

For example, you can specify the language of the e-book as English by using the following line:

```
<dc:language>en-US</dc:language>
```

The following example of the metadata.xml file shows the properties for language, creator, and title:

```
<dc:language>en-US</dc:language>
<dc:creator>The Grimm Brothers</dc:creator>
<dc:title>Household Tales</dc:title>
```

The Dublin Core properties will be covered in greater detail in Chapter 6 since this data appears in the OPF file.

Property	Meaning
Contributor	Person who contributed to the publication
Coverage	Area or time covered by the publication
Creator	Person responsible for making the publication
Date	Time associated with the publication
Description	Account of publication
Format	File format, physical medium, or dimensions of the publication
Identifier	Reference to resource within a context
Language	The language of the resource
Publisher	Entity responsible for making the publication available
Relation	A related resource
Rights	Information about rights held on the publication
Source	Related resource from where the publication was derived
Subject	Publication's topic
Title	Name given to publication
Type	Nature or genre of resource

Table 1-8 Dublin Core Properties

mimetype

The mimetype file must be in the root of the EPUB, and its content is `application/epub+zip`. The first part shows the EPUB file is a media type of application with a subtype of EPUB and ZIP. The contents must not be changed or added to with spaces or any other text or symbols.

Please note that even though the IDPF requires the mimetype file in the root with no changes, some reading systems may still show the EPUB anyway. It is best to leave this file as it should be and not try to modify it in case some systems may not handle it properly.

The Internet Assigned Numbers Authority (IANA) controls all media types. For more information, visit www.iana.org/assignments/media-types/index.html. You can also get a comprehensive list of subtypes for each media type.

Chapter 2

HTML

- Understand differences between HTML and XHTML
- Learn HTML for EPUB
- Practice XHTML in EPUB files

XHTML

When viewing EPUB documents, the material displayed on the reading system is from Extensible Hypertext Markup Language (XHTML). When creating, editing, or enhancing EPUBs, understanding XHTML is very important.

If you do not know XHTML or know only a little, don't worry. Playing around with a few EPUB files and making changes can help you learn it quickly. Keep in mind the scope of the various EPUB components is quite a bit to take in. Simply learn each chapter before moving on to another one.

NOTE

Chapter 3 builds on the skills learned in Chapter 2. Make sure you have a fair understanding of this chapter before moving on to Chapter 3.

What Is XHTML?

The Extensible Hypertext Markup Language is a form of Extensible Markup Language (XML). As you'll see, XHTML appears similar to XML since both are markup languages. One way to look at it is that XML describes the data, while XHTML describes how the data will appear. For example, XML may describe data as a book title, and XHTML describes the title is bold.

The format you will use with XHTML is as follows:

```
<tag attribute1="value1" attribute2="value2">
```

Tags may have no attributes, or may have a lot, and any number of them may be used.

With XML, every tag and possible attributes are contained within the less than (<) and greater than (>) symbols. Most tags will have an end tag to show the element has ended, while others are self-closing. Ending a tag requires a forward slash (/). Self-closing tags need no data, such as line break, which has the tag name of br. The break tag looks like this:

```
<br />
```

A quick sample of an end tag is the paragraph tag, which shows a paragraph's beginning and ending. The tag is a <p> and it looks like this:

```
<p>This is a paragraph.</p>
```

You can easily see where the paragraph starts and ends, as well as the content of the paragraph. An element consists of everything from the beginning to the end tag.

What's the Difference Between HTML and XHTML?

The tags used are all the same, but XHTML has stricter rules for the tags and attributes. With XHTML, all tags must be closed and each element nested within another element must end before the outermost one. For example, if we include bold words (<b>) within a paragraph (<p>), the bold element must close first as shown:

```
<p>The last word is <b>bold.</b></p>
```

It cannot be

```
<p>The last word is <b>bold.</p></b>
```

Also, attributes must be lowercase with values in quotes, whereas in HTML, the case and quotes don't always matter.

Finally, XHTML needs a header to indicate the file is XHTML. HTML does not require a header, but may have one. The header portion tells programs using the file, such as web browsers, that the file is XHTML. The XHTML header is as follows:

```
<?xml version="1.0" encoding="utf-8" standalone="no"?>
```

XHTML has other requirements that do not affect EPUB files, so keep in mind that as long as you understand HTML, XHTML won't be too radically different.

OPS XHTML Types

In Chapter 1, we covered information on the Open Publication Structure (OPS). The OPS is the portion of the EPUB displayed to the reader. If you look back at Table 1-5 in Chapter 1, you can see a list of the acceptable XHTML modules and the elements within each one.

Be prepared, because now we are going into the details of those tags and all available attributes.

NOTE

Not all reading devices are identical. Be aware that some tags and attributes may work on some devices and not on others. Some may not look the same either. Go to the McGraw-Hill website at www.mhprofessional.com/EPUB and download the EPUB tester file. It is an EPUB that you can place on your reading device to allow you to see how each tag on your device appears. You can also view the code in Sigil for each tag as you read for a better understanding of the coding.

Structure

The structure tags set up the whole XHTML page. These tags make up the framework of the file.

There are four tags in the structure module:

- html
- head
- title
- body

html

The <html> tag contains all the elements within the XHTML file. Any attributes in the <html> tag are inherited by all elements with the XHTML document. When using these attributes, keep in mind that these affect everything within this file.

The XHTML file is split into two sections: the head and the body (discussed next). The sections are as follows:

```
<html>
      <head>
            Place Head elements here
      </head>
      <body>
            Place Body elements here
      </body>
</html>
```

Attribute	Value	Description
id	*string*	Specifies the id of page to allow it to be linked
lang	*language type*	Specifies the language displayed by the file
version		Designates the version of XHTML used in the file
xmlns	*url*	Namespace used in the file
xml:lang	*language type*	Specifies the language displayed by the file when parsed as XML

Table 2-1 <html> Attributes

Table 2-1 lists the attributes available for the <html> tag.

Keep in mind that you can use no attributes, all of them, or just some of them. Use only what is required so problems do not arise within the EPUB because of conflicting information.

id The id is an attribute that can have a unique value within all the XHTML files within the EPUB. No two id attributes can be the same; this is very important. The value cannot be blank, but must have one or more characters. The first character must be a letter (a–z) and followed by numbers, hyphens, underscores, or periods. The value is case-sensitive when referenced by an anchor (<a>).

If we have an XHTML file that is Chapter 1 of a book, we can place the following within the document:

```
<html id="chapter1">
```

If a table of contents is made for the EPUB, then the listing for Chapter 1 in the table of contents can be linked to the individual file. This works well when each chapter is its own XHTML file.

lang Within an EPUB, the reader device should check each XHTML document to determine the language. If the device finds no language attribute, the reading system should check any XML files processed within the document. If nothing is found, the final place to determine the language is from the Open Packaging Format (OPF) file (see Chapter 6).

Table 2-2 lists the various language codes.

Language	ISO 639-1 Code	Language	ISO 639-1 Code
Abkhazian	ab	Latin	la
Afar	aa	Latvian (Lettish)	lv
Afrikaans	af	Limburgish (Limburger)	li
Albanian	sq	Lingala	ln
Amharic	am	Lithuanian	lt
Arabic	ar	Macedonian	mk
Aragonese	an	Malagasy	mg
Armenian	hy	Malay	ms
Assamese	as	Malayalam	ml
Aymara	ay	Maltese	mt
Azerbaijani	az	Maori	mi
Bashkir	ba	Marathi	mr
Basque	eu	Moldavian	mo
Bengali (Bangla)	bn	Mongolian	mn
Bhutani	dz	Nauru	na
Bihari	bh	Nepali	ne
Bislama	bi	Norwegian	no
Breton	br	Occitan	oc
Bulgarian	bg	Oriya	or
Burmese	my	Oromo (Afaan Oromo)	om
Byelorussian (Belarusian)	be	Pashto (Pushto)	ps
Cambodian	km	Polish	pl
Catalan	ca	Portuguese	pt
Chinese (Simplified)	zh	Punjabi	pa

Table 2-2 Language Codes

Language	ISO 639-1 Code	Language	ISO 639-1 Code
Chinese (Traditional)	zh	Quechua	qu
Corsican	co	Rhaeto-Romance	rm
Croatian	hr	Romanian	ro
Czech	cs	Russian	ru
Danish	da	Samoan	sm
Dutch	nl	Sangro	sg
English	en	Sanskrit	sa
Esperanto	eo	Serbian	sr
Estonian	et	Serbo-Croatian	sh
Faeroese	fo	Sesotho	st
Farsi	fa	Setswana	tn
Fiji	fj	Shona	sn
Finnish	fi	Sichuan Yi	ii
French	fr	Sindhi	sd
Frisian	fy	Sinhalese	si
Galician	gl	Siswati	ss
Gaelic (Scottish)	gd	Slovak	sk
Gaelic (Manx)	gv	Slovenian	sl
Georgian	ka	Somali	so
German	de	Spanish	es
Greek	el	Sundanese	su
Greenlandic	kl	Swahili (Kiswahili)	sw
Guarani	gn	Swedish	sv
Gujarati	gu	Tagalog	tl

Table 2-2 Language Codes (*continued*)

Language	ISO 639-1 Code	Language	ISO 639-1 Code
Haitian Creole	ht	Tajik	tg
Hausa	ha	Tamil	ta
Hebrew	he, iw	Tatar	tt
Hindi	hi	Telugu	te
Hungarian	hu	Thai	th
Icelandic	is	Tibetan	bo
Ido	io	Tigrinya	ti
Indonesian	id, in	Tonga	to
Interlingua	ia	Tsonga	ts
Interlingue	ie	Turkish	tr
Inuktitut	iu	Turkmen	tk
Inupiak	ik	Twi	tw
Irish	ga	Uighur	ug
Italian	it	Ukrainian	uk
Japanese	ja	Urdu	ur
Javanese	jv	Uzbek	uz
Kannada	kn	Vietnamese	vi
Kashmiri	ks	Volapük	vo
Kazakh	kk	Wallon	wa
Kinyarwanda (Ruanda)	rw	Welsh	cy
Kirghiz	ky	Wolof	wo
Kirundi (Rundi)	rn	Xhosa	xh
Korean	ko	Yiddish	yi, ji
Kurdish	ku	Yoruba	yo
Laothian	lo	Zulu	zu

Table 2-2 Language Codes

If an EPUB were to have a default language of French, the attribute would appear as follows:

```
<html lang="fr">
```

version This attribute is not part of the <html> tag. Rather, it precedes the <html> tag at the beginning of the XHTML file and specifies the version of the current HTML file. Since most pages are XHTML, the line needed in each XHTML file is

```
<!DOCTYPE html PUBLIC "-//W3C//DTD XHTML 1.1//EN"
"http://www.w3.org/TR/xhtml11/DTD/xhtml11.dtd">
```

The version comes before the <html> tag at the beginning of the XHTML file.

xmlns An XML namespace for the XHTML document can be specified. Some documentation may say it is required, but the default of xmlns="http://www.w3.org/1999/xhtml" is used if the attribute is left out.

You will see later in this chapter as we look at and create sample EPUB files that Sigil automatically places the default XML namespace for you. For example:

```
<html xmlns="http://www.w3.org/1999/xhtml">
```

xml:lang If your XHTML file will be treated as an XML file, then you may use the xml:lang attribute. The codes used are the same listed in Table 2-2. If you specify the lang attribute, it is best practice to also specify the xml:lang as well. See the following for the French language:

```
<html lang="fr" xml:lang="fr">
```

head

The <head> tag contains all the elements within the first section of the XHTML file called head. Elements within the XHTML head portion inherit any attributes in the <head> tag, as discussed in the previous "html" section.

Keep in mind that within the head section of the file, there must be a <title> element, covered a little later in the chapter. In addition, none of the information in the head section is displayed by the reading system.

The attributes available for the <head> tag are listed in Table 2-3.

Keep in mind that you can use no attributes, all of them, or some of them. Use only what is required so problems do not arise within the EPUB due to conflicting information.

Attribute	Value	Description
id	*string*	Specifies the id of page to allow it to be linked to
lang	*language type*	Specifies the language displayed by the file
xml:lang	*language type*	Specifies the language displayed by the file when parsed as XML

Table 2-3 <head> Attributes

dir The optional dir attribute specifies the direction of the text. It can be left-to-right (ltr) or right-to-left (rtl). By default, the text direction will be used based on the reading device, but these can be overridden.

For example, if we have an XHTML document that will display text in English, the direction would be left-to-right. In this case, the <head> tag would be:

```
<head dir="ltr">
```

id The id is an attribute that can have a unique value within all the XHTML files within the EPUB. No two id's can be the same; this is very important. The value cannot be blank, but must have one or more characters. The first character must be a letter (a–z) and followed by numbers, hyphens, underscores, or periods. The value is case-sensitive when referenced by an anchor (<a>).

If we have an XHTML file that is Chapter 1 of a book, we can place the following within the document:

```
<head id="chapter1">
```

If a table of contents is made for the EPUB, then the listing for Chapter 1 in the table of contents can be linked to the individual file. This works well when each chapter is its own XHTML file.

lang Within an EPUB, the reader device should check each XHTML document to determine the language. If no language attribute is found, the device should check any XML files that have been processed within the document. If nothing is found, the final place to determine the language is from the OPF file (see Chapter 6).

The various language codes are shown in Table 2-2.

If an EPUB were to have a default language of Italian, for example, the attribute would appear as follows:

```
<head lang="it">
```

xml:lang If your XHTML file will be treated as an XML file, then you may optionally use the xml:lang attribute. The codes used are the same listed in Table 2-2. If you specify the lang attribute, it is best practice to also specify the xml:lang. See the following for the Italian language:

```
<head lang="it" xml:lang="it">
```

title

The <title> tag specifies the title of the XHTML document. Keep in mind that this tag is required, but it can be blank. The EPUB title displayed on the reading device is not taken from this tag. The contents of the tag will have no bearing on the EPUB or be visible to the reader unless they view the XHTML files.

Table 2-4 lists the attributes available for the <title> tag.

Attribute	Value	Description
id	*String*	Specifies the id of page to allow it to be linked to
lang	*language type*	Specifies the language displayed by the file
xml:lang	*language type*	Specifies the language displayed by the file when parsed as XML

Table 2-4 <title> Attributes

id The id is an attribute that can have a unique value within all the XHTML files within the EPUB. No two id's can be the same; this is important. The value cannot be blank, but must have one or more characters. The character must be a letter (a–z) and followed by numbers, hyphens, underscores, or periods. The value is case-sensitive when referenced by an anchor (<a>).

If we have an XHTML file that is Chapter 2 of a book, we can place the following within the document:

```
<title id="chapter2">
```

If a table of contents is made for the EPUB, then the listing for Chapter 2 in the table of contents can be linked to the individual file. This works extremely well when each chapter is its own XHTML file.

lang Within an EPUB, the reader device should check each XHTML document to determine the language. If no language attribute is found, the device should check any XML files that have been processed within the document. If nothing is found, the final place to determine the language is from the OPF file (see Chapter 6).

The various language codes are shown in Table 2-2.

If an EPUB were to have a default language of Russian, the attribute would appear as follows:

```
<title lang="ru">
```

xml:lang If your XHTML file will be treated as an XML file, then you may use the xml:lang attribute. The codes used are the same listed in Table 2-2. If you specify the lang attribute, it is best practice to also specify the xml:lang. See the following for the Russian language:

```
<title lang="ru" xml:lang="ru">
```

body

The <body> tag contains all the elements within the second section of the XHTML file called body. The body section contains the elements that display the text that appears on the reading device. The body section is the true heart of the publication.

The attributes available for the <body> tag are listed in Table 2-5.

NOTE

Tables with grayed rows are deprecated in HTML 5.0. The attributes can be found in Cascading Style Sheets (CSS) or at least emulated by CSS (see Chapter 3). The attributes are listed in case you come across them in an EPUB.

Attribute	Value	Description
alink	*color*	Color of a link when it is chosen.
link	*color*	Color of unvisited links.
vlink	*color*	Color of the visited links.
background	*url*	Background image to be used as wallpaper for the XHTML file. The image is repeated continuously.
bgcolor	*color*	Color of background for XHTML file.
bgproperties	*fixed*	The background image is displayed only once and the text displayed scrolls over it.
text	*color*	Color of the text displayed.

Table 2-5 <body> Attributes

Text

The text tags will usually make up most of the XHTML tags in a document. These tags are the heart of the EPUB. There are 24 tags in the text module:

- Headers (h1, h2, h3, h4, h5, h6)
- p
- div
- span
- br
- blockquote
- pre
- address
- code
- kbd
- samp
- var
- cite
- dfn
- q
- abbr
- acronym
- em
- strong

Headers (h1, h2, h3, h4, h5, h6)

The header tags are used to start chapters and indicate titles. Text that is similar in function to a title and that needs to stand out should be a header. The headers are larger and bolder than normal text. The size ranges from the largest (h1) to the smallest (h6).

Headers are also used in Sigil to create a table of contents that a reading device can use to allow a reader to maneuver through a book, discussed in Chapter 5.

The attributes available for the header tags are listed in Table 2-6.

p

The paragraph tag, <p>, is used to signify the beginning and ending of a paragraph. The attributes available for the paragraph tag are listed in Table 2-7.

Attribute	Value	Description
align	left	Text is aligned to the left side of the display
	right	Text is aligned to the right side of the display
	center	Text is aligned in the center of the display
	justify	Text is spaced out to fill the display left to right

Table 2-6 <header> Attributes

Attribute	Value	Description
align	left	Text is aligned to the left side of the display
	right	Text is aligned to the right side of the display
	center	Text is aligned in the center of the display
	justify	Text is spaced out to fill the display left to right

Table 2-7 <p> Attributes

div

The division tag, <div>, is used to select elements and assign them a style using CSS. The <div> tag can include as many other tags as needed, even of different types.

Table 2-8 lists the attributes available for the division tag.

span

The <span> tag is used to select a portion of another tag, such as a paragraph, and apply a style to that portion.

br

The <br /> tag is used as a line break and can appear in the center of a paragraph or outside one. The attribute available for the <br /> tag is listed in Table 2-9.

id The id is an attribute that can have a unique value within all the XHTML files within the EPUB. No two id's can be the same; this is important. The value cannot be blank, but must have one or more characters. The first character must be a letter (a–z) and followed by numbers, hyphens, underscores, or periods. The value is case-sensitive when referenced by an anchor (<a>).

Attribute	Value	Description
Align	left	Text is aligned to the left side of the display
	right	Text is aligned to the right side of the display
	center	Text is aligned in the center of the display
	justify	Text is spaced out to fill the display left to right

Table 2-8 <div> Attributes

Attribute	Value	Description
id	*string*	Specifies the id of page to allow it to be linked to

Table 2-9
 Attribute

If you include a break between lines and you want to add a link to go to it, you use the following:

```
<br id="chapter1break">
```

blockquote and q

When one or more paragraphs will contain quoted text, the text can be out in paragraph tags and enclosed in <blockquote> tags. The tag should automatically include the quotation marks, so these are not placed within the <p> tags.

When a short quotation is used and the quote remains part of a paragraph, use <q> and not <blockquote>. Remember the <q> tag adds quotation marks.

The attribute available for the <blockquote> and <q> tags is listed in Table 2-10.

cite The cite attribute is used to specify the source of the quoted material. However, the reading device doesn't display the cited URL. The cite attribute is for those who may look at the XHTML code within the EPUB file. A sample blockquote would be as follows:

```
<blockquote cite="http://en.wikipedia.org/wiki/EPUB">
<p>EPUB (short for electronic publication; alternatively capitalized as ePub,
ePUB, EPub, or epub, with "EPUB" preferred by the vendor) is a free and open
e-book standard by the International Digital Publishing Forum (IDPF). Files
have the extension .epub.</p>
</blockquote>
```

A quote tag looks like this:

```
<p>Marcus Tullius Cicero said, <q cite="http://www.goodreads.com/
author/show/13755.Marcus_Tullius_Cicero">A room without books is like
a body without a soul.</q></p>
```

Attribute	Value	Description
cite	*url*	The URL source of the quoted text

Table 2-10 <blockquote> and <q> Attribute

pre

Preformatted text is text that is displayed in a fixed-width font. A fixed-width font is one where each character has the same width as all the other characters. The <pre> tag also keeps all spaces and line breaks. XHTML normally drops extra spaces and only preserves one; but in <pre>, multiple spaces are preserved. For example:

```
<pre>
This text will be displayed
exactly as it is typed with line breaks
and          extra spaces.
</pre>
```

address

The <address> tag is used to indicate the text is contact information, such as a physical address. Most reading devices will display the address in italics and add a line break before and after the address tags.

The following example shows a physical address:

```
<address>
John Doe<br />
Some Street<br />
Someplace, Some-State, 00000
</address>
```

code

The <code> tag is used to show the specified text is computer code. The code is displayed as a fixed-width font, like addresses, and may be a smaller font.

The following shows a code example:

```
<code>X=2</code>
<code>Y=4+X</code>
<code>Print Y</code>
```

kbd

The <kbd> tag is used to show that specific keys on the keyboard are pressed. The text is displayed as a fixed-width font.

The following shows a keyboard example:

```
<p>Select the program in Windows you want to shut down, then press
<kbd>ALT</kbd> and <kbd>F4</kbd></p>
```

samp

Sometimes you may need to show sample output from code. The <samp> tag allows you to do this, and the code is a small, fixed-width font.

The following shows an output sample:

```
<samp>X=1</samp>
```

var

When variables are used and need to be noted as such, the <var> tag is used. The variable will be italicized.

The following shows a variable sample:

```
<p>The <var>value</var> for the align attribute for the p tag is set
to 'Left'.</p>
```

cite

If a citation is made, then the cite tag displays the text in italics. The following shows a cited example:

```
<p>Alexandre Dumas wrote <cite>The Three Musketeers</cite>.</p>
```

dfn

When a definition is used, the word or words being defined should be marked. In this case, the <dfn> tag will be displayed in italics. If a device doesn't render the <dfn> tag properly, you can use CSS to make it appear as you wish.

The following shows a definition example:

```
<p><dfn>Example</dfn> is when a rule is illustrated. </p>
```

abbr and acronyms

Including both abbreviations and the full unabbreviated text can take up a lot of space in a document. An abbr tag can be used instead and assigned the full unabbreviated text. On a web browser, a user can place the mouse over the abbreviation, and a text box will appear with the unabbreviated text in it. Most reading devices will not do this, though. Be aware if your specific reading device renders the <abbr> tag properly.

Similar to abbreviations, including acronyms and the text they represent can take up a lot of space in a document. Like with abbreviations, on a web browser, a user can place the mouse over the acronym and a text box will appear with the full text in it.

Most reading devices will not do this, though. Be aware if your specific reading device renders the <acronym> tag properly.

NOTE

Download the EPUB tester file from the McGraw-Hill website and place the file on your device. Go to the page on the <abbr> tag and see how it works on your device.

The attribute available for the <abbr> and <acronym> tags is listed in Table 2-11.

title The title attribute is used to specify the meaning of the abbreviation that shows up in a browser when the mouse is hovered over the abbreviation. Be aware that some devices do not support this feature.

An <abbr> example follows:

```
<p>I know a guy named <abbr title="Calvin">Cal</abbr>.</p>
```

An <acronym> example is shown next:

```
<p>The chapter you are reading is about <acronym title="eXtensible
HyperText Markup Language">XHTML</acronym>.</p>
```

em

The emphasis tag will place emphasis on a word or group of words by displaying it in italicized text. For example:

```
<p>The last word has <em>emphasis</em>.</p>
```

strong

The strong tag gives the indicated word or words emphasis by displaying it in bold. For example:

```
<p>The last word is <strong>strong</strong>.</p>
```

Attribute	Value	Description
title	*String*	A string that represents the full text of the abbreviation

Table 2-11 <abbr> and <acronym> Attribute

Hypertext

The hypertext tag is used to define a link to allow access to other text or information. There is one tag in the hypertext module: a.

a

A link or hyperlink is text or an image that, when selected, moves you to the place to which the link points. The link can refer to another page, a specific place on another page, or a specific place on the same page.

To go to another page, use the href attribute as shown:

```
<a href="OtherPage.xhtml">
```

To go to a specific place on another page, an id attribute needs to be set up and the href lists the other page, then a pound sign (#), followed by the unique ID name. For example:

```
<a href="OtherPage.xhtml#somewhere">
```

To go to a specific spot in the current page, use the following:

```
<a href="#somewhere>
```

The attributes used with the <a> tag are listed in Table 2-12.

Attribute	Value	Description
href	*url*	Hyperlink reference to another place, whether it is a different XHTML file or the current one
id	*string*	A unique ID to which a hyperlink is attached
charset	*encoding*	Encoding value for the target page, such as UTF-8
type	*mime type*	Mime type value of target file
shape	circ, poly, rect	Specifies the shape of an image that references a hyperlink
cords	*circle* *X,Y,radius*	For a circular shape, three values are required indicating the center (X,Y) and the radius (r)
	rect *X1,Y1,X2,Y2*	For a rectangular shape, four values are required indicating the top-left corner (X1,Y1) and the bottom-right corner (X2,Y2)
	poly *X1,Y1,X2,Y2,...*	For a polygon, any number of coordinates (X,Y) can be specified

Table 2-12 <a> Attributes

href The reference to the hyperlink in an EPUB will be to another XHTML file or a place within the current file. Some books that have a section of all the footnotes will have a hyperlink from the word or phrase to the footnote entry. The footnote entry will have a link back to the relevant hyperlink, as shown in the example:

```
<a href="../Text/Footnotes.xhtml#F25" id="Link-25"><sup>25</sup></a>
```

The link in the footnote section would look like the following:

```
<p><a href="../Text/Chapter-1.xhtml#Link-25" id="F25">25.</a> This is
the information for Footnote 25.</p>
```

If the first example is part of Chapter 1 (called chapter-1.xhtml) and the link has an ID of Link-25, we can link back to it using that ID. The hyperlink is going to a file called Footnotes.xhtml and specifically to an ID called F25. Notice how the link is a superscript (discussed later in this chapter).

The second example is in a file called Footnotes.xhtml with an ID of F25. The link to Chapter-1 and ID Link-25 will take the reader back to the referring hyperlink. By setting it up this way, the reader does not need to maneuver around the EPUB page by page. Footnotes do not need to be placed in the same document. Footnotes may not even appear on the same page the reader is reading. Reading devices allow for font sizes to be changed, so the text on the display may not always be the same.

If the IDs were removed from the example, the reader would be taken to the beginning of the footnotes. When selecting the first example, the reader would then have to scroll down through the pages to find the specific entry needed. When the second hyperlink was chosen, they would be taken back to the beginning of Chapter-1, where they would have to scroll down to find where they had stopped reading.

id The id identifies the specific spot to which the link (href) is referencing. The id is only needed when the link points to a specific spot within a document. Within each XHTML file, the id's must be unique. If two id's are identical, the link will take the reader to the first link. An <a> tag can have both an href and an id, as shown:

```
<a href="../Text/Footnotes.xhtml#F25" id="Link-25"><sup>25</sup></a>
```

charset The hyperlink may refer to a file that does not have the same encoding as the current file. The link may specify the encoding of the linked file as follows:

```
<p>You need to go to a file encoded differently found <a
charset="utf-16" href="../Text/footnote.xhtml#25">here</a>.</p>
```

NOTE

Be aware that with some reading devices the filenames for the XHTML files are case-sensitive. If the file is called Footnotes.xhtml, you cannot put footnotes.xhtml in the href statement. It must be Footnotes.xhtml.

type The file type linked to can be specified by its media type. Chapter 1, Table 1-6, and Table 1-7 covered the various media types. For instance, if a reference is made to a picture, a hyperlink can be set to show a JPG file:

```
<p>The <a href="../images/MonaLisa.jpg" type="image/jpeg">Mona Lisa</
a> is a famous painting.</p>
```

shape Text is not the only way to use a hyperlink. Sometimes an image is used as a hyperlink, such as a picture of a button. Three options can be used to specify the shape: rectangle (rect), circle (circ), and polygon (poly).

As an example, let's assume a square button is used as a link to another file; the code would be as follows:

```
<a href="../images/MonaLisa.jpg" shape="rect" type="image/jpg"><img
alt="button" src="../Images/button.JPG" /></a>
```

In this case, the button that is displayed by the image tag (<img>), which is covered later, is a rectangle. When the button is selected, the MonaLisa.jpg file is shown.

coords If an image is to be split up into sections, you can specify coordinates for each hyperlink. The three ways to do this are rectangle, circle, and polygon. Unlike the previous example, you use the object tag (<object>), covered later.

The coordinates for a rectangle are the top-left corner (X1,Y1) and then the bottom-right corner (X2,Y2). If a rectangle is 200 pixels wide and 100 pixels tall, for example, to split the button into two equal sections, you would use the following:

```
<object alt="Button" data="../Images/Button.jpg" height="100" width="200"
shapes="shapes" usemap="#button" ></object>
 <map name="button">
    <a coords="1,1,100,100" href="../images/MonaLisa.jpg" shape="rect"></a>
    <a coords="101,1,200,200" href="../images/David.jpg" shape="rect"></a>
</map>
```

The <map> tag is covered later, but you can see the two cords attributes. The first one starts at the top left (1,1) and ends in the center bottom of the button at (100,100).

If this area is selected, a picture of the Mona Lisa appears. If the area of the right half of the image is selected (101,1)-(200,200), then an image of David is shown.

When a circle section is used, the coordinates are the center of the circle (X,Y) and then the radius of the circle (R). So the coordinates of a circle that has a center at point (50,50) and a radius of 30 would be as follows:

```
<a coords="50,50,30" href="../images/MonaLisa.jpg" shape="circ"></a>
```

If a polygon is used, a set of as many points needed is listed, as shown:

```
<a coords="1,1,50,50,100,100,50,50,100,1,1,100" href="../images/
MonaLisa.jpg" shape="poly"></a>
```

In the previous example, the coordinates would be a big X in a box with a dimension of 100 pixels by 100 pixels. If someone clicked on the X, a picture of Mona Lisa would appear.

List

The list section is a set of tags used to create bulleted lists of items. There are six tags in the list module:

- ol
- ul
- li
- dl
- dt
- dd

ol

An ordered list displays items in a specific order, such as a set of directions to get to a specific location. The items must be done in the order given or you will not arrive at your destination.

Table 2-13 lists the attributes used with the <ol> tag.

Attribute	Value	Description
start	*number*	Specifies the number of the first item when numbering the list
type	*bullet_type*	Specifies the style to use, such as bullets or numbering

Table 2-13 <ol> Attributes

Attribute	Value	Description
type	*bullet_type*	Specifies the style to use, such as bullets or no bullets

Table 2-14 <ul> Attribute

ul

An unordered list is used when the order of the items doesn't matter. For example, a shopping list may have no order and usually doesn't require it.

The attribute used with the <ul> tag is listed in Table 2-14.

li

When using an ordered or unordered list, there must be items within it. The list items, indicated by <li>, create the list itself. Once a list is designated as either ordered or unordered and the style type is set, the list can be created.

For example, consider this partial list of books by Jules Verne:

```
<ul type="circle">
      <li>Journey to the Center of the Earth</li>
      <li>20,000 Leagues Under the Sea</li>
      <li>Around the World in 80 Days</li>
</ul>
```

dl, dt, dd

The definition list is used for items such as glossaries. The list is contained by the <dl> tag. The defined term is noted by the <dt> tag and a description of the term is in the <dd> tags.

An example of using a definition list to define EPUB is as follows:

```
<dl>
      <dt>EPUB</dt>
      <dd>A free and open e-book standard by the International Digital
Publishing Forum (IDPF).</dd>
</dl>
```

Object

The object section is a set of tags used to embed objects into the document, which is different from a link. As previously discussed in the "Hypertext" section, a link can be selected to go somewhere else in the EPUB. If you wanted to have a picture or some object appear at a specific place in the text, you would use an object and not a link.

There are two tags in the object module:

- object
- param

object

The <object> tag can be used to embed images instead of the <img> tag, which is discussed later in this chapter. For EPUB 3, audio and video can be embedded into the XHTML file as an object.

NOTE

Be aware that some reading devices may not handle the object tag, so the img tag may be preferable.

The attributes for the <object> tag are listed in Table 2-15.

Attribute	Value	Description
alt	*string*	Alternate text displayed when image cannot be shown; used for visually impaired readers
data	*url*	Location and name of the object
type	*mime_type*	Specifies the MIME type of the object
shapes		If the shapes attribute is present, then <a> tags are used to specify a shaped hyperlink in the object
usemap	*url*	Specifies the image map for use with the object
align	bottom	The bottom of object should align with the bottom of the lowest element on the line
	textbottom	The bottom of object should align with the bottom of normal text on the line
	middle	The center of the object is in line with the center of normal text
	top	The top of the object should align with the top of the tallest element on the line
	texttop	The top of the object should align with the top of the tallest text on the line

Table 2-15 <object> Attributes

Attribute	Value	Description
	left	The object is on the left side of the display
	right	The object is on the right side of the display
border	*number*	Width of border box in pixels
hspace	*number*	Number of pixels on either side of the object that acts as a margin so text does not overlap the object
vspace	*number*	Number of pixels on the top and bottom of object that acts as a margin so text does not overlap the object
height	*number*	Height in pixels of the object
width	*number*	Width in pixels of the object

Table 2-15 <object> Attributes (*continued*)

alt The alt attribute gives a description of the object that should be displayed when the image cannot be shown. For visually impaired readers, this descriptive text is usually read to describe the object being embedded. The description can be as precise as you wish to make it.

```
<p><object alt="Centered button" align="middle" data="../Images/
button.jpg"></object>Text that button is centered with.</p>
```

data The value of the data attribute specifies the object, as you can see from the previous examples in the "Object" section. An example of an SVG image is similar, as shown:

```
<p><object data="../Images/face.svg"></object></p>
```

type The type of file being embedded by the data attribute can be specified by its media type. Chapter 1, Table 1-6, and Table 1-7 listed the various media types. For instance, an embedded JPG image is illustrated by the following:

```
<p><object data="../Images/MonaLisa.jpg" type="image/jpeg"></object></p>
```

shapes If an object has hyperlinks and anchors associated with one or more shaped areas, the shapes attribute must be used. Once the attribute is specified, then the <a> tags are used before the end object tag to reference the shapes. For more information, see the <a> tag in the "Hypertext" section in this chapter.

```
<object alt="Button" data="../Images/Button.jpg" height="100" width="100"
shapes="shapes" usemap="#button" ></object>
 <map name="button">
    <a coords="1,1,100,100" href="../images/MonaLisa.jpg" shape="rect"></a>
 </map>
```

In this example, the attribute is given as: shapes="shapes" for the objects tag.

usemap The usemap attribute is needed on an object with anchors and hyperlinks to specify a map name. The name starts with a pound sign (#) and is used in the map tag name attribute without the pound sign to join the object and coordinates for the hyperlinks.

```
<object alt="Clickable button" data="../Images/Button.jpg" height="100"
width="100" shapes="shapes" usemap="#button" ></object>
 <map name="button">
    <a coords="1,1,100,100" href="../Images/MonaLisa.jpg" shape="rect"></a>
 </map>
```

param

The <param> tag can be used to pass parameters to embedded objects that work as controls. For instance, the parameter can be passed to an audio control to play an audio file. The parameters allowed are dependent on the object itself, so documentation for the embedded object should be consulted for proper parameter values and attributes.

Presentation

The presentation tags are used to present the text in various ways. There are seven tags in the presentation module:

- b
- big
- small
- sub
- sup
- tt
- hr

b

The bold element is used to display text in bold lettering. There are no attributes for the bold element. An example follows:

```
<p>The last word is <b>bold</b>.</p>
```

big

The <big> tag changes text to at least one font size larger than the normal text. The size it becomes will vary depending on the reading system.

The <big> tag has no attributes, as shown:

```
<p>The last word is <big>bigger</big>.</p>
```

small

Similar to the <big> tag, the <small> tag reduces the text by at least one font size, depending on the reading system.

The small tag has no attributes, as shown:

```
<p>The last word is <small>smaller</small>.</p>
```

sub

Occasionally subscripts are needed. The <sub> tag has no attributes. An example follows:

```
<p>The chemical formula for water is H<sub>2</sub>O.</p>
```

sup

Superscripts can be handy for counting and addresses. The <sup> tag has no attributes. An example follows:

```
<p>I live on 3<sup>rd</sup> Street.</p>
```

tt

The teletype tag is used to emulate teletype text. The text is displayed in a fixed-width font, sometimes called monospace. The tag is rarely used and can be emulated with CSS, as discussed in Chapter 3.

An example follows:

```
<p>The paper showed the caption, <tt>Happy New Year!</tt></p>
```

Attribute	Value	Description
color	*color*	Specifies the color of the horizontal rule
noshade	noshade	Removes any shading, if supported; may also remove color
size	*number*	Height in pixels of the horizontal rule
width	*number*	Width in pixels

Table 2-16 <hr> Attributes

hr

In some books or other publications, a horizontal line or rule is useful to separate sections. Horizontal rules can be manipulated with a few types of attributes, as listed in Table 2-16.

NOTE

Even though the <hr> tag has attributes, it has no closing tag.

Edit

The edit tags are used to show edited material when numerous people are working on a publication. There are two tags in the edit module:

- del
- ins

del and ins

If text has been removed from the publication, the del tag will show a line through the text. The insert tag shows text that has been inserted to correct a deletion if needed and is shown as underlined. Both tags have the same two attributes available (see Table 2-17).

Attribute	Value	Description
cite	*url*	URL to the document that explains why text was deleted or inserted
datetime	*YYYY-MM-DDThh:mm:ssTZD*	Date and time when text was deleted or inserted

Table 2-17 <del> and <ins> Attributes

cite When some text has been deleted or inserted, the cite attribute points to a document that shows why the text was changed. For example, if an acronym is incorrectly identified, the website can be cited showing the correct acronym.

```
<p>The <del cite="www.idpf.org">IPDF</del><ins cite="www.idpf.
org">IDPF</ins>  created the EPUB standard.</p>
```

datetime The datetime attribute shows when the change was made. The format is *YYYY-MM-DDThh:mm:ssTZD*. There should be four digits for the year, two for the month, and two for the day. The date is then followed by a T, which is necessary, then followed by two digits for the hour on the 24-hour clock, two digits for the minutes, and two for the seconds. Finally, there is a Z showing Zulu or Greenwich Mean Time. An example follows:

```
<p>The <del datetime="2013-02-21T15:33:12Z">IPDF</del><ins
datetime="2013-02-21T15:33:12Z">IDPF</ins> created the EPUB
standard.</p>
```

Bidirectional Text

The bidirectional text tag is used to specify the direction that the text should be displayed. Not all languages are read from left to right. There is one tag in the bidirectional text module: bdo.

bdo

The bidirectional override tag is used to specify the direction of the text. There is one attribute available for the tag, shown in Table 2-18.

The <bdo> tag is usually used when embedding text from a different language. However, there are other uses, as shown:

```
<p>Sometimes it may be fun to read things backwards, such as
Hippopotamus - <bdo dir="rtl">Hippopotamus</bdo>.</p>
```

Attribute	Value	Description
dir	ltr	Text flows left-to-right
	rtl	Text flows right-to-left

Table 2-18 <bdo> Attribute

Table

The table tag is used to create tables in your publication. There are ten tags in the table module:

- table
- tr
- td
- th
- thead
- tbody
- tfoot
- caption
- col
- colgroup

table

The table tag is used to contain the contents of the table. The table is made up of a header, body, and footer. Generically, the table can consist of only the table rows. The table tag has nine attributes, as listed in Table 2-19.

Attribute	Value	Description
summary	*string*	Descriptive information about the table for speech-enabled devices
align	left	Table is to the left of the display (this is the default)
	center	Table is centered in the display
	right	Table is to the right of the display
bgcolor	*color*	Background color for the table
border	*number*	Width of a table border in pixels
cellpadding	*number*	Space between the cell edge and the cell content in pixels
cellspacing	*number*	Space between borders of cells in pixels
frame	void	No outermost border of table
	above	Outermost border on top only
	below	Outermost border on bottom only
	hsides	Outermost border on top and bottom only

Table 2-19 <table> Attributes

Attribute	Value	Description
	lhs	Table border on left side only
	rhs	Table border on right side only
	vsides	Outermost border on left and right sides only
	box | border	Border on all sides of the table
rules	none	No inner borders
	groups	Borders between groups only
	rows	Horizontal row borders only
	cols	Vertical column borders only
	all	Horizontal and vertical borders between rows and columns
width	*number*	Width of table in pixels

Table 2-19 <table> Attributes (*continued*)

summary For the visually impaired, text information can be read to them by a device with speech capability. With tables, the device will read the text listed in the summary attribute.

```
<table summary="The table shows the earnings for the fiscal year.">
```

tr

The table row tag is used to contain the data fields that will make up a row of cells for the table. Of course, the <tr> tags are contained within the <table> tags, as previously discussed. The <tr> tag is used for regular rows of data, while the <th> tag is for table headings. (The <th> tag will be covered next.) The <tr> tag has three attributes, listed in Table 2-20.

td and th

The table data tag (<td>) is used to designate a single cell of text, while the table header tag (<th>) is for the column headers. By default, the data cells are left-aligned in normal text. The headers are bold and horizontally centered by default. These two tags signify different cell types, but have the same attributes. The attributes for the <td> and <th> tags are listed in Table 2-21.

Attribute	Value	Description
align	left	Text is moved to the cell's left
	center	Text is moved to the cell's center
	right	Text is moved to the cell's right
	justified	Text within the cell fills whole cell
bgcolor	*color*	Background color for the row
valign	top	Text aligned with top of cell
	middle	Text aligned with center of cell
	bottom	Text aligned with bottom of cell
	baseline	First line of text is on the same horizontal line

Table 2-20 <tr> Attributes

thead, tbody, tfoot

Tables may not always be set up with a table header, body, and footer. By using these tags, it is easier to manipulate the look of the table's sections.

Attribute	Value	Description
align	left	Text is moved to the cell's left
	center	Text is moved to the cell's center
	right	Text is moved to the cell's right
	justified	Text within the cell fills the whole cell
bgcolor	*color*	Background color for the row
valign	top	Text aligned with top of cell
	middle	Text aligned with center of cell
	bottom	Text aligned with bottom of cell
	baseline	First line of text is on the same horizontal line

Table 2-21 <td> and <th> Attributes

NOTE

The order of the three tags are <thead>, then <tfoot>, then <tbody>.

The layout is as follows:

```
<table>
     <thead>
             Place Head elements here
     </thead>
     <tfoot>
             Place Foot elements here
     </tfoot>
     <tbody>
             Place Body elements here
     </tbody>
</table>
```

The <thead>, <tfoot>, and <tbody> tags have two attributes (see Table 2-22).

caption

Some tables need a caption to specify what the table represents. Where the caption is placed is managed by its single attribute (see Table 2-23), which appears directly after the opening table tag.

Attribute	Value	Description
align	left	Text is moved to the cell's left
	center	Text is moved to the cell's center
	right	Text is moved to the cell's right
valign	top	Text aligned with top of cell
	bottom	Text aligned with bottom of cell

Table 2-22 <thead>, <tfoot>, and <tbody> Attributes

Attribute	Value	Description
align	top	Caption is placed on the top of the table
	bottom	Caption is placed on the bottom of the table

Table 2-23 <caption> Attribute

col and colgroup

The <col> and <colgroup> tags are used to specify attributes on whole columns instead of individual cells. The <col> tag can be used individually or with <colgroup>. The tags have the same attributes shown in Table 2-24, but may be supported differently on various devices.

span When attributes need to be specified for a certain number of columns, the span attribute is used to tell how many columns are affected. If span is not used, then the <col> tag only manipulates one column. A separate <col> tag can be used for each column even if the attributes are the same. The tags are placed after the <table> tag but before the <tr> tags. For instance, if the first two columns were supposed to be yellow and the third blue, the following code could be used:

```
<col span="2" bgcolor="yellow" />
<col bgcolor="blue" />
```

If <colgroup> were to be used, it would be as shown:

```
<colgroup span="2" bgcolor="yellow">
</colgroup>
<colgroup span="1" bgcolor="blue">
</colgroup>
```

Attribute	Value	Description
span	*number*	Specifies the number of columns that are manipulated
align	left	Text in column cells are to the left
	right	Text in column cells are to the right
	center	Text in column cells are centered
	justify	Text within the cell fills the whole cell
bgcolor	*color*	Background color for the row
valign	top	Text aligned with top of cell
	bottom	Text aligned with bottom of cell
width	*number*	Width of column cells in pixels

Table 2-24 <col> and <colgroup> Attributes

Image

The image tag is used to embed images into the publication. This is useful for showing covers, pictures, maps, etc. There is one tag in the image module: img.

img

The <img> tag is used either to insert an image into the text or to display it by itself. EPUB 2 supports JPG, GIF, PNG, and SVG images. More details are given about the various formats in Chapter 4. Table 2-25 shows the image attributes.

NOTE

SVG images require a height and width value to match the image size. Otherwise, the image may be displayed with scroll bars. The SVG image will not shrink or enlarge as other image files do when the height and width are changed. Sometimes it may be best to only specify height or width but not both. In the case of an SVG image, however, both should be specified.

Attribute	Value	Description
alt	*text*	Alternate text for the image
src	*url*	The URL of the image file
usemap	*#mapname*	Name to use when making a client-side image map
align	top	Image is aligned with the top of the tallest line element
	bottom	Image is aligned with the bottom of the lowest line element
	middle	Image is centered with the line
	left	Image is to the left side of the display
	right	Image is to the right side of the display
border	*number*	Width of border in pixels
height	*number*	Height of image in pixels
hspace	*number*	Margin size in pixels to the left and right of image
vspace	*number*	Margin size in pixels to the top and bottom of image
width	*number*	Width of an image in pixels

Table 2-25 <img> Attributes

alt The alt attribute is used to specify alternate text that is displayed when an image cannot be shown. The alternate text is also used for systems that read the content out loud for visually impaired people. The <alt> attribute is required for the image tag. An example follows:

```
<p><img alt="Mona Lisa" src="../Images/Mona Lisa.jpg" /></p>
```

src The source image is the path and filename of the image itself. The src attribute is required for the tag.

```
<p><img alt="Mona Lisa" src="../Images/Mona Lisa.jpg" /></p>
```

usemap The usemap attribute is needed on an image with anchors and hyperlinks to specify a map name. The name starts with a pound sign (#) and is used in the map tag name attribute without the pound sign to join the object and coordinates for the hyperlinks.

```
<image alt="Clickable button" src="../Images/Button.jpg" usemap="#button" />
 <map name="button">
    <a coords="1,1,100,100" href="../images/MonaLisa.jpg" shape="rect"></a>
 </map>
```

Client-Side Image Map

The client-side image map tags are used to specify portions of an image to use as a hyperlink. There are two tags in the client-side image map module:

- area
- map

area

The area tag is used to signify coordinates that are clickable in an image. There are six attributes for the area tag, as shown in Table 2-26.

alt The alt attribute is used to specify alternate text that is displayed when an image cannot be shown. The alternate text is also used for systems that read the content out

Attribute	Value	Description
alt	*text*	Alternate text for the image
href	*url*	Reference to hyperlink target
nohref	nohref	Specifies that no hyperlinked reference is linked to the area
shape	circ, poly, rect	Specifies the shape of an image that references a hyperlink
cords	*circle* *X,Y,radius*	For a circular shape, three values are required indicating the center (x,y) and radius
	poly *X1,Y1,X2,Y2,...*	Lists various x,y coordinates
	rect *X1,Y1,X2,Y2*	For a rectangular shape, four values are required indicating the top-left corner (X1,Y1) and the bottom-right corner (X2,Y2)

Table 2-26 <area> Attributes

loud for visually impaired people. The <alt> attribute is required for the area tag. An example follows:

```
<img id="Image-Maps" src="../Images/Face.jpg" usemap="#Image-Maps" border="0"
width="600" height="600" alt="" />
<map name="Image-Maps">
<area shape="poly"
coords="195,165,210,196,224,177,220,144,208,141,197,152,196,163,196,181,"
href="area.xhtml#left-eye" alt="Left Eye" />
```

href The hyperlink reference designates the URL to go to when the specified area is selected. As with other targets within the publication, the link can go to a different XHTML file or to the same XHTML file within the EPUB. If a specific place within the target page is used, it must be preceded by a pound (#) sign, as shown in the example. Usually, specifying a web address in the href attribute should not be done.

```
<img id="Image-Maps" src="../Images/Face.jpg" usemap="#Image-Maps" border="0"
width="600" height="600" alt="" />
<map name="Image-Maps">
<area shape="poly"
coords="195,165,210,196,224,177,220,144,208,141,197,152,196,163,196,181,"
href="area.xhtml#left-eye" alt="Left Eye" />
```

nohref Usually, the areas of an image or object will be hyperlinked to a reference point. Some areas could be left with no "hotspot"—that is, no hyperlink. For consistency, every section can be set up, and for the sections with no links, use the nohref attribute. Later, if the section does need a hyperlink, the area is already defined and the nohref can be changed to href.

```
<area shape="poly"
coords="195,165,210,196,224,177,220,144,208,141,197,152,196,163,196,181,"
nohref="nohref" alt="Left Eye" />
```

shape Three options can be used to specify the shape: rectangle (rect), circle (circ), and polygon (poly). In the following example, we have a smiley face that has a hyperlink set up as the left eye. The shape is a polygon with given coordinates and a reference to a place within the document. The polygon can have numerous coordinates, always an even number since one is the X value and the other is the Y value.

```
<area shape="poly"
coords="195,165,210,196,224,177,220,144,208,141,197,152,196,163,196,181,"
href="area.xhtml#left-eye" alt="Left Eye" />
```

coords If an image is to be split up into sections, then you can specify coordinates for each hyperlink. The three ways to do this are by rectangle, circle, or polygon.

The coordinates for a rectangle are the top-left corner (X1,Y1) and then the bottom-right corner (X2,Y2). When a circle section is used, the coordinates are the center of the circle (X,Y) and then the radius of the circle (r). If a polygon is used, a set of the required points is needed, as shown in the example:

```
<area shape="poly"
coords="195,165,210,196,224,177,220,144,208,141,197,152,196,163,196,181,"
href="area.xhtml#left-eye" alt="Left Eye" />
```

map

The map attribute is used to connect the coordinates with the image or object. The connection is made by specifying a name for the usemap attribute and then using the same name for the name attribute. The one attribute is shown in Table 2-27.

Attribute	Value	Description
name	*text*	Name matching the usemap attribute to connect coordinates to the image or object

Table 2-27 <map> Attribute

name The map name is identical with the usemap name, but without the pound (#) sign. Within the beginning and ending map tags, the coordinates are given for each hyperlinked section, as shown in this example:

```
<object alt="Button" data="../Images/Button.jpg" height="100" width="200"
shapes="shapes" usemap="#button" ></object>
 <map name="button">
    <a coords="1,1,100,100" href="../images/MonaLisa.jpg" shape="rect"></a>
    <a coords=" 101,1,200,200" href="../images/David.jpg" shape="rect"></a>
 </map>
```

Meta Information

The meta information tag is used to place data about the publication within the EPUB file. There is one tag in the meta information module: meta.

meta

The meta tags are not necessary and usually are not used. The metadata is contained within the OPF file covered in Chapter 6. Any metadata contained within the XHTML file can usually be removed when it is already within the OPF. There are two attributes for the meta tag, shown in Table 2-28.

name and content The name attribute is used to specify a metadata name, such as author, description, etc. The content is the value given to the name, as shown in the example:

```
<meta name="author" content="Victor Hugo" />
```

NOTE

The metadata is not viewable except in an EPUB editor. The metadata that is displayed to a reader on a reading device is contained in the OPF.

Attribute	Value	Description
name	*string*	Specifies a metadata type
content	*string*	Specifies the value of the metadata type

Table 2-28 <meta> Attributes

Style Sheet

The style sheet tag is used to specify the Cascading Style Sheet (CSS) rules to apply to a specified tag. There is one tag in the style sheet module: style.

style

The style attribute is used to define a style to apply to the XHTML file. The style tag is used in the <head> section of the XHTML file. Styles can be defined for specific XHTML tags. Each XHTML file can have numerous styles for the various tags, as shown in the example:

```
<style type="text/css">
h1 {color:red;}
p {color:green;}
</style>
```

In this case, the <h1> header will be red and the paragraphs (<p>) will be green. The CSS styles will be covered in Chapter 3, and linking an external style sheet is covered next in the "Link" section. The <style> tag has two attributes, as shown in Table 2-29.

type The type attribute is used to specify the MIME type of the style sheet. It is set to text/css, as shown in the following example:

```
<style type="text/css">
```

Link

The link tag is used to link to an external document; for an EPUB, this is a CSS. There is one tag in the link module: link.

link

The link tag is placed in the <head> section at the beginning of the XHTML file. The best practice for a CSS is to place all the specific styles in a file and link the external sheet to the XHTML file. Multiple style sheets can be created, with none to all linked to an XHTML file. The CSS styles are covered in the next chapter. Table 2-30 lists the four attributes for the link tag.

Attribute	Value	Description
type	text/css	Specifies the MIME type of the style sheet
xml:space	preserve	Preserves whitespace within the XHTML file

Table 2-29 <style> Attributes

Attribute	Value	Description
charset	*encoding*	Encoding value for the target page, such as UTF-8
href	*url*	Location of linked resource
rel	stylesheet	Relationship between current document and linked resource
type	*string*	MIME type of the linked resource

Table 2-30 <link> Attributes

charset The linked document may be a file that does not have the same encoding as the current file. The character set may be as follows:

```
<link href="../Styles/Style.css" rel="stylesheet" type="text/css"
charset="utf-16" />
```

href A reference is made to the external resource—in this case, the CSS file. An example is shown:

```
<link href="../Styles/Style.css" rel="stylesheet" type="text/css" />
```

rel The relationship of the linked resource is a required attribute. It may not seem necessary, but it must exist. The value will be stylesheet to indicate what the CSS is to the current file.

```
<link href="../Styles/Style.css" rel="stylesheet" type="text/css" />
```

type The MIME type of the CSS file will be text/css. The type attribute should be placed on all link tags.

```
<link href="../Styles/Style.css" rel="stylesheet" type="text/css" />
```

Base

The base tag is used to specify a directory within the EPUB that will be considered a root. All directory paths given will be based on the specified root. There is one tag in the base module: base.

base

When specifying references from the many tags, a base directory can be specified as the root. If, for instance, the Images directory was specified as the base, then all image references would only require a filename. All other references to files outside of the Images directory would require paths originating from the Images directory, not the current folder.

Attribute	Value	Description
href	*url*	URL of new root directory

Table 2-31 <base> Attribute

The base tag is placed in the <head> tags and has one attribute, listed in Table 2-31.

href The hypertext reference (href) is the folder that is to be the root directory for all href attribute values. The reference is initially based on the current location when the href attribute is made. For instance, the Images directory is in the parent folder (..), then the Images folder (/Images).

```
<base href="../Images/" />
```

After this, an image file can be referenced as if the current folder were the Images folder, as shown:

```
<img alt="David" src="David.jpg" />
```

Practice

Probably the best way to get used to the XHTML tags is to use them. Download the EPUB tester.epub file from the McGraw-Hill website and look around in it using Sigil.

NOTE

Sigil should be installed on your system as described in Chapter 1. If you skipped Chapter 1, go back and install it, as well as 7-Zip.

You can download free EPUB files from www.ManyBooks.net and look through these books. It will be easier to learn XHTML as well as Sigil this way. Get accustomed to using Sigil and viewing the XHTML code; it will be an indispensable tool.

Figure 2-1 shows Sigil's toolbar and specifically two main buttons: Book View and Code View. The Book View is used to view the EPUB in book mode (how it should look on an EPUB device). The Code View shows the EPUB as XHTML code. Switch between the two using F2 as you make changes to see what happens.

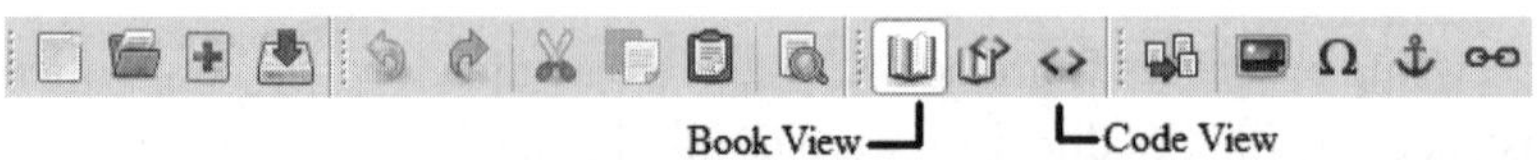

Figure 2-1 SIGIL's toolbar

Chapter 3

CSS

- Understand the importance of using CSS with XHTML
- Learn CSS coding
- Practice CSS

XHTML has been changed by the use of Cascading Style Sheets (CSS). As you may have noticed in Chapter 2, many of the attributes were grayed out. These attributes do work on EPUB devices, but it is strongly recommended that CSS be used.

Learning CSS is a very important task for working with EPUB files.

What Are Cascading Style Sheets (CSS)?

Let's assume you are working with an EPUB file, specifically a novel. Throughout the novel, the paragraph tags (<p>) are used hundreds of times. When you look back later, you decide you want to change the margins, line indentations, etc. Even with using find and replace in Sigil, it would take time to change it all. Later, you decide to tweak it a little more. The process can become time consuming and may cause mistakes in the XHTML code. So, what to do?

The answer is CSS. CSS allows a change made in a single place to occur throughout the whole text layout. The beauty is that changes do not need to be made on every XHTML file to have a consistent layout.

In the previous chapter, we covered the <style> tag. The <style> tag allows the CSS entries to be placed in the XHTML file itself. An example of the <style> tag is shown:

```
<style type="text/css">
h1 {color:red;}
</style>
```

Instead of having all of the styles within the XHTML files, all of the styles for the XHTML files can be centrally located. XHTML files can share styles, which can be changed in one place. So, every XHTML file that uses a CSS must have a link to it. The links look like this:

```
<link href="../Styles/Style0001.css" rel="stylesheet" type="text/css" />
```

The name of the style sheet is Style0001.css and it is located in the Styles directory off the parent folder.

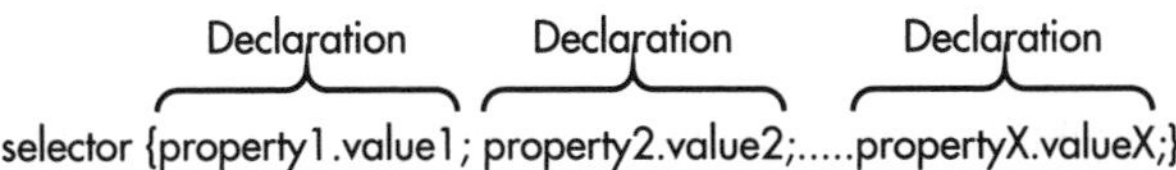

Figure 3-1 CSS format

The content of the CSS has a specific format; however, you can change it a little bit. First, the selector is specified, followed by a curly bracket, then a declaration. The declaration is made up of a property, followed by a colon, then the value assigned to the property. A semicolon is next, followed by more declarations and semicolons, if needed. Finally, a closing curly bracket is needed to end the style. A sample layout is shown in Figure 3-1.

CAUTION

Be aware that the CSS rules may not perform the same on all reading systems!

Selectors

The selector specifies either the class name of the style and/or the tag to which the declaration rules apply. When specifying a class name, the attributes are used only on elements with the specified class. If a tag name is used, the attributes are used only on the specified tags. However, if both a class and tag name are specified, the attributes are used on the tags which also have the specified class name.

Class Name Assignment

CSS styles are given a name, and it is best practice to start the name with a letter, not a number. For example:

```
.blue-text {color:blue;}
```

The example is self-explanatory. The name of the style is blue-text and it causes the associated element to have blue-colored text. In the next example, I'll assign the style to a paragraph, so all the text in the paragraph will be blue:

```
<p class="blue-text">This is a paragraph element.</p>
```

Now, looking back at the style, or class name, you can see it starts with a period. The period is important. Since nothing comes before the period, the class name can be assigned to any tag. If you assign the style to the <html> or <body> tag, for example, all the text in the entire EPUB will be blue.

NOTE

Be careful when applying styles to the <html> or <body> tag since it will be applied to every element within the XHTML body. Try to place the styles on individual tags within the body.

Now, the second way to name a style is to make it only work with a specific tag. For example, to make text centered for a style named center-text to only work on paragraph tags, the style would be:

```
p.center-text {text-align:center;}
```

In this case, the style can only be applied to paragraphs. If you tried to assign it to a span tag, it would not work. For instance, the following element would work:

```
<p class="center-text">This text is centered.</p>
```

The following example would not work with the p.center-text style:

```
<h1 class="center-text">This is a header.</h1>
```

TIP

Unless you have styles with the same class name for different tags, you could simply place a period in front of all styles.

Tag Name Assignment

Another way to name a style is to name it with a tag name only. In the following example, a style is placed on all <h1> tags. The style will center the header and make it green.

```
h1 {text-align:center; color:green;}
```

From this example, you can see that multiple properties can be placed in one class name. The properties and values are separated by a semicolon, and it is best practice (although not necessary) to end the list with a semicolon before the closing curly bracket.

Just as you can add multiple properties to one style name or tag, multiple tags can be specified. For instance, if all headers were to be centered and blue, the class would be set up as shown:

```
h1, h2, h3, h4, h5, h6 {text-align:center; color:blue;}
```

NOTE

The list of rules or declarations can be on one line separated by semicolons, or they can be on multiple lines as long as they are still separated by semicolons.

It would be appropriate to also do the following:

```
h1 {
    text-align:center;
    color:green;
}
```

Using multiple lines for the declarations makes it easier to read. The curly brackets can be placed as shown, with the first declaration, text-align:center;, on the top line as well. The closing curly bracket could be behind the second declaration. If you use Sigil, it automatically formats the sections as shown in the example.

Other possibilities exist for the selector, but we'll cover those later in this chapter. Let's get through the basics first.

Declarations

The declarations are made up of two parts. The first is the property, and the second is the value. Each property has specific values that can be assigned to it. Be aware that unlike XHTML attributes, the declaration values do not need to be in quotes.

There are nine property sections, as shown in Table 3-1. These sections can be split up in many different ways.

Section	Realm
Font	Changes font appearance
Text	Changes text appearance
Page	Manages page breaks
Color and Background	Foreground and background colors and images
Formatting	Manages aspects of the box model
Table	Controls table layout
List	Manages list formatting
Link	Handles link colors
Box Model	Allows management of box model properties

Table 3-1 Declaration Sections

Font Properties

The fonts make up the main part of the reading experience. Changing the appearance of the fonts can make a huge difference in a book. Table 3-2 shows the various properties for fonts.

Property	Value	Description
font-family	*typeface*	Specifies the font typeface to use
font-size	*absolute/relative/percent/length*	Sets the size of the font
font-size-adjust	*number/none*	Aspect of font; ratio of lowercase to uppercase letters
font-stretch	*relative/fixed values*	Width of letters
font-style	normal/italic/oblique	Applies a style to a font
font-variant	normal/small-caps	Sets uppercase letters the same size as lowercase letters
font-weight	*absolute/relative/numeric*	Declares thickness of text (bold)

Table 3-2 Font Properties

font-family Fonts are generically divided into typefaces. When specifying a family, you can name the typeface and allow the reading device to use a built-in font from the typeface style. The main typefaces are listed in Table 3-3 with an example font for each typeface.

Typeface	Sample Font
Sans-Serif	Arial
Serif	Times New Roman
Monospace	Courier
Cursive	Comic Sans
Fantasy	Impact

Table 3-3 Typefaces and Sample Fonts

The list of typefaces can be quite extensive, but most reading devices only support a few.

NOTE

Download the EPUB tester.epub file from the McGraw-Hill website at www.mhprofessional.com/EPUB, place the EPUB file in your reading device, and go to the page Font Family to determine which typefaces are supported.

Multiple typefaces can be specified, as well as multiple font family names. For example, if a CSS style named fontface was made to use the Times New Roman font family and then the Times font family and then any available Serif typeface, the line would be:

```
.fontface {font-family:"times new roman", times, serif;}
```

NOTE

Use quotes around any name that has spaces or is a CSS name or has an identical generic typeface name.

Keep in mind that reading systems on PCs will have a larger font base and can use various fonts. Mobile devices have only a few built-in fonts. If you use a specific font that most systems will not have, you need to embed the font. Font embedding is covered in Chapter 4.

font-size There are four ways to specify size for an EPUB: absolute, relative, percent, and length. It must be clear that on most reading systems, the reader has the ability to change the font size. For example, people with vision problems may enlarge the font quite a bit so that it is similar to a large-print book. When you specify a font size in the CSS, you need to be aware that you can affect the size the reader has set as the default.

What Are the Four Ways to Specify Size?

The first way to specify size is by absolute size. The options are xx-small, x-small, small, medium, large, x-large, or xx-large. The sizes are absolute from one to the next, where the next largest name produces a slightly larger font. Absolute sizes are not a specific size, but will vary depending on the reading system.

The values for relative size are either smaller or larger; again, these are not specific, but depend on the reading device.

(continued)

The third option for font size is by percent. To specify a size of 100 percent is to have the text the same size as the standard text. To double the text size, use 200 percent. For half the size, use 50 percent. Similar to the relative sizes, percent is also relative to the current text size on the reading system. It is recommended to use percent whenever possible.

Finally, the last size is by length. The *em* is based on the width of the lowercase letter *m* for the typeface. For the current font 1 em should be its normal size. So, 2 em would be twice the size, 5 em would be five times the size, etc. All of this means that 1 em is the same as 100 percent, 2 em is the same as 200 percent, and so on.

A recommendation is to use either percent or em since the size is relative to the current typeface and size.

To specify that the header 1 (h1) style be two and half times the size of normal text using percent, the coding would be:

```
h1 {font-size:250%;}
```

The code could also be specified by using em:

```
h1 {font-size:2.5em;}
```

font-size-adjust If the first choice of font-family is not selected, then the second or third may be chosen. When this happens, you may need to change the aspect ratio of the second font to match the first. That way, the fonts will be similar in size. Even if an extra font is placed in with the "normal" font, they can appear the same size, or the size can be adjusted as needed.

Usually, font size is not too important, but some fonts have a completely different size compared to another. In these cases, it may be best to adjust the size so the new font is not too large or too small.

The best way to test this problem is to download the font adjuster.xhtml file from the McGraw-Hill website. With this file, you can specify the two fonts you want to use and then change the font-size-adjust property. Once you do this, view the file in Firefox (it must be Firefox since no other browser supports font-size-adjust).

How Do I Test font-size-adjust?

For the best way to test font-size-adjust, use Notepad++. Open the font adjuster.xhtml file in Notepad++. Make the necessary changes at the top of the file. Select Run from the menu and select Launch In Firefox. Once Firefox opens, see how similar the lines are to one another in length.

Switch back to Notepad++ and modify the font-size-adjust value appropriately (increase the value to make the second line longer; decrease the value to shorten the second line). Save the file in Notepad++ by pressing CTRL-S. Switch back to Firefox and press the F5 key to refresh the page to the new settings. Once the lines are similar in length, use the font-size-adjust value in your EPUB file.

Say you set the font to Impact instead of Arial but you want the fonts to appear as equal size. The Impact font is much smaller than Arial and must be adjusted by .68 so the two fonts appear to be similar in size.

NOTE

As with some XHTML tags and attributes, not all CSS properties work on every reading system. Be very aware of this fact as you use the CSS properties. Use the EPUB tester .epub file from the McGraw-Hill website to test a specific property with a reading device.

The code to change the font size to use Impact instead of Arial in a style called adjust would be:

```
.adjust {font-size-adjust: .68;}
```

font-stretch If a font contains a different face—that is, various sizes of each letter or glyph—the font-stretch property can use the other face. The font itself is not stretched or condensed. If no other face is included in the font, then nothing will happen.

For the font-stretch properties, there is both relative and absolute sizing. Relative sizing is based on the current font size, which is called normal. To make the font larger, there is wider; to make it smaller, there is narrower. Absolute sizing has no specific size definitions; there are only the following choices: ultra-expanded, extra-expanded, expanded, semi-expanded, semi-condensed, condensed, extra-condensed, and ultra-condensed. To make a style called stretch and make it condensed, the code would be:

```
.stretch {font-stretch:condensed;}
```

It should be noted that no systems seem to currently support this property.

font-style There are three choices for font-style: normal, italic, and oblique. If a style has been changed and you wish to make it normal again, use normal. For fonts that include italic faces, these are used when you specify italic. Otherwise, if the face does not exist, you get an oblique font. Oblique fonts are those that slant to the right. In most cases, italic and oblique are the same.

For a style called italics in which all header 1 (h1) tags should be italicized, the code would look like this:

```
h1.italics{font-style:italic;}
```

font-variant The font-variant property makes uppercase letters the same size as lowercase letters. The two values are either normal or small caps.

For a style called small that produced small caps, the code would be:

```
.small{font-variant:small-caps;}
```

font-weight Specifying the thickness of text is the font weight. The values determine the "thickness" of the text. There are three ways to set the weight: absolute, relative, and numerically.

Relative is based off the current weight as either lighter or bolder. The font weight will be thicker (bolder) or thinner (lighter) than the current weight.

Absolute is either normal, the current default weight, or bold. Of course, bold is similar to bold in a word processor.

Numerically, the thickness can be given as values ranging from 100 to 900. The value of 400 is normal text and 700 is bold. Numbers over 700 are thicker than bolded text, while 900 is the maximum.

Text Properties

Once the fonts are set, then the text is the next major portion of the EPUB seen by the reader. Table 3-4 shows the various text properties.

Property	Value	Description
text-align	left/right/center/justify	Sets placement of text
text-indent	*length/percent*	Indents text
text-decoration	none/underline/overline/line-through/blink	Specifies appearance of text

Table 3-4 Text Properties

Property	Value	Description
text-transform	none/uppercase/ lowercase/capitalize	Sets case of text
text-shadow	*effects*/normal	Adds a shadow to text
white-space	normal/pre/nowrap	Sets how whitespace is displayed
letter-spacing	normal/*length*	Sets distance between letters
word-spacing	normal/*length*	Adjusts gaps between the words

Table 3-4 Text Properties (*continued*)

text-align The positioning of text can be very important. Paragraphs are usually set as justified to be similar to regular printed books. Chapter titles are sometimes centered. For example, the code to make paragraphs justified would be:

```
p{text-align:justify;}
```

If all header 1 (h1) entries were to be centered for chapter titles, the code would look like this:

```
h1{text-align:center;}
```

text-indent The first lines of paragraphs are usually indented. To specify the indentation amount, the length or percentage must be specified.

What Are the Various Length Measurements?

There are three types of measurements: relative, absolute, and percentages.

Relative measurements are based on the screen resolution or current font size. These measurements will appear differently on various reading systems. The three types of relative measurements are

- px (pixels) are the individual dots that make up the display. Depending on the resolution of the display, these can vary quite a bit.
- em refers to the width of the lowercase letter *m* of the current font.
- ex refers to the height of the lowercase letter *x* of the current font.

(continued)

Absolute values are those that remain the same between all reading devices. They are

- pt (point) is comparable to a pixel, but is a standard 1/72nd of an inch.
- pc (pica) is based off the typewriter 12-point units, which makes it 1/6th of an inch.
- in (inch) is a customary inch.
- cm (centimeter) is a metric unit based on 1/100th of a meter, or 10 millimeters.
- mm (millimeter) is a metric unit based on 1/1000th of a meter, or 1/10th of a centimeter.

Percentages are related to another factor. For instance, the font size can be a percentage of the normal font size. So, 100 percent would be like the normal-sized text, and 200 percent would be twice the height of the normal text. Likewise, 50 percent would be half the height of the normal text size.

For instance, to make the first line of all paragraphs indented by 5 percent of the total width of a screen, the code would be:

```
p {text-indent:5%;}
```

text-decoration The text-decoration property allows for the addition of an underline, overline, or line through the text. There is also an option to make the text blink, but this doesn't work on most monochrome displays. Since most monochrome displays are not refreshed until a selection is made to turn the page, the blink value does nothing.

To use a style called underlined on any tag so the text is underlined, the code would be:

```
.underlined {text-decoration:underline;}
```

text-transform Transforming text from one case to another can be useful instead of having to retype sections of a book. The options are lowercase, uppercase, and capitalize. The first two are obvious, but capitalize will capitalize the first letter of each word.

If we wanted to make sure all the chapter titles (h1) were uppercase letters, the code would look like this:

```
h1 {text-transform:uppercase;}
```

NOTE

Be aware that the capitalize value only works on lowercase letters. If the section being capitalized is already uppercase letters, it will not work.

text-shadow Shadowed text can make a great effect. Unfortunately, like other CSS properties, it is not supported on all reading systems.

The text-shadow property requires four values: x, y, blur, and color. In the CSS style sheet, these values are not separated by commas.

The first value is the x, or horizontal direction. A positive value is to the right, and a negative value to the left. A 0 value remains behind the text.

The second value is the y, or vertical direction. A positive value is down, and a negative value is up. Again, a 0 value remains behind the text.

The third value specifies the length of the blur. The smaller the value, the more clear the color specified next will be. If the blur value is large, the color will become faded.

The final value is the color. The color can be specified as red, green, blue (RGB) values or as acceptable XHTML color names.

For example, you could create a shadow on all header 1 (h1) tags in an EPUB that uses them only for chapter titles. The shadow would be to the right and down by a small bit (.2 em). The blur would be .3 em and the shadow is gray. The code would look like this:

```
h1{text-shadow:.2em .2em .3em gray;}
```

white-space The white-space property is used to determine how whitespace is handled. By using the pre property, extra spaces are kept in a line and not removed. Also, you can specify what happens to text when it reaches the end of the display. The only way to make it wrap at a specified point is use the <br /> tag. The property assures that a line or title remains on a single line.

Assume a line was to keep all the extra spaces, so a style is created called space. The code would be:

```
.space{white-space:pre;}
```

If text needed to remain on one line, a style called notwrapped could be made as shown:

```
.notwrapped{white-space:nowrap;}
```

letter-spacing If you should need to increase the spaces between the letters in the text, you can use the letter-spacing property. The value given is in any length unit, as previously discussed in the "text-indent" section, except for percent. As with all other properties, the normal value is also available. The normal value is used to set the letter spacing back to the default value. Most all of the properties have a normal value. When a different value is given to change something, these values are inherited by other text. The values must be set to normal to stop the previous change from continuing to the end of the text.

What Is Inheritance?

Inheritance is when a style is applied to a section and all text within the section is then controlled by that style. In a sense, it is inherited from the parent.

For instance, the <body> tag contains all paragraph (<p>) tags. If a style is placed on the <body> tag, then all paragraphs receive it. Let's assume we assign a style to the body that the alignment is justified. If a small section of text, such as a poem, requires left alignment, we can override the body style and place a left justify on the section. Since left justification is a default, we can simply set the style to normal to undo the justification of the <body> tag.

When some text doesn't seem to be working properly, change the settings to normal. If this doesn't work, set the properties specifically to what you need.

Always keep in mind the inheritance of properties within child tags.

If we should want the spacing between letters to spread out a little, we could use the following code:

```
body{letter-spacing:.1em;}
```

word-spacing The word-spacing property performs similarly to letter-spacing, except it changes the whitespace gap between words. The gap is set by the font, so both relative and absolute length work. Percent usually does not work for word-spacing.

If you need to increase the gap between words in an EPUB file by 3 em for a style called gapped, you would use the following code:

```
.gapped{word-spacing:3em;}
```

Page Properties

The page properties allow for the management of page breaks. Table 3-5 shows the various properties for pages.

Property	Value	Description
page-break-before	always/auto/avoid/left/right	Sets a page break before the element
page-break-after	always/auto/avoid/left/right	Sets a page break after the element
page-break-inside	auto/avoid	Manages page breaks within the element

Table 3-5. Page Properties

Property	Value	Description
orphans	*number*	Number of orphan lines for the element
widows	*number*	Number of widow lines for the element

Table 3-5. Page Properties (*continued*)

page-break-before and page-break-after When you want to start a new page, the best way to do it is to start the new page in a separate XHTML file. Some reading systems do allow for page-break-before or page-break-after to be used.

There are five values for the two page-break properties: always, auto, avoid, left, and right.

The values always, left, and right work the same way. They each force a page break as specified by the property (before or after). Left and right values are used on two-page reading systems that force a break and then make the next page be a left or right page.

The avoid value will attempt to not allow a break at the specified position, but may allow it if it is necessary.

Of course, auto allows the breaks to occur normally, and is a way to bring the page breaks back to normal.

A page-break-before occurs before the element to which the style is attached. For instance, if all header 2 (h2) tags were for chapter titles, the EPUB could be placed in one XHTML file and a style set to cause a page break before each chapter title, as shown:

```
h2 {page-break-before:always;}
```

If a chapter were to end with double <br /> tags, the style could allow for the page breaks to occur after the double tags, as shown:

```
br+br{page-break-after:always;}
```

TIP

The sample code shows a combination of two <br /> tags, demonstrating the special selectors that can be used, which is discussed later in this chapter.

page-break-inside Some elements may require a paragraph to remain as a whole. For example, a quote may require all the text remain on a single page so it can all be read at once without “flipping” the page to finish it. The following code would allow for this in a style called no-flip:

```
.no-flip{page-break-inside:avoid;}
```

The only two values for the page-break-inside property are avoid and auto. Avoid will prevent a break, while auto allows it as normal.

orphans and widows Orphans and widows are similar in an EPUB. Orphans are the lines of an element left at the end of a page. Widows are the lines left at the beginning of a page.

Let's assume that we do not want any paragraphs where one line is at the bottom of one page and the rest on the next. Also, a paragraph cannot be on one page with only a single line on the beginning of the next. We would use the following code to achieve this:

```
body{orphans:2; widows:2;}
```

The code shows that in the body, all the displayed text in an XHTML must have two lines at the end of a page and at least two lines at the beginning of each page. The number value is the total number of lines required. It, of course, requires that an element, such as a paragraph, have more lines than the value given.

NOTE

As shown in the example code, the properties and values may all be on one line.

Color and Background Properties

The color and background properties allow for the setting of foreground and background colors and images. See Table 3-6 for the various properties.

Property	Value	Description
Color	*name/#rgb*	Specifies foreground color
background-color	*name/#rgb*	Specifies background color
background-image	*url*	Image file to display as background
background-attachment	fixed/scroll	If background image is stationary or scrolls
background-repeat	repeat/ repeat-x/repeat-y/ no-repeat	If background image appears once or multiple times
background-position	*percentage*/*length*/left/ right/center/top/bottom	Placement of background image

Table 3-6 Color and Background Properties

color Different colors produce different grays (see Chapter 4) and this is something you need to take into account. Since some EPUB devices are monochrome, setting color options may not produce the desired results. Be aware that if the background is white and the text is lightened, it may be very difficult to read.

Color values are chosen either from a set of XHTML color names or by using RGB values (see Chapter 4). For instance, if we needed a style called red-text that makes the foreground color red, the code would be one of the following:

```
.red-text{color:red;}
.red-text{color:#FF0000;}
```

To use the style on a paragraph, the code would be:

```
<p class="red-text">This text is red.</p>
```

background-color Changing the background color can make things look different, but be careful. If the background color is too dark and the text is black, it may be hard to read. The color values are chosen from a set of XHTML color names or by using RGB values (see Chapter 4).

For example, a style called blue-text sets the background color to blue, as shown:

```
.blue-text{background-color:blue;}
```

background-image This property is used to place an image in the background. Remember that this image will be behind the text. If the image colors and text color are similar, the text may be difficult to see.

For example, if an image called image1.jpg is placed on every page within the EPUB, the code would be:

```
body{background-image:url("../Images/image1.jpg");}
```

background-attachment The background-attachment property determines how the image is "attached" to the page. One choice is to specify the image as fixed. This causes the image to remain in place as the text is scrolled. The other choice is scroll, which allows the image to move with the text when it is scrolled.

NOTE

Most EPUB devices do not scroll, or move line by line; instead, they page. Paging is the process of displaying a page at a time and moving directly to the next page. If the device pages, then the image should appear at the same spot on every page.

If the image from the background-image example were used and set to scroll with the text, the code would be:

```
body{background-image:url("../Images/image1.jpg"); background-attachment:scroll;}
```

background-repeat When using the background-repeat property, there are four values: repeat, repeat-x, repeat-y, and no-repeat.

To repeat an image over and over horizontally and vertically, use the value of repeat. Repeat-x causes the image to repeat horizontally only, and repeat-y repeats the image vertically. To stop an inherited image from repeating, use no-repeat.

For example, to cover the background with an image called image3.svg, the code would be:

```
body{background-image:url("../Images/Image3.svg"); background-repeat: repeat;}
```

background-position So far, all the settings have placed images in a specific way. If you need to place the image in a specific spot, then the background-position property is required.

The first value allowed is by percentages. The values set are first horizontally and then vertically by percent. For example, if you want an image to appear three-fourths of the way across the screen (75 percent) and then down the screen halfway (50 percent), the code would be:

```
.imageposition{background-position:75% 50%;}
```

Another way to specify the positioning of the image is by pixel position along the *x* and *y* axes. First the values are listed horizontally (*x*) and then vertically (*y*). For example, to place an image 10 pixels to the right and 50 pixels down, the code would be:

```
.imageposition{background-position:10px 50px;}
```

Finally, you can specifically place an image using the left, right, top, bottom, and center values. These values have meanings similar to percent, as shown in Table 3-7.

Value	Direction	Percent
top	Vertical	0%
bottom	Vertical	100%
center	Vertical/horizontal	50%
left	Horizontal	0%
right	Horizontal	100%

Table 3-7 Positional Values

When using the values from Table 3-7, they are given as horizontal, then vertical. For example, if you wanted to place an image halfway across the screen (center) and way down (bottom), the code would be:

```
.imageposition{background-position:center bottom;}
```

Formatting Properties

The formatting properties allow for the control of elements. Table 3-8 shows the various formatting properties.

Property	Value	Description
visibility	visible/hidden/collapse	Determines visibility of an element
display	none/block/inline/inline-block/inline-table/list-item/run-in/table/table-row/table-cell/table-caption/table-column/table-column-group/table-row-group/ table-header-group/table-footer-group	Changes formatting of elements
position	static/relative/absolute/fixed	Controls position of element box
float	left/right/none	Controls movement of element box
z-index	*number*/auto	Sets depth of overlapped boxes
vertical-align	*length/percentage*/baseline/ bottom/middle/sub/super/text-bottom/text-top/top	
top/bottom	*length/percentage*/auto	Sets vertical position from top/bottom of elements
left/right	*length/percentage*/auto	Sets horizontal position from left/right of elements
clear	none/left/right/both	Side of element box not adjacent to floating box
overflow	hidden/visible/scroll/auto	Sets display of container element that is too small
clip	rect/auto	Sets visible portion of element

Table 3-8 Formatting Properties

visibility Sometimes elements need to be hidden from view. For instance, with Sigil, a table of contents can be created using the headers (h1 to h6) within the XHTML files. If the chapter titles are created using images, then the headers will not exist. Placing a hidden header under the images will allow Sigil to create the table of contents.

When using the visibility property and a value of hidden, the space is still used by the hidden element. A blank line or area where the object was still exists. See the following "display" section for other options to hide elements.

The value of visible will, of course, make the element visible.

The collapse value is used when you want tables to collapse, or hide, a row or column. Simply specify collapse in a style and place it in the <tr>, <col>, or <colgroup> tag.

For an EPUB with image titles, header tags can be placed to help create the table of contents, but they need to be hidden. If the titles are all h2 tags, we can create the following style:

```
h2{visibility:hidden;}
```

display The display property has values that cover many aspects of XHTML. The none value is used in a similar fashion as visibility:hidden. When the display value is none, the element is hidden, but no space is used. No blank line or area remains as a placeholder. Instead the box around the element is removed.

The block value allows an inline element to be treated as a block element.

What Is the Difference Between Inline and Block?

The concept of inline and block is not too difficult—it just sounds that way.

The block elements create an invisible box around them. The box then can be manipulated to change its dimensions, and the element can be moved around inside the box. Another way to look at it is that a block element has a line break before and after it; for example, <p> and <div> tags.

An inline element fits within another element; for example, <b> and <sub> go in <p>. Inline elements go inside another element and are, therefore, in the same line, or inline.

Block elements are <address>, <blockquote>, <br>, <dd>, <div>, <dl>, <dl>, <h1>, <h2>, <h3>, <h4>, <h5>, <h6>, <hr>, <li>, <ol>, <p>, <pre>, <table>, and <ul>.

Inline elements are <abbr>, <acronym>, <b>, <bdo>, <big>, <blink>, <cite>, <code>, <del>, <dfn>, <em>, <i>, <img>, <ins>, <kbd>, <map>, <q>, <samp>, <small>, <span>, <strike>, <strong>, <sub>, <sup>, <textarea>, <tt>, <u>, and <var>.

When an element is set to block, it basically takes an inline tag and makes it act like a block tag. If you created a style to make all code (<code>) tags behave like block elements, each section of code would now have a line break before and after it. Within the XHTML files attached to the CSS, all code would be on its own line, as shown:

```
code{display:block;}
```

The inline value works the other way, by making a block tag act like an inline tag. For instance, when two paragraphs are placed one after the other, there is a gap between them. If the paragraphs were set to act inline, then the gap would disappear and they would appear as one paragraph. The code shows an example:

```
p{display:inline;}
```

Inline-block can be a little confusing. It takes block objects and makes them inline, but still allows them to be treated as a block element. For example, if an unordered list (<ul>) was made and the list items (<li>) were set to inline-block, they would be lined up horizontally. The list items could still be manipulated as they were before, but they would be horizontal, not vertical, as shown in the following code:

```
li{display:inline-block;}
```

The inline-table value allows you to set up a table-like format using inline tags, such as <span>. An example follows:

```
span {width:50px;display:inline-table;}
```

As shown by this example, all <span> tags would now have a width of 50 pixels and be considered a table format.

The list-item changes an inline item like span to a list item in a list. The elements can then be managed like a list, as shown in the example:

```
span {display:list-item; list-style:inside disc; }
```

Now all span tags associated with the CSS style will be seen as list items and be preceded by a disc-shaped bullet.

The run-in value allows block elements to join together as one. For instance, if a header tag (<h2>) were followed by a paragraph (<p>) tag, the two would be on separate lines even if both tags were together on one line, as shown:

```
<h2>This is a Header 2</h2><p>This is a paragraph tag.</p>
```

If a CSS entry made the header 2 tag (<h2>) a run-in, the two lines would now be on one line, as would all other tags following a header 2 tag (<h2>):

```
h2 {display:run-in;}
```

The table values work in a similar way as the XHTML table tags. Remember to order them in the same way as is required by the table tag. An example follows that shows a caption and two cells. The first column is set to blue and the second is red. Table headers and footers are not in the example, but they work the same way as the tags.

```
<div style="display: table;">
      <div style="display:table-column;background-color:blue;"></div>
      <div style="display:table-column;background-color:red;"></div>
      <div style="display:table-caption;">Caption</div>
      <div style="display: table-row;">
            <div style="display: table-cell;width:100px;">
                  Cell 1
            </div>
            <div style="display: table-cell;width:100px;">
                  Cell 2
            </div>
      </div>
</div>
```

These CSS types are placed inline to show all the needed properties.

NOTE

Instead of creating a CSS, the properties and values can be placed in the tag like an attribute. It only requires a style= followed by the properties and values separated by semicolons and all enclosed in double quotes. It is best to use CSS on a separate sheet so all settings can be changed in a single place.

position Positioning block items other than with the standard flow can be a little tricky and require a little practice for some. There are four properties for position: static, relative, absolute, and fixed.

Static is the normal or default value. A block item that is set to static will be placed where it normally should be placed. Positioning values such as top, bottom, left, and right have no effect on a static box. Width and height do allow for the box to have a different size. For example, in this code, the line "Static Box" will appear in the normal flow of any surrounding text:

```
<div style="position: static;width:100px;height:100px;">
      <p>Static Box</p>
</div>
```

Relative is similar to static, but allows for the use of top, bottom, left, and right, as well as width and height. The box will start at the normal flow position, but then be moveable. In this example, the text "Relative Box," with dimensions of 50 pixels by 75 pixels, is moved down 50 pixels and to the right 100 pixels:

```
<div style="position:relative;top:50px;left:100px;width:50px;height:75px;">
      <p>Relative Box</p>
</div>
```

The absolute value creates an element with its start position based within the container it is in. If it is the main element, it is based off the display, just like a fixed value. If it is inside another element, it is based off that element's position, as shown. If we use the previous example and place a small box within it that is 20 pixels square and move it down 10 pixels and to the right 20 pixels, we would have the following code:

```
<div style="position:relative;top:50px;left:100px;width:50px;height:75px;">
<p>Relative Box</p>
      <div style="position:absolute;top:10px;left:20px;width:20px;height:20px;">
            <p>Absolute Box</p>
      </div>
</div>
```

The fixed value places the element in a moveable box. The box's position is based on the display as a parent container and not another block element. So the fixed value allows for the element to be placed anywhere on the screen, even over other elements.

```
<div style="position:fixed;top:50px;left:100px;width:100px;height:100px;">
      <p>Fixed Box</p>
</div>
```

float The float property has three values: left, right, or none. None is the default and all blocks act normally.

If left or right is used, then the element boxes are moved to the right or left of the container that the element is inside. Float can be used with the position property to cause the box to move to the left or right of the parent container. We can use this property to float text around an image. The text is floated right and the image is floated left. The image tag is placed within the text, not before or after, the text will flow around the image, as shown in the following code:

```
<p style="float:right;">A bunch of text is placed here. <img
alt="button1" src="../Images/button1.JPG" style="float:left;" /> More
and more text, on for a few lines more.…  Then ends here.</p>
```

This isn't the best way to get text around a box, but that is covered more in Chapter 4.

z-index Z-index values can either be a number or set to auto. Images placed in a display at specific coordinates (absolute or fixed) can overlap one another. The images can then be given a depth value to place certain images on top of others. Images with a value of –1 will be placed behind text and act like a background image.

When the value is set to auto, the z-index value for the image is the same as the container it is in. For example, to place an image as a background image, the Z-index would be –1, as shown:

```
<img alt="button1" src="../Images/button1.JPG" style="z-index:-1" />
```

vertical-align Vertical alignment controls the vertical placement of inline elements. Using CSS lengths, the element can be raised (positive value) or lowered (negative value). Percent can also be used to specify its distance compared to the line height.

Other values include the baseline. The baseline is the default to which the bottom of the text is placed. Another value is bottom. This refers to the lowest element on the line. Middle is the center of the parent container. The value sub makes the element act like a subscript, while super makes the element act like a superscript. Text bottom is the bottom of the parent container's font, while text top is the top of the parent container's font. Top places the top of the element even with the top of the tallest element on the line.

If, for example, we needed a span to be called centered so we could align the text within the span to be vertically centered, the code would be:

```
span.centered{vertical-align:middle;}
```

top, bottom, left, and right These properties are used to place elements in specific locations when using the position property. The values may seem a little strange at first, but it isn't too hard to catch on.

Top places the item at the top, but the value given, whether it is length or percentage, is how far down from the top. The left property specifies how far from the left, and so forth. If an element must be at the top of a parent container, then the value would be 0px, or 0 percent. Negative values are allowed, and none of the properties work on static positioning.

To make a header 1 (<h1>) tag's position absolute and then move it up 10 pixels from its normal flow position, the code would be:

```
h1 {
position:absolute;
top:10px;}
```

clear The clear property lets you specify whether floats are allowed to the sides of the current element. The property clear has four values: none, left, right, and both.

None declares that no clear is present and floats are allowed on either side of the element. Left specifies that no floats are allowed on the left side; right disallows floats on the right side. Both removes floats from both sides of the current element. If an image is floated to the left of text but the next paragraph should be moved to the image's bottom and then displayed, the paragraph should be cleared of floats, as shown:

```
<p style="float:right;">A bunch of text is placed here. <img
alt="button1" src="../Images/button1.JPG" style="float:left;" /> More
and more text, on for a few lines more..... Then ends here.</p>
<p style="clear:both">The second paragraph of text after the image.</p>
```

overflow Sometimes when specifying the box size, the box may be too small for the content. This produces overflow. The default value is visible. Visible shows all content, even that which is outside the box. If the box has a background color or a border, it will be obvious that the content has overflowed.

Hidden is another value that will hide the overflow; unfortunately, this causes the missing content to not be viewable.

The value of scroll places scroll bars to allow the reader to scroll the content to view it.

NOTE

Be aware that scroll bars do not work on all EPUB devices.

The auto value clips off the overflow and places a scroll bar on the box to view the overflow.

The example that follows creates a green box and places text within it. The overflow property is set to scroll and causes scroll bars to appear.

```
<div style=" background-color:green;width:100px;height:75px;overflow:s
croll;">This text should appear with a green box and cause scroll bars
to appear.</div>
```

clip If an image is too large for its containing box, the clip property allows you to clip an absolute positioned image. If the overflow property is set to visible, then clip does not work. The auto value is the default and causes no clipping to be applied to the image.

The rect value allows you to specify a rectangular area. The values are top, right, bottom, and left. The top value is the number of pixels from the top to clip off. The right value is the number of pixels from the left to keep (the image portion after the number of pixels is clipped off). Then the number of pixels from the top to the bottom is specified and the bottom section is clipped off. Finally, the left side indicates the number of pixels from the left to clip off.

For example, if we have an image that is 200 pixels wide and 100 pixels tall and we want to clip off 10 pixels all around the image, keeping only the center, the code would be:

```
clip:rect(10px,190px,90px,10px);
```

Table Properties

The table properties allow for the control of table elements. Table 3-9 shows the various table properties.

Property	Value	Description
table-layout	auto/fixed	Sets table to fixed width or not
border-collapse	collapse/separate	Indicates if borders should be collapsed
border-spacing	*length*	Distance between adjacent cells
empty-cells	hide/show	Manages how empty cells are handled
caption-side	top/bottom	Placement of caption

Table 3-9 Table Properties

table-layout In some cases, each cell in a table will have different widths. The width of the table can be fixed or allowed to shrink or enlarge as needed.

When the value of table-layout is set to auto, the column width is determined by the widest cell in the column—that is, the unbreakable part that has no spaces. Text in cells can be split at spaces, hyphens, and other elements.

The value of fixed sets the column widths to be able to account for them all within the table width.

The following example shows a style called fixed-table that has a fixed width:

```
.fixedtable{table-layout:fixed;}
```

border-collapse The border-collapse property allows you to set up a table where each cell has its own border, or, if adjacent cells, they share the same border. To have separate borders, use the value separate. For cells to share a border, use collapse.

The following example shows a style set for all tables to have the borders collapsed and therefore shared by all cells:

```
table {border-collapse:collapse;}
```

border-spacing When table cells are set to have separate borders, the gaps between the borders can be controlled. The border-spacing property can have one length (cm, px, pc, etc.) specified or two. If one length is specified, then it is used for both horizontal and vertical spacing of borders. If two lengths are specified, the first is for the horizontal spacing and the second for vertical spacing.

For example, if all tables were to have a 5-pixel horizontal spacing and a 10-pixel vertical spacing, the code would be:

```
table{border-collapse:separate;border-spacing:5px 10px;}
```

empty-cells Another property useful for a table with separate borders is empty-cells. When a cell is empty, this property allows the cell and its background to be either hidden or shown. The default is for the empty cell to be shown, or with the value of show.

To hide the empty cell, use the value of hide. A cell is considered empty if the cell has no content; has its visibility property set to hidden; or contains tabs, line feeds, or blank spaces.

The following example shows a style set to hide all empty cells in all tables:

```
table{border-collapse:separate;empty-cells:hide;}
```

caption-side The caption-side property is used to specify the location of the table caption. It can be placed on the top or bottom of the table. Usually only top or bottom is allowed, but some systems do allow the value of left or right.

NOTE

Stick to top and bottom since some reading systems may not support the left and right values. If a system does not support left and right, then the caption should appear at the top by default.

The following example shows all table captions set to be at the bottom of the table:

```
table{caption-side:bottom;}
```

List Properties

The list properties allow for the control of list elements. Table 3-10 shows the various list properties.

Property	Value	Description
list-style-type	*style-name*	Sets table to fixed width or not
list-style-image	*url*/none	Distance between adjacent cells
list-style-position	inside/outside	Indicates if borders should be collapsed

Table 3-10 List Properties

list-style-type When lists are made, each list item (<li>) can be preceded by a bullet as we saw in Chapter 2. The style of the bullet can be changed as shown in Table 3-11.

Style	Definition
none	No marker is shown
circle	Bullet is a circle
disc	Bullet is a filled circle (this is the default for <ul>)
square	Bullet is a square
armenian	Bullet is traditional Armenian numbering/lettering
georgian	Bullet is traditional Georgian numbering/lettering
cjk-ideographic	Bullet is plain ideographic numbers
decimal	Bullet is a number (1, 2, 3, etc.) (this is the default for <ol>)
decimal-leading-zero	Bullet is a number with leading zeros (01, 02, 03, etc.)
hebrew	Bullet is traditional Hebrew numbering
hiragana	Bullet is traditional Hiragana numbering
hiragana-iroha	Bullet is traditional Hiragana iroha numbering
katakana	Bullet is traditional Katakana numbering
katakana-iroha	Bullet is traditional Katakana iroha numbering
lower-roman	Bullet is lower-roman numbering (i, ii, iii, iv, v, etc.)
upper-roman	Bullet is upper-roman numbering (I, II, III, IV, V, etc.)
lower-alpha	Bullet is lower-alpha lettering (a, b, c, d, e, etc.)
upper-alpha	Bullet is upper-alpha lettering (A, B, C, D, E, etc.)

Table 3-11 CSS list-style-types

Style	Definition
lower-greek	Bullet is lower-Greek lettering
lower-latin	Bullet is lower-Latin lettering (a, b, c, d, e, etc.)
upper-latin	Bullet is upper-Latin lettering (A, B, C, D, E, etc.)

Table 3-11 CSS list-style-types (*continued*)

The following example sets all bullets to lower roman for all tables:

```
li{list-style-type:lower-roman;}
```

list-style-image Instead of using a built-in style, you can supply an image of your own to use. All that is required is a supported image type (PNG, GIF, JPG, or SVG). It is best to use a small image with a width of 1 em and a height of 1 em. The width can be more, but it is best to keep the image size more of a square. Of course, the 1 em is based off the current font being used. Technically, any image will do, but the smaller ones work better. The larger the image used, the larger the space that appears between the list items.

The following example uses an image called arrow.jpg for all unordered lists (<ul>):

```
ul {list-style-image:url("../Images/arrow.jpg");}
```

list-style-position The position of the list style can be inside or outside the element's box. By default, the position is outside the element box.

The following example specifies that all list items (<li>) will have the list styles placed inside the element box:

```
li{list-style-position:inside;}
```

Link Properties

The link properties allow for the control of links. Table 3-12 shows the various link properties. Technically, these are not properties, but specific style names.

Property	Description
a:link	Link that has not been visited yet
a:visited	Link that has been visited
a:active	Link that is being clicked

Table 3-12 Link Properties

a:link The a:link, a:visited, and a:active styles allow you to specify color, fonts, sizes, etc., for a link. The three must appear in the order shown in Table 3-12.

For example, to specify that a link should be blue and bold, a visited link should be green and italics, while an active link should be purple and normal, use the following code:

```
a:link{color:blue; font-weight:bold; font-style:normal;}
a:visited{color:green; font-weight:normal;font-style:italic;}
a:active{color:purple; font-weight:normal; font-style:normal;}
```

NOTE

On a monochrome EPUB display, the color makes little difference, but other properties may be set.

Box Model Properties

The box model properties allow for the control of dimensions, margins, padding, borders, and outlines. Table 3-13 shows the various box model properties.

Property	Value	Description
height	*length/percentage/*auto	Height of box element
max-height	*length/percentage/*none	Maximum height of box element
min-height	*length/percentage*	Minimum height of box element
width	*length/percentage/*auto	Width of box element
max-width	*length/percentage/*none	Maximum width of box element
min-width	*length/percentage*	Minimum width of box element
margin-top	*length/percentage/*auto	Top margin
margin-bottom	*length/percentage/*auto	Bottom margin
margin-left	*length/percentage/*auto	Left margin
margin-right	*length/percentage/*auto	Right margin
margin	*all/top right bottom left*	All margins
padding-top	*length/percentage*	Top margin
padding-bottom	*length/percentage*	Bottom margin

Table 3-13 Box Model Properties

Property	Value	Description
padding-left	*length/percentage*	Left margin
padding-right	*length/percentage*	Right margin
padding	*all/top right bottom left*	All padding
border-top-color	*color*/transparent	Color of top border
border-bottom-color	*color*/transparent	Color of bottom border
border-left-color	*color*/transparent	Color of left border
border-right-color	*color*/transparent	Color of right border
border-color	*color*/transparent	Color of border
border-top-style	none/hidden/dotted/ dashed/solid/ double/ groove/ridge/inset/ outset	Style of top border
border-bottom-style	none/hidden/dotted/ dashed/solid/ double/ groove/ridge/inset/ outset	Style of bottom border
border-left-style	none/hidden/dotted/ dashed/solid/ double/ groove/ridge/inset/ outset	Style of left border
border-right-style	none/hidden/dotted/ dashed/solid/ double/ groove/ridge/inset/ outset	Style of right border
border-style	none/hidden/dotted/ dashed/solid/ double/ groove/ridge/inset/ outset	Style of border
border-width	thin/medium/thick/*length*	Width of border
outline-style	none/dotted/dashed/ solid/double/ groove/ ridge/inset/outset	Outline style
outline-color	*color*/invert	Outline color
outline-width	thin/medium/thick/*length*	Width of outline

Table 3-13 Box Model Properties (*continued*)

Figure 3-2 shows a sample box. The center is the content, such as an image, header, paragraph, or other element. Around the content is an area that is padding. The padding separates the content from the border, however thick the border may be, if it exists. Outside this section is the margin that separates the content and border from other objects. Surrounding the margin area, if it exists, is the outer edge of the box. Even when a border is placed around content, it doesn't include the margin area. When margins are set to 0, then borders can touch.

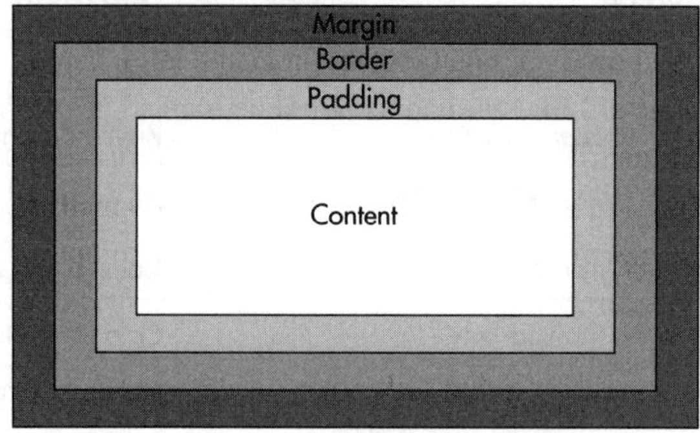

Figure 3-2 Box model

For all of the properties listed in Table 3-13, keep Figure 3-2 in mind to better understand the concepts that deal with it.

height, max-height, and min-height These properties affect block-level elements to specify the height, maximum height, and minimum height of a block. The measurements specified only affect the content and not the padding or margins. The maximum height specifies the maximum height of the box, and the minimum height is the smallest the box can be. If the height goes beyond these boundaries, then the value will stop at the minimum or maximum.

All three values can be given as lengths or percentages, as discussed previously in this chapter under "What are the four ways to specify size?". Height also has an option for auto. Auto allows the size to be calculated automatically for the size it needs, if the container it is inside can hold it. Max-height has a possible value of none which is default and allows the height to go to any value. Min-height has a default value of 0.

NOTE

Content out of the defined box is controlled by overflow values.

If the height of a division is set to 100 pixels and the overflow is set to clip off any extra part of the image after 100 pixels, the code would be

```
div{height:100px;overflow:hidden;}
```

width, max-width, and min-width These properties affect block-level elements to set the width, maximum width, and minimum width. Measurements do not affect padding or margins, only the content portion of the box. The maximum width sets the maximum value of width and minimum width sets smallest value of width. Minimum width by default is 0 while maximum width default is set to none. If width should be larger than the maximum or smaller than the minimum, the width will be set to the max or min value as needed.

All three values can be given as lengths or percentages as discussed previously in this chapter in the "What Are the four Ways to Specify Size?" sidebar. Width also has an option for auto. Auto allows the size to be calculated automatically for the size it needs, if the container it is inside can hold it.

NOTE

Content out of the defined box is controlled by overflow values.

If a division were made with a width of 75 percent and the overflow is shown, the code would be:

```
div{width:75%;overflow:visible;}
```

margin-top, margin-bottom, margin-left, margin-right, and margin Values can be set to modify the margin for the box. They can be set for each side as needed. The auto value is used to allow the reading system to determine margin values to allow the box to fit in its container.

For example, if all images in an EPUB were to have a margin of 2 pica all around it, the code would be as follows:

```
img {margin-top:2pc;margin-bottom:2pc; margin-left:2pc;margin-right:2pc;}
```

If all margins were to be the same, then the property margin can be used with one value for all sides, as shown:

```
img {margin:2pc;}
```

If the margins are somewhat different, they can be specified as top, right, bottom, and left. The values start at the top and continue around the box clockwise. The following example sets an image margin for the top and bottom of 3 em, a left margin of 5 pt, and a right margin of 3 percent, as shown:

```
img {margin:3em 3% 3em 5pt;}
```

padding-top, padding-bottom, padding-left, padding-right, and padding The values for these properties specify the padding on the relevant side of the box. The value is either a length, as discussed earlier, or a percentage of the parent container. The default padding value is 0.

If a paragraph were to have padding above and below set to 5 em and padding to the left and right of 15 percent, the code would be:

```
p{padding-top:5em; padding-bottom:5em; padding-left:15%; padding-right:15%;}
```

Padding also has a property called padding that allows you to set all four sides at once if the padding values are the same, as shown:

```
p{padding:5%;}
```

Padding also allows for all four sides to be set starting at the top value, then moving to the right, bottom, and left. If, for example, the padding for an image was to be 1 inch for the top, .5 inches for the bottom, 3 em for the right, and 2.5 em for the left, the code would look like this:

```
img{padding:1in 3em .5in 2.5em;}
```

border-top-color, border-bottom-color, border-left-color, border-right-color, and border-color The color is set individually for each side. The color can be specified with an RGB value or a supported color name. The default value is transparent, which causes the border to allow the background to come through.

In the following example, the top is red, the bottom is black, the left is blue, and the right is green:

```
img{border-top-color:red;border-bottom-color:#000000;border-left-
color:rgb(0,0,255);border-right-color:green;}
```

The border color can specify all sides at once, or specify all four sides, starting with the top and going clockwise around the box. For example, if you wanted all sides to be blue, the code would be:

```
img{border:blue;}
```

If all sides are different, we can use a previous example. For an image border, if the top is red, the bottom is black, the left is blue, and the right is green, the code would be:

```
img{border:red green black blue;}
```

border-top-style, border-bottom-style, border-left-style, border-right-style, and border-style The border style can be specified for each side or all sides at once. The border styles are listed in Table 3-14.

Style	Description
none	No border
dotted	Dotted border
dashed	Dashed border
solid	Solid border
double	Two border lines
groove	3-D grooved border
ridge	3-D ridged border
inset	3-D inset border
outset	3-D outset border

Table 3-14 Border Styles

The following example indicates a border around all division sections but no border to the left or right and a single solid border on top with a double line on the bottom:

```
div{border-style-top:solid;border-style-bottom:double;border-style-
left:none;border-style-right:none;}
```

Use a single value to place a border on all sides of the box. The following example shows a dotted border for all sides:

```
div{border-style:dotted;}
```

If each side is to be specified individually, then the style names can be used, starting with the top and going around the box in a clockwise direction, as shown:

```
div{border-style:solid none double none;}
```

border-top-width, border-bottom-width, border-left-width, border-right-width, and border-width To set border widths, the border style must be set, since it defaults to none. The width is given as thin, medium, or thick and can also be specified by CSS length values. Percentages are not allowed.

For example, to set the width of an image for the top and bottom to 3 pixels and the left and right to 2 em, the code would be:

```
img{border-top-width:3px;border-bottom-width:3px;border-left-
width:2em;border-right-width:2em;}
```

To specify all sides, starting with the top value and going around the box in a clockwise direction, the code would be:

```
img{border-width:3px 2em 3px 2em;}
```

If all sides are to be the same, such as 3 px, the code would be:

```
img{border-width:3px;}
```

outline-style The style for the outline is similar to that for a border. See Table 3-14 for the style names.

For example, to set a ridged outline around all tables, the code would be:

```
table{outline-style:ridge;}
```

TIP

Since the default outline style is none, always set the style first for an outline, and then set color and/or width.

outline-color An outline is similar to a border except that it overlays the box and takes up no room. So this means that the outline does not add height or width to the box. The outline appears outside the border, touching it. Regardless of the thickness of the border, the outline is still outside it.

The outline-color property is used to specify the color of the outline in any of the aforementioned ways. Invert can also be used to invert the color, making sure the outline is visible.

For example, to specify an outline around an image that is blue, the code would be:

```
img{outline-style:solid;outline-color:blue;}
```

outline-width Borders can have a width specified, and so can outlines. The values are thin, medium, thick, and the normal CSS measurements, except percent.

To set an outline around a specific paragraph called outlined that is a solid style and a width of 1 em, use the following code:

```
p.outlined{outline-style:solid;outline-width:1em;}
```

Special Selectors

Many selectors have been covered already, but a few more exist that enable you to perform some fancy CSS manipulation. If you come across something you may not understand in CSS, it most likely is some type of selector (unless it is in curly brackets).

ID Selector

The ID selector is another type of "normal" selector. It works just like the class selector, but works with ID attributes.

ID styles in CSS start with a pound (#) sign. The style is then assigned (without the pound sign) as an ID value. For example, if an ID selector is named bold-text and then applied to a paragraph, the code would look like this:

```
CSS: #bold-text{font-weight:bold;}
XHTML: <p id="bold-text">This is all bold.</p>
```

All Tags

All tags can be selected by using the asterisk (*). Be aware that this affects every element connected with the CSS style sheet. For example, if we wanted all text to be green, the code would be:

```
* {color:green;}
```

Multiple Elements

If multiple elements will have the same settings, such as header 1 (h1) and header 2 (h2), they can be separated by commas. We can place as many elements as we want together as long as they are separated by commas. For example, let's make h1 and h2 elements underlined, as shown:

```
h1,h2{text-decoration:underline;}
```

Child

If you want to put styles on elements that only exist with other elements, you can use the selector element1>element2. Here, element2 must exist within element1. For example, if you wanted all image elements within a division to have a yellow outline, the code would be:

```
div>img{outline-style:solid;outline-color:yellow;}
```

Descendant

You can manage an element within another element, such as italics (<i>) within a paragraph (<p>). We can then make the italicized element a larger font as follows:

```
p i {font-size:200%;}
```

Adjacent Sibling

If every element after another element needed special styles, it can be done using element1+element2. Here, element2 must follow directly after element1. For example, in an EPUB, if chapter titles are header 2 (h2) and the first paragraph after the header should have no indentation, the code would be:

```
h2+p{text-indent:0px;}
```

If you needed to indent the second paragraph after the header 2, not counting the one directly after it, you would use:

```
h2+p+p{text-indent:3px;}
```

Attribute and Value

To find a specific value of an attribute, you can search for a match. For example, you can search for all tags with a property of title that is set to MonaLisa, as shown:

```
[title=MonaLisa] {border-width:3px;}
```

If we wanted to select and apply a style to all tags with a partial attribute and value, we can use this selector. For instance, to find all tags with the language beginning with "fr," we can apply an italics style, as shown:

```
[lang|=fr] {font-style:italic;}
```

We can also check for text contained in the value by using ~=. The selection must be an exact match—partial matches do not count. If the search is for "frog," for example, "frogs" will not be found, although "green frog" will. If we wanted to select all tags with a title containing the word "frog" and create a border around it with a thickness of 2 px, the code would be:

```
[title~=frog] {border-style:solid;border-width:2px;}
```

Values may also begin with specific text. For instance, to find all tags that have a class beginning with "text-" and highlight them in yellow, we can do the following:

```
[class^="text-"] {background-color:yellow;}
```

If we want to change the style for any attributes that end with specific text, such as any JPG files that can have a border, we use the following code:

```
[src$=".jpg"] {border-style:solid;border-width:3px;}
```

We can also find values that contain specific text in the middle. For example, if links to McGraw-Hill.com needed to be underlined, the code would be:

```
a[src*="mcgraw-hill"] {text-decoration:underline;}
```

First Letter

To select the first letter of a specific element, such as a paragraph tag (<p>), you use element:first-letter. For example, to make the first letter of all paragraphs a bold font, use the following code:

```
p:first-letter{font-weight:bold;}
```

These selectors can be combined. For example, if an EPUB had all chapter titles as header 2 (<h2>) and the first letter of each paragraph right after the header should be made twice as big as the other letters, the code would be:

```
h2+p:first-letter {font-size:200%;}
```

First Line

Similar to first letter, the first line element affects the entire line. The actual portion of the line may vary, depending on the reading device, since default font size, screen size, etc., may cause the first line to vary in length. Again, note that the selectors can be combined.

For example, for any paragraph following a header 2 (<h2>), we can cause the first line to have an overline as shown:

```
h2+p:first-line {text-decoration:overline;}
```

First Child

The first child element is the first occurrence of a specific tag within another element. In the following example, the first paragraph tag that occurs in the body and any div tags should be orange, as shown:

```
p:first-child{color:orange;}
```

We can also style the first bold (<b>) tag in each paragraph to be underlined, as shown:

```
p:first-child b{text-decoration:underline;}
```

In addition, the first child of each ordered list can be bold:

```
ol>:first-child{font-weight:bold;}
```

Content Before and After

Content can be placed before and after specific elements. If text needed to be placed after tags, for example, and you did not want to have to do it manually, you can use this property instead. If all of the header 2 (<h2>) tags need to have -= placed before it and =- after it, the code would be:

```
h2:before {content:"-= ";}
h2:after {content:" =-";}
```

Within the curly brackets, other styles can be set for the content to be added, such as color, font weight, etc.

General Siblings

To style every element after another element of specific types, use the general siblings selector. For example, to style every paragraph after a header 2 (<h2>) to be indented by 2 em, the code would be:

```
h2~p {text-indent:2em;}
```

This will indent every paragraph after the header that is not part of a <div>. The style will continue to the end of the XHTML file.

First of Type

First of type is used to set styles for elements that are the first of its type within a parent. For example, if every first emphasis (<em>) element is to be underlined as well, use the following code:

```
em:first-of-type{text-decoration:underline;}
```

Last of Type

Last of type is used to set styles for elements that are the last of its type within a parent. For example, if all final emphasis (<em>) elements are to be overlined as well, use the following code:

```
em:last-of-type{text-decoration:overline;}
```

Only of Type

If only one tag is used within a parent, you can set styles for that element. For example, if you wanted the only <strong> element to have a line through it as well and a parent, such as a paragraph, has only one <strong> element, the code would look like this:

```
strong:only-of-type{text-decoration:line-through;}
```

Only Child

The only child selector sets a style for the specified element that is the only child element of a parent.

A style is set up where the paragraph (<p>) is being looked for as the only child within an XHTML file. If a span (<span>) and (<p>) paragraph exist within a division (<div>), then neither is the only child and both are ignored. If a division (<div>) has a paragraph (<p>) only, then the paragraph would be given the style. The code would be:

```
p:only-child{background-color:gray;}
```

nth Child

The nth child element allows you to specify odd or even and apply a style to those items. It is best used with lists and tables that are set up in a linear fashion and do not have extra elements mixed in. In an EPUB, if I specified the even paragraphs (<p>) to be red and the odd ones to be blue, they may not be every other one as expected. The nth child counts all elements, not just the specified tags. An algebraic formula is used to specify the selected items otherwise. For example, if every third paragraph were to be blue, the code would look like this:

```
p:nth-child(3n) {color:blue;}
```

Instead of specifying 3n, you can use odd or even, as long as you keep the aforementioned caveat in mind.

nth of Type

The nth of type is a very useful tool that we'll talk about more in Chapter 4. The nth of type element works similar to nth of child, but it only counts the specified selector. This way, you get exactly odd and even when you want it.

For example, if every even paragraph is blue and the odd ones are purple, the code would be:

```
p:nth-of-type(even) {color:blue;}
p:nth-of-type(odd) {color:purple;}
```

nth Last Child

Instead of selecting every so many children, you can select the last item or the nth last element. For example, to apply a style to a paragraph that is the third last paragraph, use the following code:

```
p:nth-last-child(3) {color:orange;}
```

If no number is specified, the very last selector type is selected. Like nth child, this selector counts every element, not just the specified types, as explained in "nth Child."

nth Last of Type

Similar to nth last child, this picks only a specified type and does not count every element. Otherwise, it works the same as nth last child.

We'll use the same example to demonstrate this, but depending on the paragraphs and elements involved, they may change the color of different paragraphs, as shown:

```
p:nth-last-of-type(3) {color:orange;}
```

Last Child

The last child selector allows you to select the very last element of a parent. Be aware that if the last element is a break (<br />), no visible changes could be made, since this element has no visible attributes. If the selected element is not the last element, then nothing happens.

```
p:last-child {border-style:single;}
```

Root

Root allows you to set CSS settings for all the XHTML files connected to the CSS style sheet. The :root selector specifies settings to place on the <HTML> tag that affects the entire file.

For example, to set all margins to a default of 5 pixels, use the following code:

```
:root{margins:5px;}
```

Of course, this is a simple example, but as many settings as you wish can be placed in the brackets to set up your XHTML files within the EPUB.

Empty

To select all empty elements of a specified type, you can use the empty selector with the required tag. For example, if you wanted to find all empty paragraph tags and remove them from the display (meaning no line break), use the following code:

```
p:empty{display:none;}
```

Practice

I know this chapter may seem overwhelming if you do not know CSS. Be aware that you may not use many of the properties and selectors discussed here, but it is helpful to be familiar with them. In the following chapters we'll go over examples that will help you to understand CSS much better. Keep referring to the EPUB tester file from McGraw-Hill's website. You can view it in Sigil to see how things work. You can also change things in the tester to try things out. Just remember to keep a backup copy or to discard the changes when you exit Sigil.

Chapter 4

Fonts, Images, and Colors

- Understand how to embed and use fonts
- Understand how to embed and use images
- Learn about SVG images
- Learn about the various color schemes
- Learn how to determine grayscale from colors

Any EPUB can greatly depend on fonts to enhance it. Fonts need to be included within the EPUB file so all readers can have access to it. Images are also important. Many books include pictures, not counting the cover picture. There are many uses for pictures, including in comic books and magazines.

Scalable Vector Graphics (SVG) images are very small image files that can be useful in an EPUB.

Even though monochrome reading devices have no real need for color, using color is important. Colors will be displayed in various shades of gray. There is also the ability to know what color will look like in grayscale. In some cases, two colors may be similar when converted to grayscale and then will not be distinguishable from each other.

Fonts

Dealing with fonts in an EPUB can be one of the biggest differences in a reading experience. Imagine if, like on a PC, you could change your text to any font you wish. Well, it can be done with an e-reader. Most e-readers support True Type Fonts (TTF) and Open Type Fonts (OTF). Others may support SVG fonts and Web Open Font Format (WOFF).

TIP

It is usually best to stick with True Type Fonts to be assured of compatibility.

In an EPUB, fonts can be used to change all the text, certain sections of text, specific letters, or just to add flair. Some fonts may look great, but then some are not easy to read. Certain script fonts can be so embellished as to be undecipherable. Don't go overboard with changing fonts.

Embedding Fonts

Hopefully, you have had time to look around in the Sigil application as shown in Figure 4-1. The left pane with the folders for Text, Styles, Images, etc., is the Book Browser pane. The right pane is the Table Of Contents pane. The lower pane is the Validation Results pane. The upper central pane is where you have access to the Code View and Book View. The Code View allows you to see the code for the XHTML file selected in the Book Browser pane. The Book View lets you see how the code may appear in an EPUB reading system. I say "may" because not all devices manage the XHTML and CSS code in the same manner, just as all browsers do not show content the same. To switch between Book and Code View, use the F2 key.

In the Book Browser pane you see a folder called Fonts. It is here that you place your fonts to be used by the EPUB. Of course, it's not that simple; there is more to it. Now to get a font, you need to go to www.dafont.com. At the top of the page, do a search for "Great Victorian." A font should be found called "Accents Euro Great Victorian," and you

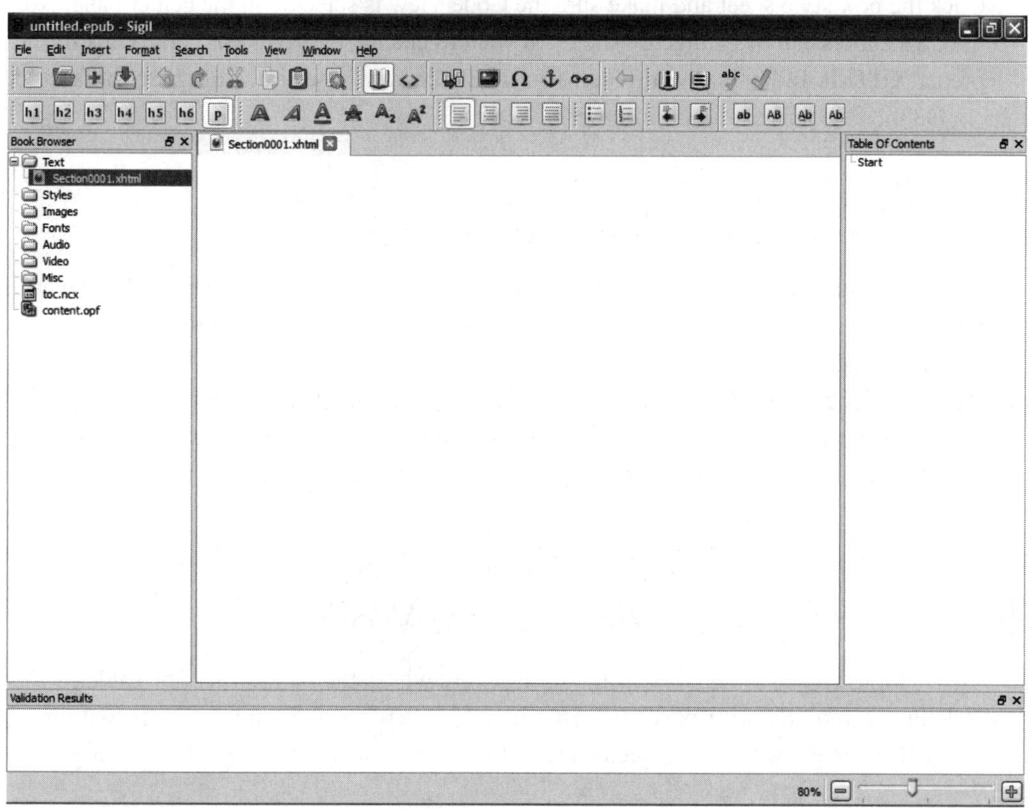

Figure 4-1 Sigil's main screen

should download it. If you cannot find it, download another font to use. The fonts are OTF, but should work fine on EPUB devices. The font file is compressed as a ZIP, but you can use 7-Zip to open it. Double-click the ZIP file, select GreatVictorian-Standard.otf, and drag it to a folder on your system. Back in Sigil, right-click the Fonts folder in the Book Browser pane and select Add Existing Files. In the box that pops up, find your font file and select Open. The font is now part of the EPUB.

CAUTION

Do not rename the font file. Fonts have an internal name that matches the filename. When the EPUB device accesses the font, it uses the font's name, which is sometimes used as the internal name as well. If the two don't match, the font may not work properly.

Now to make the font part of the EPUB, we need to create a style sheet and add the font to it. Right-click the Styles folder in the Book Browser pane and then select Add Blank StyleSheet. There should now be a CSS sheet called style0001.css in the folder. Click the new style sheet and make sure the Code View is selected in the center pane. Now the CSS entries can be changed. When you want to change the XHTML code, click the proper XHTML file in the Text folder. You should be able to see how things are organized.

On the CSS sheet, add the following code:

```
@font-face {
font-family: "victorian";
src: url("../Fonts/GreatVictorian-Standard.otf");}
```

Every embedded font in an EPUB will have a similar section. They should be one after the other in any order. The @font-face should be placed in the CSS before all styles.

The font-family is how this font will be referred to within the XHTML files linked to the CSS. It is best practice to keep the font-family name small and, of course, unique. The source (src) is the location of the font file itself. In the example, the file is found in the parent folder (..), then in the Fonts folder where the font file itself is named.

How Does the Directory Structure Work?

File locations can be thought of as the file structure within the EPUB file. The folders listed in the Book Browser pane all exist within the OEBPS folder in the EPUB. Within the OEBPS are the folders you need—at least the ones that contain files. If you are using an XHTML file in the Text folder and want to reference an image in the Images folder, you must go up to the parent folder or the OEBPS folder. To do this, the two dots are used (..). Then, you go to the Images folder next, but the folder and filename must be separated by forward slashes (/). Once the proper folder is reached, then the file itself must be named, including the extension after the period.

Be aware that case can be important. For Linux systems that are running an EPUB app, the file structure names are case-sensitive. This includes filenames and extensions.

The font is now embedded and ready to use, so let's set up a CSS style to use it. Let's make a style called "fancy" that will set up no other styles with it, but uses the font:

```
.fancy {font-family: "victorian";}
```

This font-family name *must* match the one from font-face. If multiple fonts are used, make sure you use the correct font-family name from the correct font-face entry.

Switch over to the text files, select section0001.xhtml, and make sure it is in Code View. Add the following two lines to the body:

```
<p>This is Line 1.</p>
<p class="fancy">This is Line 2.</p>
```

You can see the second line should be using our new font, but we have one more thing to change. At this point, our XHTML file is not linked to the style sheet. Without it being linked, the XHTML file cannot access the styles we specify. So, to fix this, right-click the XHTML file and select Link Stylesheets. Next a window should appear listing the style sheets available (there should be only the one), so place a check in the box next to it. Select OK and make sure you are in Book View to see the new font.

It's a little small, so let's make a simple change. Add the following line to the "fancy" style in CSS:

```
font-size:3em;
```

When you look back at the Book View, the line should be easier to read and should look different from the first line. If you have problems, look back over the code to make sure everything is typed correctly. If there is still a problem, download c04-01.epub from the McGraw-Hill website (www.mhprofessional.com/EPUB) and try it. If it doesn't work, try a different EPUB viewer. If you are using an application, an app on a tablet, or other device, since they all work differently, a different app or device may work better.

What If My TTF File Doesn't Work?

If this happens, the file most likely has been renamed. You may try to get another copy of it to make sure it wasn't corrupted during a download.

The best thing is to get a free font maker program (I suggest Type Light 3.2). Type Light Free can be downloaded from www.cr8software.net/typelight.html. You need to pay for the full version.

Open the font in the font program and then on the menu, choose Font and then Rename Font. The default name should be listed after Family Name. Clear this box and then select File and Save As. Enter the name listed under Family Name. Delete the font file in your EPUB that doesn't work and re-embed it with the new name. Change the CSS entry for the font-face style, and it should work now. If, for any reason, it doesn't, check all of your CSS entries to make sure the font-family name is the same for the font face and the style you are using it in. Also, check the class name to make sure they match. Of course, make sure the path and filename of the font file itself is properly listed in the source (src).

If nothing works, try a different font. If the second font works, then something is wrong with the first one.

Any option for managing the font text can be included in the CSS fancy style. The style can include margins, indents, padding, and any other CSS properties that you need to have on all the text displayed. Try to always keep it simple by placing all the properties in one place.

If you need to use multiple style sheets, you can link an XHTML file to them. When you select the option to link a sheet, click more than one sheet to link it. Be aware that fonts should be loaded one time. Do not place a font face on multiple sheets and have one XHTML file linked to both. If both font faces were given the same family name, then they would not be unique. If multiple sheets are used, have one sheet for the fonts only and link all necessary XHTML files to it. Add other sheets as needed. See the example file c04-02 .epub from the McGraw-Hill website.

If you right-click a style sheet, you can rename it. When you rename it in Sigil, it automatically changes the name in all the links as well. This is also true of fonts and images, but do not rename the fonts this way. Right-click the XHTML files to rename them.

Now let's try something a little different. Suppose we want to use the new font to change the first letter of each paragraph in a chapter. So, let's start a new EPUB by going to File and selecting New in Sigil. Create two XHTML pages, each with a header 2 title: Chapter 1 and Chapter 2 (you can rename the XHTML file accordingly). Add two paragraphs after the headers. Embed in the font as we did previously (you'll have to add a style sheet and link both XHTML files to it).

Hopefully, everything is good so far. Now in the CSS, add the following code, which should make sense now after the previous chapter:

```
h2 {text-align:center;}
h2+p:first-letter {font-family: "victorian";font-size:300%;}
```

As you can see, we are controlling the <h2> headers by centering them. Then we are taking the paragraph following any <h2> headers (we should only use them for chapter titles) and assigning them a style. The style indicates that the first letter of the paragraph will use the embedded font and be three times larger than the normal text. There are two reasons for making the text larger using a percentage. First, we want to make it larger so it stands out from the other text. More importantly, a percentage is used because we do not know the specific size on any device. Some people may set their EPUB device to default to small print. Others select a size closer to what a large-print book may be, and if we selected a specific size, our first letter may end up half the size of the rest of the text.

This can be seen in the example file c04-03.epub.

Some devices may not support the first:letter selector. In this case, you may need to create a workaround by spanning the first letters, as shown in the following code or in the example c04-04.epub file:

```
CSS:   .fancy-letter {font-family: "victorian";font-size:300%; }
XHTML: <p><span class="fancy-letter">T</span>his is Line 1 of Chapter 1.</p>
```

The changes should make it all work the same, except you have to go to each chapter and set the span on the first letter. This may be time-consuming, but should work on any reading system unless it does not support embedded fonts.

Shouldn't All EPUB Systems Support Embedded Fonts?

Technically, they should. Unfortunately, they don't. The main reason is that some tablet apps or PC applications are not fully International Digital Publishing Forum (IDPF)–compliant for the EPUB. Most companies in this case simply need time to update their programs to get everything working.

If you come across an app that doesn't support what you need, find another one. Most of the best ones will be from device manufacturers that emulate their reading devices.

Important: The second generation Nooks from Barnes and Noble, do not support embedded fonts at the time of writing this book.

Font Type	Normal Size	Zipped EPUB Size
TTF	18,452	10,456
OTF	20,232	14,516
SVG	18,753	5,171
WOFF	10,828	10,776

Table 4-1 Font File Size Differences

Other than using fonts that will be compatible on as many systems as possible by using TTF, another factor needs to be considered. File sizes can play an important part. TTF again does well here, even though SVG fonts do the best, but they do not have a wide range of support. For a better example, see Table 4-1.

Many changes can be made to an EPUB using embedded fonts. What it comes down to is that like any programming code, even HTML and CSS, the ability is limited only by your imagination.

Images

Images help enhance any book. EPUB 2 supports PNG, GIF, JPG, and SVG images. Most of these image formats are straightforward, but some people have not dealt with SVG. To play around with SVG, download InkScape for free from www.inkscape.org.

TIP

It is usually best to stick with JPG images to be assured of compatibility. SVG images are not fully supported yet by all devices.

Embedding Images

Embedding images is the same as embedding fonts within the EPUB. To start, you right-click on the Images folder, select Add Existing Files, and then select your image files to add. Now the images are embedded within the EPUB. Don't forget to save the file.

To place images within an XHTML file, you use the <img> tag. To make things simpler, however, you can select the Insert Images button. Place your cursor over each image in the menu, and a tooltip will pop up telling you what the button does.

Using the Insert Images button causes a window to appear that lists all embedded images. If you select the image on the left, an area on the bottom right shows the image dimensions, file size, and whether the image is color or grayscale, as well as its color depth. An SVG image will not show the image itself, but the XML code for the image.

By selecting an image with the Insert Images button, the following would be placed within the XHTML code:

```
<img alt="Smiley" src="../Images/Smiley.svg" />
```

As you can see, Sigil fills in the necessary properties and values for the selected image. Keep in mind that if an image is renamed, all links to it in the image tags will also be renamed.

How Do I Get Dimensions of an SVG Image?

In Sigil, when you select the SVG image file, the code is displayed in the Code View. Somewhere in the top section you'll see two lines showing width= and height=. The two values given in double quotes are the width and height in pixels.

Flowing Text

As discussed in Chapter 3, sometimes text needs to flow around an image. Usually, text will stop at the top of the image and continue at the image's bottom. Some images that are small can have text flow around them. To start, place your image where you want it; then place the image tag within a division with a style called "illustration," as shown:

```
<div class="illustration">
<img alt="Smiley" src="../Images/Smiley.svg" />

</div>
```

Now, to set up the text flow, we need to set up the illustration style in CSS and make sure the XHTML file is linked to it. The CSS code follows:

```
div.illustration{
width: 50% !important;
float: left;
margin: 3px 3px 3px 0 !important;}
```

The image is set to a width of 50 percent of the screen, but the value should match your image. The !important declaration makes sure the image width is not overridden by any other style. The image is then floated to the left, although it could be floated to the right as well. The margins are then set for the image to 3 pixels on the sides that are next to text. Again, the margins are set with the !important declaration so they are not overridden by another style.

Text should flow around the image just as it would in a book or magazine.

What About CSS Order of Precedence?

Normally, the order in which CSS styles have precedence is

- **Inline styles** Styles placed within the tag itself using a style= attribute
- **Embedded styles** Styles placed in the XHTML <style> section at the beginning of the XHTML file
- **External styles** Styles placed in the external CSS file

An inline style overwrites an embedded style, which overwrites an external style. When there are two styles for the same selector, such as <p>, the last one from the beginning of the external CSS style sheet overwrites the first.

The selectors have an order of precedence over one another. The first has priority over the second, which has priority over the third, and so on, as follows:

- **ID selector** #style used in XHTML as id="style"
- **Attribute selector** The search selector [title=MonaLisa]
- **Class selector** The .style-name selectors
- **Child selector** Selector that selects an element of another (div > p); for example, a paragraph inside a division
- **Adjacent sibling selector** Elements next to each other (h2+p); for example, a paragraph after a header 2
- **Descendant selector** An element within another element (p i); for example, an italics element inside a paragraph element
- **Type selector** Styles set for a tag (img); for example, a style set for all images

If a style isn't working properly, check the order of precedence to see where the problem may lie. If you cannot correct the problem, place an !important declaration on the properties you do not want changed.

Cover Image

In an EPUB, you will want to add a cover if it doesn't have one. Images should be 600 pixels wide and 800 pixels tall. They can be in color, since monochrome devices can usually display color images in grayscale.

NOTE

If you need to resize an image, try to keep the size in the same aspect ratio so the image is not "squeezed" in one direction. Most programs allow you to adjust the size and keep the aspect ratio intact. If needed, download a program called Pixresizer at www.bluefive.pair.com. It works well and allows you to also change the format.

EPUB Note

In Sigil, it is usually best to keep all sections of the book separate. The cover, chapters, introduction, etc., should be individual XHTML files, which assures that a page break occurs between files. The title page should come after the cover and include the title in an <h1> tag. Chapter titles should use <h2> tags. Of course, this is all personal preference, but there are reasons for this that will be covered in Chapter 5.

If you have an existing XHTML file that you want to split into chapters, place the cursor where the break should be between files, and press CTRL-ENTER. Pressing CTRL-ENTER causes the file to end at that position and the remaining text to go to the next file. Right-click an XHTML file to rename it.

Section Breaks

Another issue with regular printed books is the section breaks. Some books just have a blank line, while others may use one or more asterisks (* * *) or some other method of signifying a section break. The main thing is that they are plain, and much couldn't previously be done because of the cost. But now in the digital world, the choices are limitless. Look at Table 4-2 and you may see some familiar titles. A symbol also is included that represents the book. Some books may not have a symbol come immediately to mind, but usually there is something if you think about it long enough.

NOTE

Be careful with images from the Internet, as some may be copyrighted. For free images, try www.openclipart.org.

Book	Symbol
Robin Hood	bow and arrow
Snow White	apple
Moby Dick	whale
Three Musketeers	sword
From the Earth to the Moon	rocket

Table 4-2 Books and Possible Symbols

In the EPUB, these images could be shrunk down to a height of around 100 pixels or less (keeping the aspect ratio). These can then be placed in as a section break with a margin above and below to give some blank space around it. The image can also be centered. An example follows:

```
XHTML:        <img alt="Moby Dick" src="../Images/Whale.jpg"/>
CSS:          img {display:block;margin:1em auto 1em auto;}
```

When the margin-left and margin-right values are set to auto, then both sides are calculated and made equal. This causes the block element, set by the display:block, to be centered.

Some devices may not support this centering feature, but you can achieve this manually, as shown:

```
XHTML:      <p class="center"><img alt="Moby Dick" src="../Images/Whale.jpg"/></p>
CSS:        .center{text-align:center;}
            img {margin:1em auto 1em auto;}
```

Both of these together should work on most, if not all, systems.

NOTE

To see an example of a full e-book, download Nada The Lily.epub from the McGraw-Hill website. It includes examples on images, fonts, and chapter layouts. It is also a great read.

Another option is to alternate pictures between every other section break. This may not work on all devices, but it is a cool trick for the devices it does work on.

First, pick two images and embed them in the EPUB. Then set up the image tags for each section break as shown:

```
<img alt="" title="placepic"/>
```

If needed, place the code in paragraph tags to allow it to be centered as previously described. You should notice there are not enough attributes for the image tag, especially the source attribute. Don't worry yet; we'll take care of it.

You then need the following CSS styles:

```
img {display:block; margin-left:auto; margin-right:auto;}
img[title=placepic]:nth-of-type(2n+1) {content:url("../Images/
bowarrow.jpg"); width: 71px; height: 100px;}
img[title=placepic]:nth-of-type(2n){content:url("../Images/Bullseye.
jpg"); width: 87px; height: 112px;}
```

The nth-of-type value of 2n+1 is for odd values and 2n is for even. Of course, these can be replaced with "odd" and "even" values. Also, you can see that code is set for img by itself, which centers the image. The content code is added to the HTML <img> coding for the even and odd images, overwriting any properties that are the same.

What happens is the content is added to the <img> that it finds in the XHTML files. It also sets the width and height for each image as needed. An example is given in c04-05 .epub on the McGraw-Hill website. Another example is also given in the EPUB to show a second way to place the images without depending on nth-of-type.

NOTE

By using the content attribute to complete the image tag, when you perform an EPUB validation check, it will show errors.

Comic Books

Color EPUB devices have built-in support for comic books (CBZ). CBZ, or Comic Book Zipped, is a ZIP file containing scanned images of the comic book. The built-in support allows for the images to be zoomed in. Older devices do not support this feature. The best way to handle this feature is to digitally cut out each square on each page and make it a single page. The images can then be enlarged for ease of reading. For an example, see c04-06.epub, which is a Robin Hood comic book. Public-domain comic books can be downloaded from www.comicbookplus.com.

Magazines

Magazines are usually set up similar to the CBZ files. The magazine is scanned as JPG files and placed in separate XHTML files. The main difference is that the magazine is usually left as a single page, requiring a newer device that can zoom in to view portions of the whole page.

Colors

Colors can be an important part of EPUB. As I've mentioned before, even on a monochrome device, colors appear as shades of gray. Don't be afraid to use colors; just be aware how they look both in color and on a monochrome device.

Displaying Colors

There are five ways to express colors in an EPUB: six-digit hex, three-digit hex, RGB integers, RGB percents, and color names. Use whichever method you feel more comfortable with.

Six-Digit Hex

Hexadecimal values range from 00 to FF, which is 0 to 255 in standard numerals. Conversion from one to another can be accomplished by using a scientific calculator. Usually, you select decimal (DEC) and type in the number you want to convert to hex and then press the hexadecimal (HEX) key. The hex value should be shown on the display. Remember that hex counts 0 to 9 and then uses letters A to F for 10 to 15.

Hex values are ordered specifically based on red, green, blue (RGB) values. Each has an allowable range of 0 to 255 (00 to FF). The hex numbers are preceded by a pound (#) sign.

For example, red would be #FF0000, green would be #00FF00, and blue would be #0000FF. Then, of course, mixing colors like blue and red to make purple would be #FF00FF. Using a value of FF; produces a pure color and #FF00FF would be a dark purple. To lighten it to a medium purple, you would use a less-than-pure color, such as #880088.

Three-Digit Hex

Three-digit hex is similar to six-digit hex, but it uses only one hex value for each color. For example, red would be #F00, green is #0F0, and blue is #00F. Values are 0 through 9, then A through F. The higher the value, the more pure the color will be. For example, #F00 would be a bright true red, while #500 would be a deep dark red, almost black.

RGB Integers

The RGB value is similar to hex, but you can use the decimal values, which are separated by commas. For example, red is RGB(255,0,0), green is RGB(00,255,00), and blue is RGB(00,00,255). Mixing colors is achieved by setting values for more than one color. Purple, for example, would be RGB(255,0,255).

RGB Percents

RGB percents use percentages to represent the RGB values. Percentages can include a decimal and range from 0.0 percent to 100.0 percent. For example, red would be RGB(100%,0%,0%), green would be RGB(0%,100%,0%), and blue would be RGB(0%,0%,100%).

As before, the colors can be mixed to produce any color you wish to use.

Color Names

IDPF states that a device may render the XHTML 1.1 color names, of which there are 16. The reading system may render the CSS 2.0 color names as well, for a total of 147 color names. The 16 are listed here; the full 147 color names are listed in c04-07.epub. Also provided are examples using the different color expressions. The 16 colors are black, white, aqua, blue, fuchsia, gray, green, lime, maroon, navy, olive, purple, red, silver, teal, and yellow.

Grayscale

Converting to grayscale is a simple task. For my Nook device, the conversion looks like this:

```
Grayscale Value = (.28 * Red) + (.60 * Green) + (.12 * Blue)
```

If we have a color such as purple—RGB(255,0,255)—we would get a grayscale value of 102. Now we create a new RGB value of RGB(102,102,102). The gray produced by the grayscale value should match up perfectly to the purple if they were side by side on my Nook.

You may be wondering how I create the values for my device. Using the c04-08.epub file, you look through the color tables shown for red, green, and blue. Start with red and find where the colors match as perfectly as possible. Take that number—assume it is .28 in this example— and the equation would start with .28 * red. Do the same for blue—we'll assume it is .60. Now, taking these two numbers and adding them (.28 + .60), we get .88. We then subtract this from 1.0 and get .12, which should be the number for blue. Be aware that blue is dark and most lower values all match. All three numbers found must add up to 1.0, so just subtract it from 1.0 and it should work. Now you have your own equation for your device. You can edit the end of c04-08.epub with Sigil to change the Rainbow section. Once done, place it on your device and all the colors should match perfectly. If, for some reason, they seem a little off, try the process again; be a little more careful—it takes some practice.

A listing of the grayscale values is shown in Figure 4-2.

NOTE

The equation may produce a decimal value, such as 192.8. Drop the decimal place and round it as needed to 193.

0	32	64	96	128	160	192	224
1	33	65	97	129	161	193	225
2	34	66	98	130	162	194	226
3	35	67	99	131	163	195	227
4	36	68	100	132	164	196	228
5	37	69	101	133	165	197	229
6	38	70	102	134	166	198	230
7	39	71	103	135	167	199	231
8	40	72	104	136	168	200	232
9	41	73	105	137	169	201	233
10	42	74	106	138	170	202	234
11	43	75	107	139	171	203	235
12	44	76	108	140	172	204	236
13	45	77	109	141	173	205	237
14	46	78	110	142	174	206	238
15	47	79	111	143	175	207	239
16	48	80	112	144	176	208	240
17	49	81	113	145	177	209	241
18	50	82	114	146	178	210	242
19	51	83	115	147	179	211	243
20	52	84	116	148	180	212	244
21	53	85	117	149	181	213	245
22	54	86	118	150	182	214	246
23	55	87	119	151	183	215	247
24	56	88	120	152	184	216	248
25	57	89	121	153	185	217	249
26	58	90	122	154	186	218	250
27	59	91	123	155	187	219	251
28	60	92	124	156	188	220	252
29	61	93	125	157	189	221	253
30	62	94	126	158	190	222	254
31	63	95	127	159	191	223	255

Figure 4-2 Grayscale with decimal values

Chapter 5

Navigation Center eXtended (NCX) and Open Packaging Format (OPF)

- Understand how the navigation system works
- Learn how to edit the NCX
- Learn how to edit the OPF
- Learn how to check the validity of the NCX and OPF

All EPUB files require the existence of one Navigation Center eXtended (NCX) and Open Packaging Format (OPF) file. The NCX file allows for navigation through the file. For EPUB reading systems, for example, a table of contents can be opened for the reader to navigate the publication. The navigation comes from the contents of the NCX file. In Sigil, the NCX contents are shown in the right pane labeled Table Of Contents.

The OPF file keeps a list of all files, provides the metadata, manages reading order, specifies the NCX, and provides fallback information for the EPUB. Sigil produces the NCX and OPF files for you, but you can edit them manually as needed.

NCX Introduction

The NCX is a required UTF-8 encoded file located in the OEBPS directory. The filename can be almost anything, as long as the extension is .ncx; usually, it is toc.ncx.

The NCX has five sections. We'll go over each section individually. As I stated, Sigil creates the file for you, so there may be no need to ever edit the file, but it is best that you understand the contents.

NOTE

If needed, open one of the sample files from Chapter 4 in Sigil and view the NCX file.

Header

As with any XML-based file, there needs to be a header. The NCX has specific requirements maintained by the DAISY (Digital Accessible Information System) Consortium. As you can see in the following code, the DOCTYPE is set to the DTD (Document Type Definition) from www.daisy.org.

```
<?xml version="1.0" encoding="UTF-8" standalone="no" ?>
<!DOCTYPE ncx PUBLIC "-//NISO//DTD ncx 2005-1//EN"
 "http://www.daisy.org/z3986/2005/ncx-2005-1.dtd">
```

The header is a requirement for the NCX file. Do not omit or change any part unless the International Digital Publishing Forum (IDPF) or DAISY should update the NCX standard.

<ncx>

The next section is the main section that contains the rest of the NCX. You can think of it as being similar to the XHTML <body> section. It begins with the following:

```
<ncx xmlns="http://www.daisy.org/z3986/2005/ncx/" version="2005-1">
```

After all the other sections have completed, the <ncx> section ends with the following:

```
</ncx>
```

Make sure both of these lines exist in any NCX file.

<head>

The next section is the <head>, which contains metadata, as shown:

```
<head>
    <meta content="urn:uuid:3a4fb55f-b38e-4d83-b75b-3c39bfb3c97f" name="dtb:uid"/>
    <meta content="3" name="dtb:depth"/>
    <meta content="0" name="dtb:totalPageCount"/>
    <meta content="0" name="dtb:maxPageNumber"/>
</head>
```

The urn:uuid is a Uniform Resource Name (URN) that is a unique identifier and must match the UUID contained in the OPF file. The UUID (Universally Unique Identifier) is a string of 16 octets or 12 bytes. The numbers are hexadecimal and should be unique to the EPUB. Sigil creates its own unique IDs so you do not need to worry about it.

The DTB stands for Digital Talking Book. The depth represents the levels in the table of contents. In the sample listed, it shows a value of three. The value shows how many levels and sublevels exist.

In previous chapters, I mentioned how Sigil can use the header tags to create a table of contents (TOC). Do not confuse the TOC with a page of hyperlinks in the EPUB that shows a list of chapters. Selecting one would take you to that specific chapter, but these can be cumbersome to navigate. The TOC we are talking about is a "digital" TOC. The reading system allows you to navigate to specific pages or chapters in a similar way. You should be able to access this TOC on your display and allow a simple selection to move around the EPUB.

Sigil creates the TOC in the NCX from header tags. If you list a book title as an <h1> tag, for example, and each chapter as an <h2> tag, then there would be two levels. In the previous sample code from an NCX, it showed a depth of three. The three levels show that Sigil used <h1>, <h2>, and <h3> tags as titles. The example is from Nada The Lily.epub, which can be downloaded from McGraw-Hill's website at www.mhprofessional.com/EPUB.

The totalPageCount and maxPageNumber are required entries that are often set to zero. They often have no bearing on anything but still must be present in the NCX.

<doctitle>

The next section is the <doctitle>, which includes the entry for the book's title. Reading systems do not use the listed title, but it is a requirement of the NCX. The coding follows:

```
<docTitle>
<text>Nada the Lily</text>
</docTitle>
```

The title of the EPUB is Nada the Lily, and should match dc:title in the OPF. The entry is like all other entries in the NCX, which Sigil makes. Changing it will not affect anything, but it may be best not to make changes unless needed.

<navMap>

The navigational map is the heart of the NCX. It stores all the important information. The structure is set for each header tag in Sigil and is set up like this:

```
<navMap>
    <navPoint id="navPoint-1" playOrder="1">
        <navLabel>
            <text>NADA THE LILY</text>
        </navLabel>
        <content src="Text/Title.xhtml"/>
        <navPoint id="navPoint-2" playOrder="2">
            <navLabel>
                <text>DEDICATION</text>
            </navLabel>
            <content src="Text/Dedication.html#sigil_toc_id_2"/>
        </navPoint>
        <navPoint id="navPoint-3" playOrder="3">
            <navLabel>
               <text>PREFACE</text>
```

```
            </navLabel>
            <content src="Text/Preface.html"/>
        </navPoint>
        <navPoint id="navPoint-4" playOrder="4">
            <navLabel>
                <text>INTRODUCTION</text>
            </navLabel>
            <content src="Text/Introduction.html"/>
            <navPoint id="navPoint-5" playOrder="5">
                <navLabel>
                    <text>CHAPTER I</text>
                </navLabel>
                <content src="Text/Chapter_001.html"/>
            </navPoint>
      ......more lines
        </navPoint>
    </navPoint>
</navMap>
```

navPoint

The navPoint is a section that includes navLabel and content. Other entries may be nested within it (a sublevel) or after the end navPoint tag (level). By nesting the entries, you add another depth, counted by dtb:depth.

The id and playOrder attributes must be unique within the <navMap>. For a good example, look at the NCX in Nada the Lily. The depth of the <navMap> is three, and there are 36 chapters.

The id is a unique identifier, while playOrder is a consecutive listing of the sections' order. The playOrder should match the itemref order of the spine in the OPF.

NOTE

Some items in the NCX may not appear in the spine of the OPF. The spine is a listing of main files, the XHTML files, while the NCX may list subsections of files.

navLabel

The navLabel attribute contains a text element. The text element includes the title or text within the header tag. If you look at Nada The Lily.epub, you will see the Title.XHTML has an <h1> tag. The <h1> element contains the text "Nada the Lily," which is in the navLabel text element. If you look at other XHTML files, you will see the pattern from these files is similar to the list in the navLabel.

The second navLabel is for the dedication. You can see from the previous code listing that the Dedication navLabel is indented to the right. The greater indentation is due to the fact that it is an <h2> tag.

The first <h3> tag is for Chapter 1. If you look further down the listing, you can find Chapter 1 and see it is indented more than the Dedication.

content

The content element lists the source (src) file associated with the navPoint. All the information within the navPoint pertains to the source file. The file's location with the OEBPS is shown with the filename itself.

Looking at Nada the Lily, you see the content can point to an anchor, as shown:

```
<navPoint id="navPoint-2" playOrder="2">
      <navLabel>
            <text>DEDICATION</text>
      </navLabel>
      <content src="Text/Dedication.html#sigil_toc_id_2"/>
</navPoint>
```

Anchors are allowed in the content elements, even though they are not allowed in the OPF, as you'll see in the next chapter.

How Do I Know If the NCX Is Valid?

Sigil includes the EPUB Validator with FlightCrew. Normally, the icon, a large green check mark, is at the top right in Sigil. Once you select it, Sigil will validate the currently loaded EPUB and show any errors in the bottom Validation Results pane. If no errors occur, then you should see the message "No problems found!" Errors that do exist are listed with the filename and the line number where they occur.

Be aware that the Validator checks not only the NCX, but the whole EPUB, with the exception of the CSS.

OPF Introduction

The Open Packaging Format (OPF) is a portion of the three parts of the EPUB standard. The OPF is a required UTF-8 encoded file found in the OEBPS directory with the NCX. The filename can be almost anything as long as the extension is .OPF—usually, it is named content.opf. The OPF file must be referenced by the meta-inf/container.xml file discussed previously in Chapter 1.

The OPF is an XML file that has six parts: the header, package, metadata, manifest, spine, and guide.

NOTE

If needed, open one of the sample files from Chapter 4 in Sigil and view the OPF file.

Header

Being an XML file, the OPF requires a header. The header is the standard XML header, as follows:

```
<?xml version="1.0" encoding="UTF-8" standalone="yes" ?>
```

The header has been described previously in Chapter 1.

<package>

The <package> section contains the rest of the OPF contents. It also must specify the namespace of www.idpf.org/2007/opf and have a version of 2.0. If the version is omitted, the EPUB must be processed as an Open E-Book Publication Structure (OEBPS) 1.2 book. An example of the <package> section follows:

```
<package version="2.0" xmlns="http://www.idpf.org/2007/opf">
      …rest of OPF contents
</package>
```

The remaining sections are placed between the package tags. To see the whole file, look at a sample EPUB from Chapter 4.

<metadata>

The metadata is the section containing the EPUB metadata. An example follows of the metadata for Nada The Lily.epub:

```
<metadata xmlns:dc="http://purl.org/dc/elements/1.1/"
xmlns:opf="http://www.idpf.org/2007/opf">
      <dc:identifier id="BookId">urn:uuid:3a4fb55f-b38e-4d83-b75b-
3c39bfb3c97f</dc:identifier>
      <dc:title>Nada the Lily</dc:title>
      <dc:creator opf:role="aut">H. Rider Haggard</dc:creator>
      <dc:language>en</dc:language>
      <dc:publisher>ManyBooks.net</dc:publisher>
</metadata>
```

Other entries may exist in the metadata, such as a modification timestamp and the EPUB editor used to change the file, but this can be ignored.

In the example, you can see the Dublin Core properties listed in Chapter 1. Sigil creates these when editing the file. Enter the information in the Metadata Editor by pressing F8 and then filling in the data.

<manifest>

The manifest section is a listing of all files within the EPUB. The list includes three things: the filename, an id, and the media type. A partial example follows from Nada the Lily:

```
<manifest>
      <item href="Text/Chapter_027.html" id="Chapter_027.html" media-
type="application/xhtml+xml"/>
      <item href="Text/Chapter_017.html" id="Chapter_017.html" media-
type="application/xhtml+xml"/>
      <item href="Images/cover.jpg" id="cover" media-type="image/jpeg"/>
      <item href="Text/Chapter_008.html" id="Chapter_008.html" media-
type="application/xhtml+xml"/>
      <item href="Styles/stylesheet.css" id="css" media-type="text/css"/>
      <item href="toc.ncx" id="ncx" media-type="application/x-dtbncx+xml"/>
      <item href="Fonts/Tribal.ttf" id="Tribal.ttf" media-type="application/x-
font-ttf"/>
      <item href="Images/Lily-small.jpg" id="Lily-small.jpg" media-type="image/
jpeg"/>
      <item href="Styles/Footnotes.css" id="Footnotes.css" media-type="text/
css"/>
      <item href="Images/Introduction.jpg" id="Introduction.jpg" media-
type="image/jpeg"/>
      <item href="Images/Chapter%2001.jpg" id="Chapter_01.jpg" media-
type="image/jpeg"/>
</manifest>
```

As you can see, the files are not listed in any specific order. They are listed with the path inside the OEBPS folder. The value of the id is the same as the filename by default. The media-type is set as required in Chapter 1.

NOTE

The items listed in the manifest can have the attributes in any order: id, href, type, and fallback.

You can see from the listing there are entries for XHTML, fonts, CSS, images, and the NCX. Every file must be listed only once. If a file is not listed in the manifest, it will not be accessible by most reading devices.

The id values must be unique due to the use of fallback. An example follows:

```
<manifest>
        <item href="toc.ncx" id="ncx" media-type="application/x-dtbncx+xml"/>
        <item href="Text/Start.xhtml" id="Start.xhtml" media-type="application/
xhtml+xml"/>
        <item fallback="Fallback.doc" href="Misc/Fallback.txt" id="Fallback.
txt" media-type="text/plain"/>
        <item fallback="Fallback.pdf" href="Misc/Fallback.doc" id="Fallback.
doc" media-type="text/plain"/>
        <item fallback="Fallback.XHTML" href="Misc/Fallback.pdf" id="Fallback.
pdf" media-type="text/plain"/>
        <item href="Misc/Fallback.xhtml" id="Fallback.XHTML" media-
type="application/xhtml+xml"/>
        <item href="Text/End.xhtml" id="End.xhtml" media-type="application/
xhtml+xml"/>
    </manifest>
```

NOTE

Most reading systems do not support fallback. Use c05-01.epub to test the fallback capabilities of a reading system.

In this example, the first file to be loaded is start.xhtml, listed as the href. When the next page is displayed, the reading system should attempt to load a text file. If the device does not support the text file, then it will attempt the fallback id of Fallback.doc.

The Fallback.doc id is for the Fallback.doc file, listed in the href as Misc/Fallback.doc. Again, if the reading device does not support a Word document, it will then go to the fallback with the id of Fallback.pdf.

At this point, the PDF file will be loaded if it is supported. If not, the fallback will be to the Fallback.xhtml file. Of course, being XHTML, it should be supported by all EPUB devices. If not, the reading device should create a warning and exit the EPUB.

<spine>

The spine section specifies the reading order to the reading systems. In this section, only full filenames can be listed, not anchors. The files are then displayed from the first to the last. The first file is displayed when its end is reached, the next file is displayed from the list. The process continues until the end of the spine is reached.

The spine section must exist and contain at least one reference to a file in the <manifest>. The documents referenced must be OPS documents, as listed in Chapter 1. If the item is not an OPS document, there must be a fallback chain. Every item in the <spine> can appear there only once, since loops in the chain are not allowed.

A sample spine follows from the c05-01.epub example:

```
<spine toc="ncx">
      <itemref idref="Start.xhtml"/>
      <itemref idref="Fallback.txt"/>
      <itemref idref="End.xhtml"/>
</spine>
```

The idref has a value to match the id value in the manifest (look at the <manifest> section in the fallback code listing).

The <spine> includes the NCX file referenced by the id from the <manifest>, as shown:

```
<item href="toc.ncx" id="ncx" media-type="application/x-dtbncx+xml"/>
```

Another attribute used is the linear attribute. Usually, this attribute is ignored by most reading systems. The linear attribute is used to specify when an entry in the <spine> is required to be in the reading order and when it should be skipped. The IDPF standards indicate that a reading system may ignore the attributes and assume they are all required to be displayed.

The values for the linear attribute are either yes or no. The value is yes when the file is required in the linear order and no when it can be skipped. The attribute and value are placed in the <spine>, as follows from the example c05-02.epub:

```
<spine toc="ncx">
      <itemref idref="Title.xhtml" linear="yes"/>
      <itemref idref="Start.xhtml" linear="yes"/>
      <itemref idref="Heads.xhtml" linear="no"/>
      <itemref idref="Tails.xhtml" linear="no"/>
      <itemref idref="End.xhtml" linear="no"/>
</spine>
```

The first two XHTML files should be displayed in order. For a reading system that supports the linear attribute, the last three XHTML files should not be displayed. Instead, they should be accessible from hyperlinks. In this manner, an EPUB could be created allowing for a person to read a few pages and then make a decision. A new page would be displayed and more decisions made until the reader comes to a page with no more hyperlinks and the story is ended. Unfortunately, on most devices, this does not work and the reader can simply change the page to a spot they wish to go to. The reader is not required to get to a specific page by hyperlinks only.

<guide>

The guide section is used to identify components of the EPUB. The guide is not required by any reading system. If the <guide> exists, however, it must contain one or more elements and can contain anchors.

Each element has one href, which references an item in the <manifest>. The title attribute can have a value of anything; usually, it may be the title in the file (header) or the same name as the type. The type is a reference taken from the 13th edition of the *Chicago Manual of Style* and listed in Table 5-1.

Type	Description
cover	The book cover(s), jacket information, etc.
title-page	Page with possibly title, author, publisher, and other metadata
toc	Table of contents
index	Back-of-book-style index
glossary	List of terms
acknowledgements	Author's expression of gratitude
bibliography	List of book references
colophon	Publisher's emblem
copyright-page	Page displaying copyright information
dedication	Words with which the book is dedicated
epigraph	Short quotation suggesting a theme
foreword	Short introduction by the author
loi	List of illustrations
lot	List of tables
notes	Listing by author of facts
preface	Introduction to book stating subject and scope
text	First "real" page of content (e.g., "chapter 1")

Table 5-1 List of Guide Types

The following example comes from c05-02.epub. The types are generated by Sigil when they are applied by the user. To create them, right-click an XHTML file in the Book Browser pane, select Add Semantics, and then choose the type.

```
<guide>
      <reference href="Text/Title.xhtml" title="Title Page"
type="title-page"/>
      <reference href="Text/Start.xhtml" title="Text" type="text"/>
      <reference href="Misc/Heads.xhtml" title="Text" type="text"/>
      <reference href="Misc/Tails.xhtml" title="Text" type="text"/>
      <reference href="Misc/End.xhtml" title="Text" type="text"/>
</guide>
```

These items are not necessary. The <guide> section is the only one not required in the OPF.

Chapter 6

Converting EPUB Files

- Understand how to convert from EPUB to other formats
- Learn how to convert from other formats to EPUB

The majority of reading devices and systems support EPUB. Unfortunately, not all systems support EPUB and not all formats are EPUB compatible. EPUB is usually an easier format to manipulate, so being able to convert other formats to EPUB helps. The opposite is true as well. If you need another format, EPUB is easier to manipulate and convert to the other format.

Not all conversions are 100 percent perfect. Some need a little tweaking, but with all the information from the previous chapters, it should be simple.

Getting Ready to Convert

For this chapter, you'll need Calibre. Calibre is an e-book manager. It lets you organize the books into categories and series. The main thing about Calibre is its ability to convert files.

A list of input formats is shown in Table 6-1, and the output formats are in Table 6-2.

Format	Description
CBZ	Comic Book Zipped; compressed images of comic books
CBR	Comic Book RAR; compressed images of comic books
CBC	Comic Book Collection; compressed images of comic books
CHM	Compiled HTML Help files; compressed HTML files used as a help manual
DJVU (djv)	Extremely compressed scanned documents
EPUB	Compressed HTML, images, etc., with OPF
FB2	Fiction Book (OpenXML) XML–based e-book format
HTML	Hypertext Markup Language
HTMLZ	Compressed HTML, images, OPF

Table 6-1 Calibre Input Formats

Format	Description
LIT	Microsoft e-book format
LRF	Sony Portable Reader e-book format (compile to LRX files)
MOBI	MobiPocket Reader format; predecessor of Kindle AZW
ODT	OpenDocument Text document from OpenOffice
PDF	Adobe Portable Document Format
PRC	MobiPocket e-book format; compatible with Kindle
PDB	Palm Desktop Database for Palm-based PDA
PML	Palm Markup Language; can be made into PDB
RB	RocketBook format; compressed HTML files with images
RTF	Rich Text Format
SNB	E-book format for Shanda Bambooks
TCR	E-book for Psion Series 3
TXT	Standard text file
TXTZ	Compressed text, images, and OPF

Table 6-1 Calibre Input Formats (*continued*)

Format	Description
AZW3	E-book format for Kindle (KF8)
EPUB	Compressed HTML, images, etc., with OPF
FB2	Fiction Book (OpenXML) XML–based e-book format
HTML	Hypertext Markup Language
HTMLZ	Compressed HTML, images, OPF
LIT	Microsoft e-book format
LRF	Sony Portable Reader e-book format (compile to LRX files)

continues

Table 6-2 Calibre Output Formats

Format	Description
MOBI	MobiPocket Reader format; predecessor of Kindle AZW
OEB	Open E-Book file format; superseded by EPUB
PFF	Formatta Portable Form file format; similar to PDF
PDB	Palm Desktop Database for Palm-based PDA
PML	Palm Markup Language; can be made into PDB
RB	RocketBook format; compressed HTML files with images
RTF	Rich Text Format
SNB	E-book format for Shanda Bambooks
TCR	E-book for Psion Series 3
TXT	Standard text file
TXTZ	Compressed text, images, and OPF

Table 6-2 Calibre Output Formats (*continued*)

In most cases, a format from the input list can be converted to the output format. However, a problem may arise if any security is enabled on the input (see Chapter 7).

Once a book has been converted, it may be necessary to review the output file. Sometimes certain items may not convert as desired. Some formatting may be changed or lost.

A good example is converting from PDF, which does not store the information about paragraph starting and ending points. Because of this, some paragraphs are not output as complete paragraphs. Sometimes the paragraphs are joined with others or split up into multiple paragraphs.

Converting to EPUB

Start Calibre after you install it. E-book files can then be dragged and dropped onto the window, or click Add Books on the tool menu. Once files are added, you will see them listed in the Book List pane. If you select a book from the list, the right pane shows the cover (if it exists), the author, the file formats, and a hyperlink to the file path.

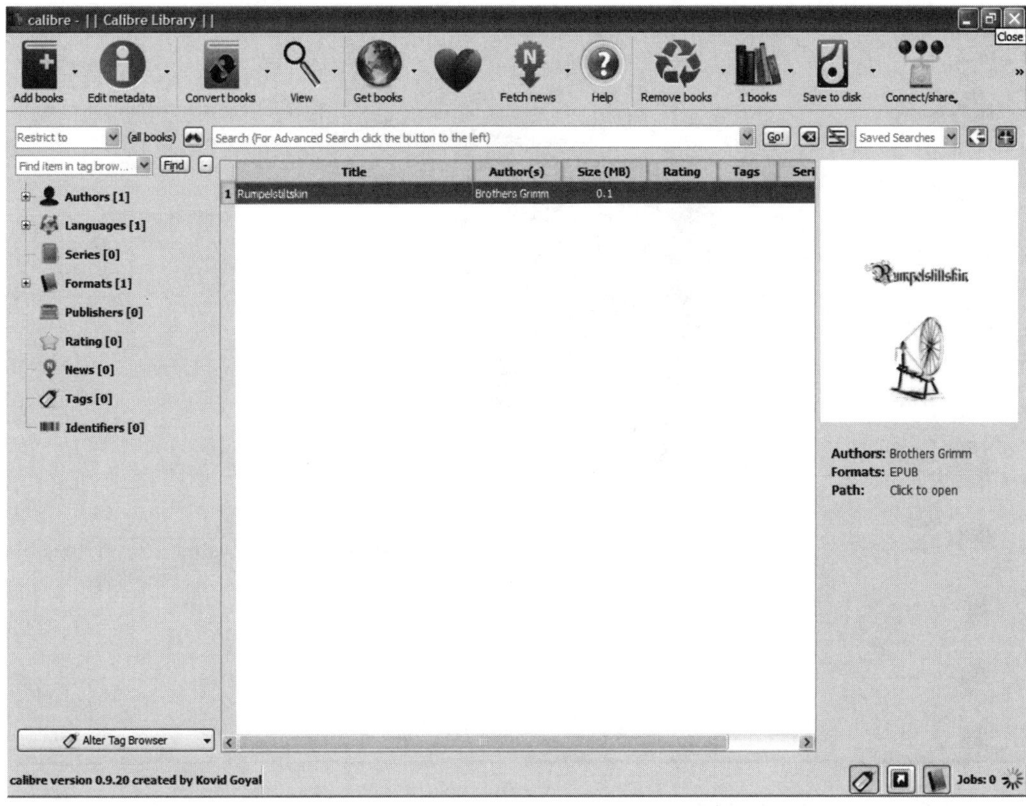

Figure 6-1 Calibre screen showing *Rumpelstiltskin*

An example is shown in Figure 6-1 showing Calibre with the information for *Rumpelstiltskin* to the right.

Now, download *The Three Musketeers* from www.ManyBooks.net, but download it in the FictionBook2 (fb2) format. Add the new file to Calibre and select it. To the right, you should see the format listed as FB2. With the book selected, click Convert Books from the toolbar. A new window should appear as shown in Figure 6-2.

NOTE

If you open the FB2 file in an editor, you can see it is an XML file similar to XHTML. There are no header tags, only paragraph tags.

In the upper-right corner of the Conversion box, the output format needs to be EPUB.

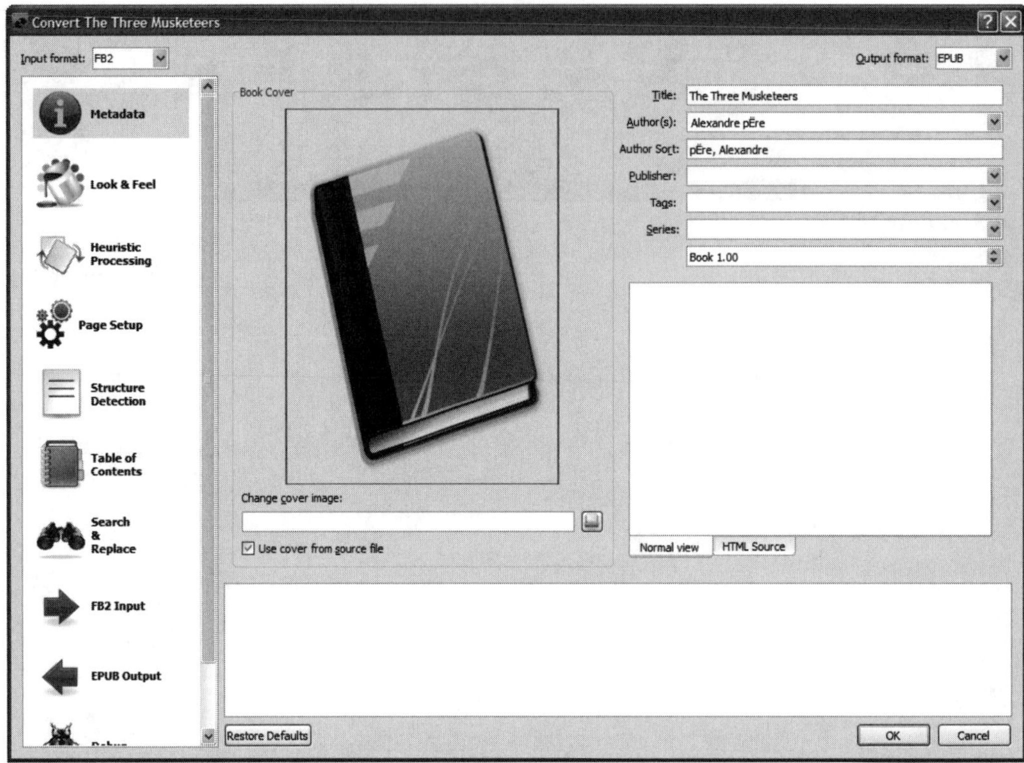

Figure 6-2 Converting in Calibre

The only suggestions I can make here is to change the following:

- **Look & Feel** Clear the UnSmarten Punctuation box. This removes the slanted quotation marks and the like, making them regular quotes.
- **Page Setup** Select your EPUB device from the output profile. This assures your EPUB is more suited for your device.

Make other adjustments based on your preference. I mainly "unsmarten" the punctuation so it is easier to search in Sigil. The "smartened" quotes are not the same ones on the keyboard.

Select the OK button in the bottom-right corner. The main screen should reappear showing Jobs: 1 in the lower-right corner. Once this is done, you should have EPUB listed next to the format for *Three Musketeers*.

NOTE

Be aware that some conversions may take a long time to complete. If you single-click the Jobs: area, a new window will appear displaying the progress of any running jobs.

Keep in mind that the file formats are stored in the Calibre Library directory. To save a copy at a different location, right-click the format you wish to save. So, right-click the EPUB link on the format line for *The Three Musketeers.* Select Save The EPUB Format To Disk. Choose where you want to save it, and select OK. Now you can go to the location where the file was saved and open it in Sigil.

If you look at the CSS style sheet, you should see the styles are usually called "calibre" with a number following it. When you see the calibre styles, you know it has been converted with Calibre.

The best thing to do at this point is to clean up the EPUB as best as you can. Hardly any conversion is 100 percent exact.

Now, you may be thinking that it would have been easier just to download the EPUB version. In this case, that would be true. Sometimes, however, you may come across a book that is not in the format you need it in. You'll need to perform a conversion and usually tidy it up a bit.

Let's try another one. Download the MOBI version of *The Island of Doctor Moreau* by H.G. Wells. Perform the same steps as when you converted *The Three Musketeers.* Once it has been converted to an EPUB, open it in Sigil.

Now begins the work. I start by separating the chapters into individual XHTML files and naming them appropriately. Make sure the chapter titles are header <h2> tags. Modify the cover page as needed, and set up a title page. If there is a legal section for Gutenberg, set it aside in its own XHTML file. Do not forget to check the Metadata Editor (press F8) and make any changes.

I usually also remove all styles and start over. Before you remove styles, make sure there are no special italics and bold styles, or the like.

NOTE

Be aware that most e-books are usually from Project Gutenberg. Because of this, most formatting is nonexistent unless someone has added it. It may take a little time to enhance the look, but in the end you'll have a nice book for your collection. Also, the more of these you do, the easier it gets. You can get some files from Gutenberg that have formatting in them, especially if they are EPUB or Kindle formats.

Special formatting tags may be used in the standard text files to signify italics. For example, some texts may enclose words in forward slashes (/), "He ran /fast/." should appear as "He ran *fast.*" Other e-books may have words which should be italicized in all caps.

Take a look at c06-01.epub (located at www.mhprofessional.com/EPUB) and you'll find an example of *The Island of Doctor Moreau* converted from the MOBI format to EPUB and slightly enhanced. This version was downloaded from www.Gutenberg.org.

You may need a little practice, but the process gets easier the more you convert and enhance the EPUB files.

Converting from EPUB

You may recall that back in Chapter 1 I made reference to the Amazon Kindle. Well, here we are. Sometimes it is easier to manipulate a file as an EPUB and convert it to the Kindle format (AZW, MOBI).

Other formats are available, as you have seen in Table 6-2. It seems that from the list, the Kindle format would be the most popular to convert from EPUB.

NOTE

Keep in mind that most MOBI and AZW files can usually have the extension changed to the other without any problems. The difference is that Amazon uses a different security than MOBI. So a secured AZW file is different from a secured MOBI file. AZW files have a few enhancements over MOBI, such as compression, etc.

The process of converting from EPUB is the same as when converting to EPUB. Right-click an e-book in Calibre, select Convert, and change the output format to AZW3.

Before you start, be aware that the cover image used for the new e-book is the same one shown on the right side of the Calibre screen when you select an e-book. If the image is already in the e-book you are converting from, it will now be in the new e-book twice. To fix this issue, right-click the cover image on the right side of the screen and select Remove Cover. You only need to worry about this for covers of the e-books you will convert. You can get a new book cover image by selecting a book and clicking the Edit Metadata icon. When a new window opens, click Download Cover. Of course, you'll need to be connected to the Internet. After some time, you should be shown covers. Choose the cover you like and select OK.

TIP

To edit any files in Calibre, right-click the file in the book list and select Open Containing Folder. Once the folder opens, select the file type you want to edit and open it in your editor.

The sample file c06-02.epub is an EPUB file of "Rikki-Tikki-Tavi" taken from Rudyard Kipling's *The Jungle Book.* The sample files c06-03.azw3 and c6-03.mobi show the EPUB files converted to the Kindle format following the steps previously mentioned.

To convert EPUB to Kindle KF8 (AZW3), you can also use KindleGen and Kindle Previewer.

The Kindle Previewer application allows you to emulate the Kindle display on various Kindle devices: Kindle Paperwhite, Kindle, Kindle DX, Kindle Fire, Kindle Fire HD, and the Kindle Fire HD 8.9". You can also emulate the Kindle App for iOS for the iPad and iPhone.

Since there is a slight difference in the MOBI and AZW formats, Calibre supports two different types of MOBI. The "old" MOBI is the MOBI version 6 format before AZW. A "new" MOBI format is technically AZW3 (KF8). Table 6-3 shows the various Kindles and the format support. A third MOBI option is listed as "Both," which contains both the old and new formats in one file. The new format will be used unless not supported, and the old format is a fallback.

The sample files for c06-03.mobi are split up as c06-03-old.mobi for the MOBI 6 format. The c06-03-both.mobi file contains both old and new styles, while the c06-03-new.mobi is the KF8 format. All of these can be tested on a Kindle device if you have one; otherwise, use the Kindle Previewer.

		MOBI		
Kindle	AZW3	Old (MOBI 6)	Both	New (AZW3)
Kindle Paperwhite	Yes	Yes	Yes	Yes – Format issues
Kindle	No	Yes	Yes	Yes – Format issues
Kindle DX	No	Yes	Yes	Yes – Format issues
Kindle Fire	Yes	Yes	Yes	Yes
Kindle Fire HD	Yes	Yes	Yes	Yes
Kindle Fire HD 8.9"	Yes	Yes	Yes	Yes
iOS iPad app	Yes	Yes	Yes	Yes
iOS iPhone app	Yes	Yes	Yes	Yes

Table 6-3 Kindle Format Support

Converting to MOBI is the same as converting to AZW3, except for one small difference. When using Calibre to convert to MOBI, there is a screen called MOBI Output, as shown in Figure 6-3.

The following figures show various outputs for "Rikki-Tikki-Tavi." Figure 6-4 is a screenshot from a Barnes and Noble Nook (first edition), and Figure 6-5 is a second-edition device.

The Nook first edition shows embedded fonts, while the second edition does not. As you will see, the same is true of the Kindle devices. The Nook HD devices show embedded fonts as well.

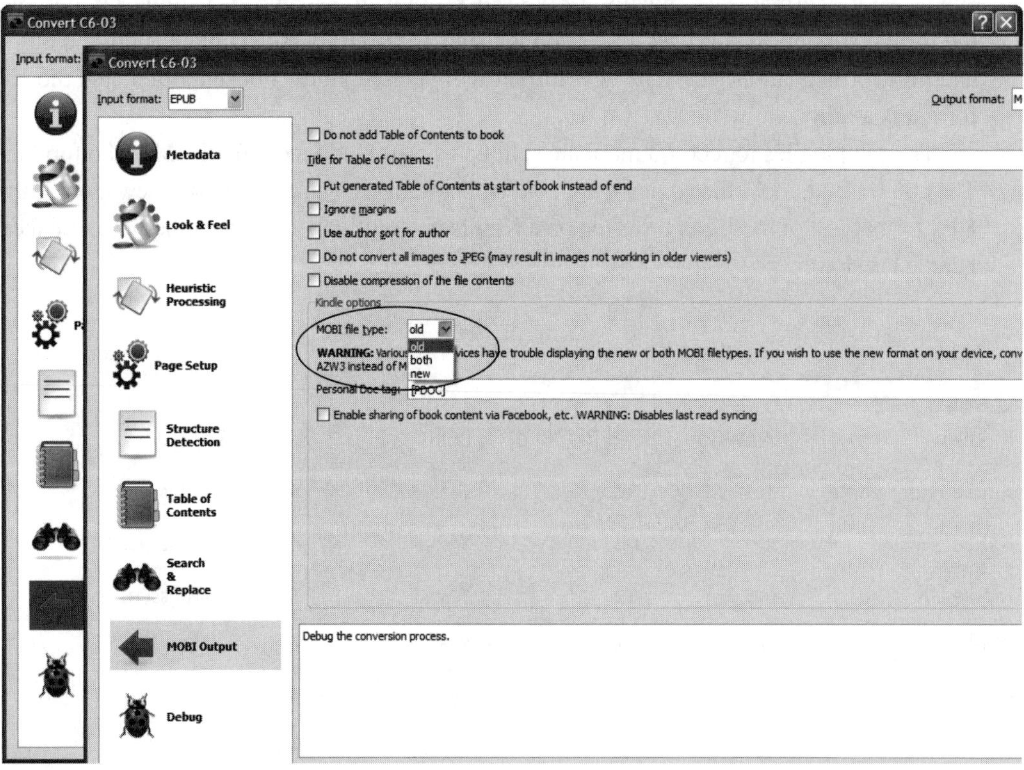

Figure 6-3 Calibre MOBI output

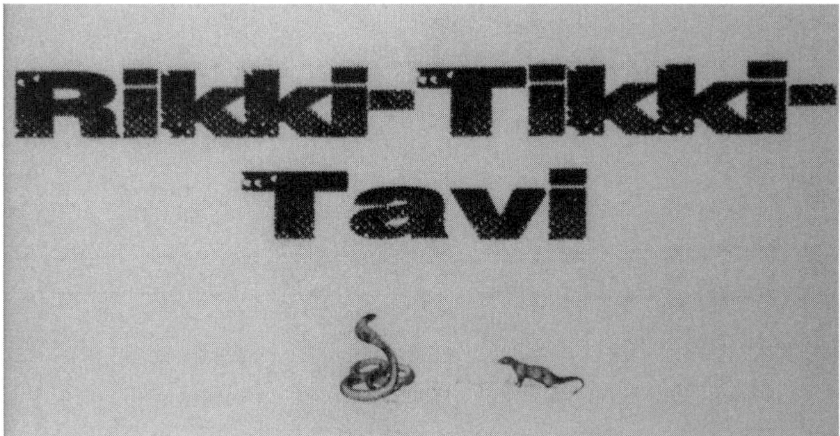

Figure 6-4 Nook first edition

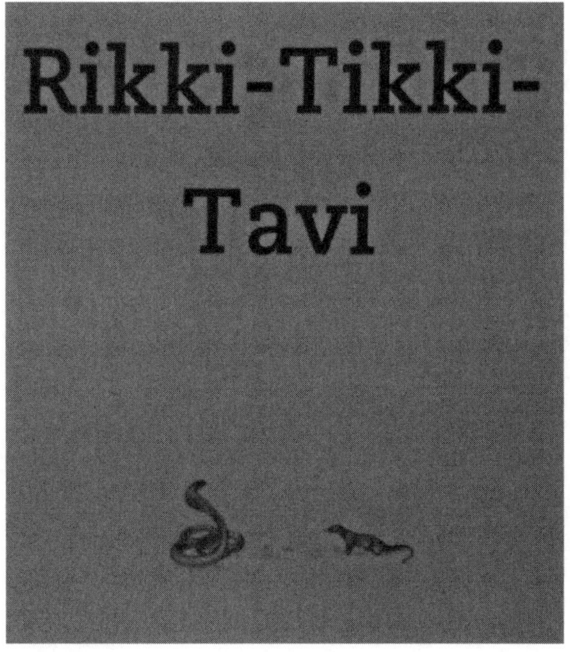

Figure 6-5 Nook second edition

Figure 6-6 Kindle Paperwhite

For the Kindle, Figure 6-6 shows the Kindle Paperwhite, Figure 6-7 is the Kindle, the Kindle DX is in Figure 6-8, and the Kindle Fire is shown in Figure 6-9. The Kindle images are from the Kindle Previewer using MOBI 6 and AZW ("Both").

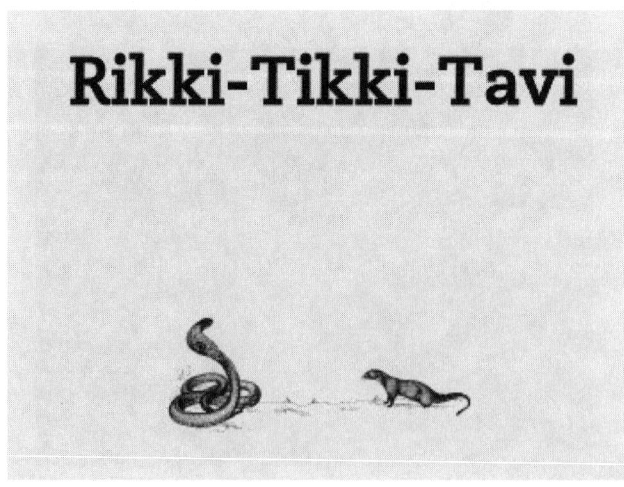

Figure 6-7 Kindle

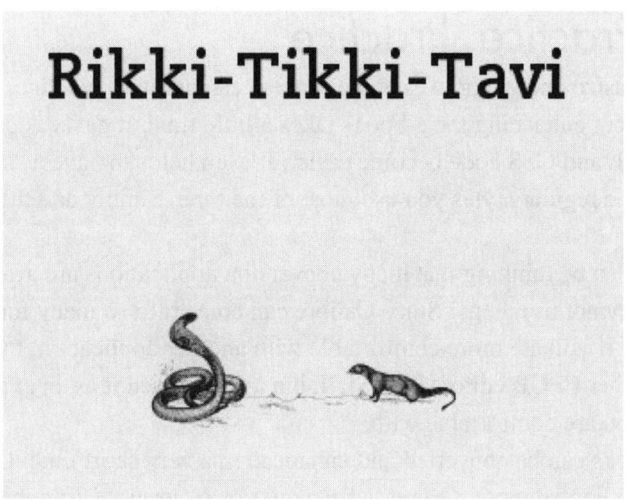

Figure 6-8 Kindle DX

You can see that the images are similar for the Paperwhite, Kindle, and DX. The embedded fonts are not available on these devices, even if you use an AZW format. The Kindle HD devices all look similar as well.

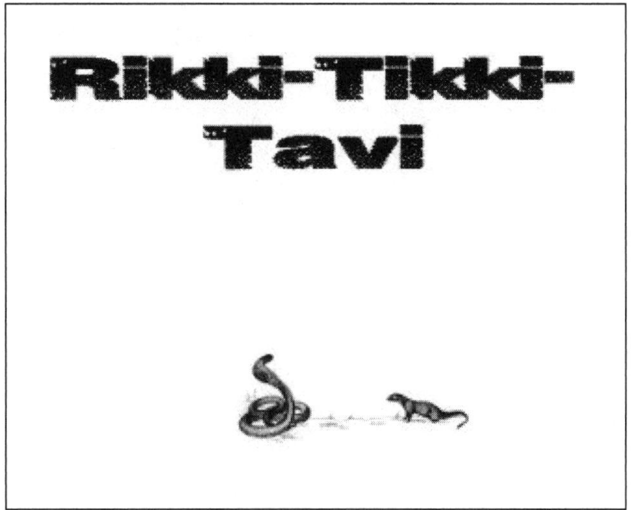

Figure 6-9 Kindle HD

Practice, Practice, Practice

I cannot emphasize enough how easy the process can get with practice. Converting files is a simple task, but enhancing the e-books takes a little time. It gets easier the more you do it. The XHTML and CSS code become easier. It even helps to have a "standard" CSS file that contains the regular styles you use most of the time. Simply add the CSS and link the files to it.

You may also be thinking that many conversion applications are available on the Internet, so why not use them? Since Calibre can convert to so many formats, I used it as an example. If you are more comfortable with another application, by all means, use it. There are other EPUB editors than Sigil, but again, I used it as an example. Use the applications you are comfortable with.

Most e-books can be converted and enhanced in a very short time. Others may take a very long time. For example, *Grimm's Fairytales* or *Household Tales* has over 200 short stories and takes a long time to split into separate files. With practice, however, it won't take long for you to create your own library for your reading device.

Chapter 7

EPUB Security

- Understand the various security methods for EPUB
- Understand how security affects EPUB
- Learn how to secure embedded fonts
- Learn how to know when EPUB contents have changed

New books can be purchased for your EPUB reading systems. These newly released books need to prevent readers from sharing the published work with everyone else on the Internet. EPUB files can be secured to prevent them from easily being shared.

With nonsecured EPUB files, the embedded fonts can be secured to prevent anyone from extracting the fonts. Once a font is extracted, it could be shared on the Internet. Sharing the font may not be allowed if the font is copyrighted.

It can be important for readers to know when the contents of an EPUB file have changed. Readers can even know if contents have been added or removed by signing the EPUB.

Introduction to EPUB Security

Most security is put into place by digital publishers. If you create an e-book and submit it to a publisher to be sold, they may choose to encrypt the file. Since the file is encrypted, it cannot be shared among readers on the Internet. By allowing sharing, the author of the EPUB and the publisher lose revenue because more readers are getting the book for free.

Security limits the purchaser from easily sharing the EPUB and is called digital rights management (DRM).

NOTE

It should definitely be noted that encryption schemes can be cracked by knowledgeable programmers. Removing encryption is beyond the scope of this book and is currently illegal. The issue is hotly debated, however. Purchasers of EPUB books argue that if they purchase the book, they should have the right to decrypt the book and convert it to another format.

Remember from Chapter 1 that the ZIP file cannot be encrypted nor can the META-INF folder and its contents. With an encrypted EPUB, the META-INF directory can contain three extra files: rights.xml, encryption.xml, and signatures.xml.

You may be asking how it all works. Well, let's look at it a piece at a time.

Public Key Infrastructure and RSA

Usually, everything starts when an account is set up on a web server. Let's say you want to download an EPUB from your local library.

Online Libraries

Most local libraries are connected to online libraries. You can ask your local librarian, or go to the website for your local library.

There should be a link somewhere to allow access with your library card. If not, try going to www.search.overdrive.com and clicking Library Search. Enter your ZIP code and then find your library on the list. Once you click your library, you should be taken to a page that shows information about it. On this page should be a link to a digital library associated with your local one.

Books can be downloaded in a variety of formats, including audiobooks. The digital books are usually for Adobe Digital Editions (ADE), which is a free download to view ADE PDFs and EPUBs. These files contain DRM security, but can be viewed for a limited time.

Another format sometimes available is Open EPUB. An Open EPUB file is a standard EPUB file with no security.

To download an e-book, you are required to set up an account. When this account is set up, the server uses your information to generate encryption keys. One key is kept on the server, while the other is for your reading system.

The keys generated are part of the public key infrastructure (PKI), which is an asymmetric key cryptography. More specifically, the portion of PKI is the public-key cryptography standards (PKCS). The PKCS has various encryption methods, but DRM uses PKCS #1, the Rivest, Shamir, and Adleman (RSA) standard.

The two keys, or certificates, are referred to as a public key, which is kept by the server, and a private key, which is kept by you on your reading system. Only the specific private key can decrypt the data encrypted by the public key. (This is just a basic explanation—this is a detailed topic that could require a whole book to explain fully.) DRM is not managed by individuals but by companies. There are currently no applications to download that allow an individual to apply DRM to their own content.

When you get a book from the server, it encrypts the book using the public key, or digital certificate, it generated. The encryption method is a very in-depth mathematical algorithm that obscures the original content. Once the e-book is downloaded and opened, your reading system will use the private key it received to decode the file for viewing.

Within an EPUB, all XHTML, CSS, images, and fonts can be encrypted. Every file can be encrypted, or only a few, but not the mimetype, META-INF folder, and the OPF file.

Once a file is opened, it is decrypted using the private key received from the server. Your application can check with a certificate authority (CA) to validate that your key is still active. If your key has been revoked, then the book will not open. If a key is revoked but you have purchased the EPUB, you need to contact the seller and have the certificate renewed.

Once it has been approved, then other factors are checked, such as the expiration date. Similar to a regular library book, a digital book can be viewed only for a certain time. Once the time expires, the e-book can no longer be viewed. Another factor checked can be on how many devices the e-book is loaded. You are also prohibited from printing or converting the e-book.

There may be more or fewer limitations, depending on the publisher of the book and from where it was downloaded.

Advanced Encryption Standard

Another security method used is Advanced Encryption Standard (AES). The data is put through matrices and encrypted using a complicated algorithm. AES is used to change the data so that no one can easily open and read the EPUB contents. If they could, the EPUB could be shared on the Internet.

The files are encrypted and placed into the ZIP file and renamed to EPUB. The encryption.xml file is generated, as discussed later in this section, and placed into the EPUB as well.

The key generated earlier by PKI is used to alter the files and encrypt them. The private key placed on your reading system is used to decrypt the file so the reading system can display a readable publication.

AES is followed by a number, which refers to the size of the key. DRM uses AES-128.

EPUB Security Files

As mentioned in Chapter 1, the three files for DRM are rights.xml, encryption.xml, and signatures.xml. The files are located in the META-INF folder.

There are two main EPUB DRM schemes: Adobe and Apple. We'll deal with the Adobe DRM scheme to show how the files are set up. Each file has a different use, and we can cover them individually.

rights.xml

The rights file is used to specify the rights a user has to view a specific EPUB. The rights .xml file is stored unencrypted in the META-INF folder.

The best way to learn about the rights.xml file is to view one. Here are the contents of a rights.xml file:

```
<?xml version="1.0"?>
<adept:rights xmlns:adept="http://ns.adobe.com/adept">
      <licenseToken xmlns="http://ns.adobe.com/adept">
            <user>urn:uuid:56b0c84e-261f-4e70-95cc-568d378925dc</user>
            <resource>urn:uuid:408082f9-82bb-406f-af59-256f3ff6fc98</resource>
            <resourceItemType>application/epub+zip</resourceItemType>
            <deviceType>standalone</deviceType>
            <device>urn:uuid:c32972ad-17ea-45f8-cecb5-916f30f49b5b</device>
            <voucher>ContentReserveID:88AFBDDD-54E9-45CF-A36B-…</voucher>
            <licenseURL>https://nasigningservice.adobe.com/licensesign</licenseURL>
            <operatorURL>http://acsepub.contentreserve.com/fulfillment</operatorURL>
            <fulfillment>0a3a8d52-1842-4a8e-a03d-e4e373e50e42-00071039</fulfillment>
            <distributor>urn:uuid:f1227b83-f91b-4f30-9ae2-0f65ffeea9ac</distributor>
            <encryptedKey keyInfo="user">TDsahTgXC…</encryptedKey>
            <permissions>
                  <display>
                        <loan>0a3a8d52-1842-4a8e-a03d-e4e373e50e42-00071039</loan>
                        <until>2013-03-15T21:51:17Z</until>
                  </display>
                  <excerpt>
                        <loan>0a3a8d52-1842-4a8e-a03d-e4e373e50e42-00071039</loan>
                        <until>2013-03-15T21:51:17Z</until>
                  </excerpt>
                  <print>
                        <loan>0a3a8d52-1842-4a8e-a03d-e4e373e50e42-00071039</loan>
                        <until>2013-03-15T21:51:17Z</until>
                  </print>
            </permissions>
            <signature>GjcPUMLsyFSuEyUsTb…</signature>
      </licenseToken>
      <licenseServiceInfo xmlns="http://ns.adobe.com/adept">
            <licenseURL>https://nasigningservice.adobe.com/licensesign</licenseURL>
            <certificate>MIIEvjCCA6agAwI…</certificate>
      </licenseServiceInfo>
</adept:rights>
```

The first line—<?xml version="1.0"?>—denotes that the file is an XML file.

The second line is a section that contains the rest of the file. It shows that the file is protected by Adobe Adept: <adept:rights xmlns:adept="http://ns.adobe.com/adept"> and the distribution server is at http://ns.adobe.com/adept.

After this, we get into the token information at <licenseToken xmlns="http://ns.adobe .com/adept">. Again, we see the information about the distribution server for checking the token information.

The next few lines are about the purchaser and device of the e-book:

```
<user>urn:uuid:56b0c84e-261f-4e70-95cc-568d378925dc</user>
<resource>urn:uuid:408082f9-82bb-406f-af59-256f3ff6fc98</resource>
<resourceItemType>application/epub+zip</resourceItemType>
<deviceType>standalone</deviceType>
<device>urn:uuid:c32972ad-17ea-45f8-cecb5-916f30f49b5b</device>
<voucher>ContentReserveID:88AFBDDD-54E9-45CF-A36B-…</voucher>
<licenseURL>https://nasigningservice.adobe.com/licensesign</licenseURL>
<operatorURL>http://acsepub.contentreserve.com/fulfillment</operatorURL>
<fulfillment>0a3a8d52-1842-4a8e-a03d-e4e373e50e42-00071039</fulfillment>
<distributor>urn:uuid:f1227b83-f91b-4f30-9ae2-0f65ffeea9ac</distributor>
<encryptedKey keyInfo="user">TDsahTgXC…</encryptedKey>
```

Starting with the first line, we have the user ID, resource ID (ID of the e-book), resource type (EPUB), device type (standalone), device ID, voucher ID, URL of license server, URL of operator, fulfillment ID, distributor ID, and finally the encryption key.

Next we get into the permissions allowed for the EPUB:

```
<permissions>
      <display>
            <loan>0a3a8d52-1842-4a8e-a03d-e4e373e50e42-00071039</loan>
            <until>2013-03-15T21:51:17Z</until>
      </display>
      <excerpt>
            <loan>0a3a8d52-1842-4a8e-a03d-e4e373e50e42-00071039</loan>
            <until>2013-03-15T21:51:17Z</until>
      </excerpt>
      <print>
            <loan>0a3a8d52-1842-4a8e-a03d-e4e373e50e42-00071039</loan>
            <until>2013-03-15T21:51:17Z</until>
      </print>
</permissions>
```

The permissions allow the display of the EPUB until the specified time. Here the time is until 2013-03-15T21:51:17Z, which is March 15, 2013, at 21:51:17 Zulu time. The reader may also take excerpts and print from the EPUB until the expiration date.

Finally we come across the following:

```
      <licenseServiceInfo xmlns="http://ns.adobe.com/adept">
            <licenseURL>https://nasigningservice.adobe.com/licensesign</licenseURL>
            <certificate>MIIEvjCCA6agAwI…</certificate>
      </licenseServiceInfo>
</adept:rights>
```

The license service info section shows the license server URL (Uniform Resource Locator) and the certificate associated with the server. The certificate is used to make a connection between the server and its public key. This allows verification of the certificate and authentication of server.

encryption.xml

The encryption.xml file is used to specify the encryption of the EPUB contents. It gives more detailed data about the EPUB than the rights.xml file. The file is stored unencrypted in the META-INF directory.

Like the rights.xml file, it is best to view one in order to better understand it. Here is a portion of the encryption.xml file that goes with the rights.xml file covered in the previous section.

NOTE

Some data is the same in each file, as we will soon see. The repetitions are removed to give you a more concise example.

```
<?xml version="1.0"?>
<encryption xmlns="urn:oasis:names:tc:opendocument:xmlns:container">
      <EncryptedData xmlns="http://www.w3.org/2001/04/xmlenc#">
            <EncryptionMethod Algorithm="http://www.w3.org/2001/04/xmlenc#aes128-
            cbc"></EncryptionMethod>
            <KeyInfo xmlns="http://www.w3.org/2000/09/xmldsig#">
                  <resource xmlns="http://ns.adobe.com/adept">urn:uuid: 408082f9-
                  82bb-406f-af59-256f3ff6fc98</resource>
            </KeyInfo>
            <CipherData>
                  <CipherReference URI="228_split_000.html">
                  </CipherReference>
            </CipherData>
      </EncryptedData>
      <EncryptedData xmlns="http://www.w3.org/2001/04/xmlenc#">
            <EncryptionMethod Algorithm="http://www.w3.org/2001/04/xmlenc#aes128-
            cbc"></EncryptionMethod>
            <KeyInfo xmlns="http://www.w3.org/2000/09/xmldsig#">
                  <resource xmlns="http://ns.adobe.com/adept">urn:uuid: 408082f9-
                  82bb-406f-af59-256f3ff6fc98</resource>
            </KeyInfo>
            <CipherData>
                  <CipherReference URI="cover.jpg">
                  </CipherReference>
            </CipherData>
      <EncryptedData>
      <EncryptedData xmlns="http://www.w3.org/2001/04/xmlenc#">
            <EncryptionMethod Algorithm="http://www.w3.org/2001/04/xmlenc#aes128-
            cbc"></EncryptionMethod>
            <KeyInfo xmlns="http://www.w3.org/2000/09/xmldsig#">
                  <resource xmlns="http://ns.adobe.com/adept">urn:uuid: 408082f9-
                  82bb-406f-af59-256f3ff6fc98</resource>
            </KeyInfo>
            <CipherData>
                  <CipherReference URI="stylesheet.css"></CipherReference>
            </CipherData>
```

```
        </EncryptedData>
        <EncryptedData xmlns="http://www.w3.org/2001/04/xmlenc#">
              <EncryptionMethod Algorithm="http://www.w3.org/2001/04/xmlenc#aes128-
              cbc"></EncryptionMethod>
              <KeyInfo xmlns="http://www.w3.org/2000/09/xmldsig#">
                    <resource xmlns="http://ns.adobe.com/adept">urn:uuid: 408082f9-
                    82bb-406f-af59-256f3ff6fc98</resource>
              </KeyInfo>
              <CipherData>
                    <CipherReference URI="toc.ncx"></CipherReference>
              </CipherData>
        </EncryptedData>
</encryption>
```

As usual, the first line specifies that the file is an XML file.

The next line is the <encryption> section, which contains the rest of the elements. The <encryption> line includes the XML namespace information of the file.

After this, there are a number of <EncryptedData> tags, which are used to specify each file within the EPUB that is encrypted. For the listed example, the repetitions of the various HTML files have been removed as well as the images. Let's look at the first one:

```
<EncryptedData xmlns="http://www.w3.org/2001/04/xmlenc#">
      <EncryptionMethod Algorithm="http://www.w3.org/2001/04/xmlenc#aes128-
      cbc"></EncryptionMethod>
      <KeyInfo xmlns="http://www.w3.org/2000/09/xmldsig#">
            <resource xmlns="http://ns.adobe.com/adept">urn:uuid: 408082f9-
            82bb-406f-af59-256f3ff6fc98</resource>
      </KeyInfo>
      <CipherData>
            <CipherReference URI="228_split_000.html">
            </CipherReference>
      </CipherData>
</EncryptedData>
```

All of the other files are identical in nature except for the CipherReference URI.

The first line shows the namespace for the encrypted data scheme. You can go to www.w3.org/2001/04/xmlenc# to see more information. The next line is the encryption method: AES-128.

The next section is the key information. The information listed here is the resource server and resource ID. The resource ID here matches the resource ID in the rights.xml file.

The next section contains the cipher reference, which relates to the file being encrypted; the data from the rights.xml file can be used to decrypt the data. Each file that is encrypted in the EPUB must be listed an "Encrypted Data" section. As you can see from the sample listed, you can encrypt XHTML, images, CSS, NCX, and fonts.

Within an EPUB 3 file, audio and video files can also be encrypted.

Font Mangling

Font mangling is used to encrypt fonts within the EPUB. The main reason to do this is to protect copyrighted fonts. As we discussed in Chapter 1, an EPUB is nothing more than a ZIP file. Since the ZIP file cannot be encrypted itself, the files are available to anyone who can open a ZIP file and extract the contents. If the fonts can be extracted, then they can be freely used. If the fonts are copyrighted, however, then they must be protected in some manner.

Look at the sample file c07-01.epub (located at www.mhprofessional.com/EPUB). It is *Rumpelstiltskin* from Chapter 6. This time, the font is encrypted. If you extract the EPUB and remove the TrueType Font file, you cannot open it in a font viewer. If you open the EPUB in a reading system that supports embedded fonts, however, you should be able to view the fonts.

Once the font is "mangled," as it is called, the encryption.xml file is created in the META-INF directory. The file has the following contents taken from c07-01.epub:

```
<?xml version="1.0" encoding="UTF-8"?>
<encryption xmlns="urn:oasis:names:tc:opendocument:xmlns:container"
xmlns:enc="http://www.w3.org/2001/04/xmlenc#">
      <enc:EncryptedData>
            <enc:EncryptionMethod Algorithm="http://www.idpf.org/2008/embedding"/>
            <enc:CipherData>
                  <enc:CipherReference URI="OEBPS/Fonts/Medi - best Ruritania.ttf"/>
            </enc:CipherData>
      </enc:EncryptedData>
</encryption>
```

The contents are similar to those we saw in the encryption.xml example. The encryption method is listed as a website address of http://www.idpf.org/2008/embedding. This means the font-mangling algorithm is from the International Digital Publishing Forum (IDPF).

The only file being encrypted in this case is the medi - best Ruritania.ttf file in the OEBPS/Fonts directory. Multiple font files can be encrypted, or none at all—in this case, only one was embedded in the file.

To encrypt fonts, you need to open your EPUB file in Sigil. Once the font is added, right-click the font and select Font Obfuscation. After the menu opens, select Use IDPF's Method. The font is now encrypted; make sure you save the file.

NOTE

If the EPUB is opened by anyone using Sigil, they can turn off the obfuscation and then extract the font.

Signing an EPUB

EPUB files can be signed to let a person know when they have been modified. Specific files within the EPUB can be entered in the signatures.xml file and checked for validity. If the files are not valid—that is, they have been modified—then the reader knows the publication has been changed.

Signing the files requires the use of the Digital Signature Algorithm (DSA) standard. The standard uses the Secure Hash Algorithm (SHA-1) to generate a value representing the files.

Secure Hash Algorithm

A hash is used to determine the contents of a file. The hash is a string of characters that is generated by running a file through an algorithm. The resulting value is the digest or hash value. A file can be checked by the reading system by generating another hash value and checking it against the hash value in the file. If the values match, it can be concluded that the file is intact and not corrupted or changed.

The digest with SHA-1 is 160 bits, or 20 bytes, or 40 hex characters. The resulting value, or hash, produced by the algorithm on the data is used to verify the current data against the original. Every time the hash is produced, it must always be the same, unless something within the data has changed. In this way, SHA is used to determine that files have not been altered, deleted, or added. Some EPUB security systems may allow for alteration, addition, and deletion of certain files, while others may not.

NOTE

The 20 bytes or 40 hex characters may look strange. One ASCII character, or byte, has a value of 2 hex characters. For example, the letter A has an ASCII hexadecimal value of 41. So A is 1 byte, and in hex, the 41 is 2 bytes.

signatures.xml

First, let's start with a sample file from the IDPF:

```
<signatures xmlns="urn:oasis:names:tc:opendocument:xmlns:container">
    <Signature Id="AsYouLikeItSignature" xmlns="http://www.w3.org/2000/09/xmldsig#">
        <SignedInfo>
            <CanonicalizationMethod Algorithm="http://www.w3.org/TR/2001/REC-xml-c14n-20010315"/>
            <SignatureMethod Algorithm="http://www.w3.org/2000/09/xmldsig#dsa-sha1"/>
            <Reference URI="#AsYouLikeIt">
                <DigestMethod Algorithm="http://www.w3.org/2000/09/xmldsig#sha1"/>
                <DigestValue>…</DigestValue>
            </Reference>
        </SignedInfo>
```

```
        <SignatureValue>…</SignatureValue>
        <KeyInfo>
            <KeyValue>
                <DSAKeyValue>
                    <P>…</P>
                    <Q>…</Q>
                    <G>…</G>
                    <Y>…</Y>
                </DSAKeyValue>
            </KeyValue>
        </KeyInfo>
        <Object>
            <Manifest Id="AsYouLikeIt">
                <Reference URI="OEBPS/As You Like It.opf">
                    <Transforms>
                        <Transform Algorithm="http://www.w3.org/TR/2001/REC-xml-c14n-20010315"/>
                    </Transforms>
                    <DigestMethod Algorithm="http://www.w3.org/2000/09/xmldsig#sha1"/>
                    <DigestValue></DigestValue>
                </Reference>
                <Reference URI="OEBPS/book.html">
                    <Transforms>
                        <Transform Algorithm="http://www.w3.org/TR/2001/REC-xml-c14n-20010315"/>
                    </Transforms>
                    <DigestMethod Algorithm="http://www.w3.org/2000/09/xmldsig#sha1"/>
                    <DigestValue></DigestValue>
                </Reference>
                <Reference URI="OEBPS/images/cover.png">
                    <DigestMethod Algorithm="http://www.w3.org/2000/09/xmldsig#sha1"/>
                    <DigestValue></DigestValue>
                </Reference>
            </Manifest>
        </Object>
    </Signature>
</signatures>
```

The first line shows the file is an XML file and uses the namespace of xmlns="urn:oasis:names:tc:opendocument:xmlns:container".

The second line is <Signature Id="AsYouLikeItSignature" xmlns="http://www.w3.org/2000/09/xmldsig#"> and shows a signature ID. The signature ID matches the following line from the OPF file: <link rel="xml-signature" href="../META-INF/signatures.xml#AsYouLikeItSignature"/> located in the <metadata> section.

The <SignedInfo> section references the signed data and specifies the algorithm used to sign it.

The next line, <CanonicalizationMethod Algorithm="http://www.w3.org/TR/2001/REC-xml-c14n-20010315"/>, shows the XML requirements, which include line order, line spacing, etc.

Following this, we come to the information on the signature schema: <SignatureMethod Algorithm="http://www.w3.org/2000/09/xmldsig#dsa-sha1"/>. The algorithm specifies the methods and parameters to generate a signature.

An important line is <Reference URI="#AsYouLikeIt">. The ID makes a reference to the upcoming manifest section, which contains all the files being signed.

After we specify the signatures schema, we need to specify the digest method that is being applied. The line is <DigestMethod Algorithm="http://www.w3.org/2000/09/xmldsig#sha1"/> and shows that SHA-1 is being used.

The following line lists the digest value. For SHA-1, the value will be a 40-hex byte string of data. For example, the <DigestValue> could be D4BC0B471C65C3013D1247DE19A55B8DB981503C.

The next line is the <SignatureValue>, which is a binary-to-text encoding of the signed information (<SignedInfo>) section data.

The next section is the <KeyInfo> section:

```
<KeyInfo>
      <KeyValue>
            <DSAKeyValue>
                  <P>...</P>
                  <Q>...</Q>
                  <G>...</G>
                  <Y>...</Y>
            </DSAKeyValue>
      </KeyValue>
</KeyInfo>
```

This section contains the information on the public key used to decrypt the data. The sections <P>, <Q>, <G>, and <Y> contain the elements of the public key or certificate. It is up to the application to check the validity of the key and the signature file. Once this information is verified, the signature information can be used to check the specified files and verify they have not been modified.

Finally, we get to the <Object> section, which contains the list of the files that are signed. The manifest is listed here and has the ID as referenced by the Reference URI from the <SignedInfo> section. The manifest section begins with <Manifest Id="AsYouLikeIt"> and contains references to each file signed.

The files referenced are listed one at a time, as shown:

```
<Reference URI="OEBPS/As You Like It.opf">
      <Transforms>
            <Transform Algorithm="http://www.w3.org/TR/2001/REC-xml-c14n-20010315"/>
      </Transforms>
      <DigestMethod Algorithm="http://www.w3.org/2000/09/xmldsig#sha1"/>
      <DigestValue></DigestValue>
</Reference>
```

The file signed here is the OPF. The file structure shows it is located within the OEBPS folder and called As You Like It.opf.

The transform algorithm is the same value as the <CanonicalizationMethod Algorithm>. The section has requirements for line order, line spacing, etc. Again we come to a digest method algorithm that specifies the use of SHA-1.

We complete the section with the SHA-1 value of the specified file. For the sample file from IDP, the As You Like It.opf would be F90F4B008E059569C8EB73DAD63D4EDB7580283E.

There will be one <Reference> section for each file that is signed.

Validation

An EPUB, when opened by a reading system, should have the signatures checked to verify that all files match the signature. When they do match, then the files have not been modified or corrupted. The files are intact as they were when they left the distribution server. Keep in mind that not all systems may validate the files against their signatures.

Chapter 8

EPUB 3

- Learn the differences between EPUB 2 and 3
- Understand the new navigation file
- Set up cover images
- Learn MathML
- Understand fixed layouts
- Learn how to embed audio and video
- Cover the ability to synchronize voice and text
- Look into Flash

EPUB 2 has been updated to include new features in the third version, called EPUB 3. For the most part, everything you've learned so far still applies to EPUB 3. The changes are mainly additions to allow for new features.

Differences Between EPUB 2 and EPUB 3

Everything you learned up to this point on EPUB 2 is still useful for EPUB 3. The main thing that has been dropped between EPUB versions is the Navigation Center eXtended (NCX) file. The NCX file can be removed from an EPUB 3 file, or it can remain for backwards compatibility.

Removing the NCX file cannot be done in Sigil. If the NCX file is deleted, Sigil will create a new one. It is best to delete it from your compression program. Once deleted, do not forget to remove the NCX line in the Open Packaging Format (OPF) file that lists the NCX in the <manifest>.

You may want to leave the NCX file in in case someone loads the file on an older EPUB 2 device. In this case, most of the information should be bypassed and allow a device to read the information generated by the XHTML code (if anything is generated).

Another difference is the MathML support. MathML is supported under EPUB 2, but it has its flaws. EPUB 3 works better with MathML.

Viewing EPUB 3 Files

The best way to view EPUB 3 files and get the most features supported is to use Readium. Readium is an EPUB 3 viewer created by the International Digital Publishing Forum (IDPF) that runs on Google Chrome and Chromium.

First, you need to install Chrome or Chromium on your system. From Chrome or Chromium, go to www.Readium.org and select Install From Chrome Web Store. Once the extension is installed, you can add EPUB 2 and EPUB 3 files to your Readium library.

When opening an EPUB file in Readium, you may notice in the Library view that the title, author, and EPUB version are listed. Everything up to this point should show "ePUB 2.0." To change the value to 3.0, the version="2.0" in the OPF <package> tag should be changed to "3.0."

New Navigation File

The new navigation file is basically set up as an ordered list (remember that from Chapter 2?). It is an XHTML file containing an order list of each chapter. The file is similar to the following:

```
<?xml version="1.0" encoding="UTF-8" standalone="no" ?>
<html xmlns="http://www.w3.org/1999/xhtml" lang="en" xml:lang="en"
xmlns:epub="http://www.idpf.org/2007/ops">
	<head>
		<title>New Book</title>
		<meta charset="utf-8"/>
	</head>
	<body>
		<nav epub:type="toc">
			<h1>Contents of New Book</h1>
			<ol>
				<li><a href="title.xhtml">Title</a></li>
				<li><a href="chapter001.xhtml">Chapter One</a></li>
			</ol>
		</nav>
	</body>
</html>
```

The <manifest> entry in the OPF should appear as follows:

```
<item id="toc" href="toc.xhtml" properties="nav" media-
type="application/xhtml+xml"/>
```

Contents of New Book

Title

Chapter One

Figure 8-1 Sample navigation

The properties="nav" shows it is used for navigation, like the NCX, and the filename can be anything you choose with an XHTML extension. The header should include the EPUB XML namespace: xmlns:epub="http://www.idpf.org/2007/ops. The namespace allows the use of <nav epub:type="toc">. As you saw in the previous example, the contents within the <nav> section showed up in the table of contents. Make sure the links to each file are valid using <a href= " ">.

The sample is shown in Figure 8-1.

Cover Image

Cover images appear when scrolling through your library, and each reading device manages cover images differently. It's simple to set up cover images in Sigil.

An XHTML file must be created that contains only the image file used for the cover. This can be done in Sigil and saved. Once the image and XHTML file are present in the EPUB, then the OPF needs to be edited.

The first section to add an entry to is the <metadata>, as shown:

```
<meta name="coverxhtml" content="coverimage" />
```

Within the <manifest> section, the entry for the XHTML and image file need to be edited as shown:

```
<item href="Text/MainCover.xhtml" id="cover" media-type="application/xhtml+xml" />
<item href="Images/Cover.jpg" id="coverimage" media-type="image/jpeg" />
```

Finally, the <spine> section of the OPF needs the following:

```
<itemref idref="cover" linear="no" />
```

The IDs, cover and coverimage are case-sensitive and can be any unique names you wish. See any sample file from this chapter for ideas.

NOTE

Setting up the cover image can be done in EPUB 2 files as well, but keep in mind that every device handles cover images differently. Some require the image file to be named the same as the EPUB (except the extension) and placed in the same directory.

MathML

Mathematics Markup Language (MathML) is used to display math and chemical formulas in an EPUB. This can be useful for math and chemistry textbooks that require proper displaying of formulas.

Each section within the MathML starts with $and ends with$.

The MathML tags are shown in Table 8-1.

Tag	Arguments	Description	Example
<mi>	n/a	Identifiers (variables)	<mi>a</mi>
<mn>	n/a	Numbers	<mn>4</mn>
<mo>	n/a	Operators	<mo>+</mo>
<mtext>	n/a	Text	<mtext>The value is:</mtext>
<rmrow>	0+	Row of items	<mrow><mi>x</mi><mo>+</mo><mn>3 </mn></mrow>
<msup>	2	Superscript	<msup><mi>b</mi><mn>2</mn></msup>
<msqrt>	1*	Square root	<msqrt><mi>x</mi></msqrt>
<mroot>	2	Base square root	<mroot><mi>x</mi><mn>3</mn>
<mfrac>	2	Fraction	<mfrac><mi>x</mi><mn>3</mn></mfrac>
<mfenced>	0+	Bracketed items	<msup><mfenced><mi>x</mi><mo>+ </mo><mn>3</mn></mfenced><mn>2 </mn></msup>
<menclose>	1*	Enclose in a division symbol	<menclose><mn>3</mn><mi>x</mi> </menclose>
±	n/a	A plus/minus sign	±<mn>2</mn>
π	n/a	Pi	<mn>2</mn>⁢<mn>π</mn>
→	n/a	Yields (chemistry)	<mtext>Na</mtext><mo>+</mo><mtext>Cl</mtext>→<mtext>NaCl</mtext>
⁢ or ⁢	n/a	Multiply two values	<mn>3</mn>⁢<mi>a</mi>

Table 8-1 MathML Tags

It is possible to create a tag that uses two arguments but each argument consists of only one element. For example, to show a fraction of 1 over x, the code would look like this:

```
<mfrac><mn>1</mn><mi>x</mi></mfrac>
```

The <mrow> is used to create one argument from many. If the fraction were 1 + x over 5 – x, the code would be:

```
<mfrac><mrow><mn>1</mn><mo>+</mo><mn>x</mn></mrow><mrow><mn>5</
mn><mo>-</mo><mi>x</mi></mrow></mfrac>
```

Each section is placed into an <mrow> making it one argument. Placing the 1 + x in an <mrow> makes it a single argument.

For an item with 1* arguments, such as <msqrt>, the code would be:

```
<msqrt><mrow><mi>x</mi<mo>+</mo><mn>3</mn></mrow></msqrt>
```

Here the x + 3 is a single argument, which is what is required for the square root tag.

The tags should be self-explanatory, except the ⁢. When two values are multiplied together, such as 3 and x to get 3x, the invisible multiplication needs to be placed between them as shown:

```
<mn>3</mn>&InvisibleTimes;<mi>x</mi>
```

NOTE

If you use <mfenced>, the section between the two tags should be in an <mrow>. If <mrow> is not used, then a comma can appear between each child element within the <mfenced>.

For examples of MathML, see the c08-01.epub file (which you can download from www.mhprofessional.com/EPUB). The file also contains an example of a new navigation file called toc.xhtml.

Fixed Layouts

With EPUB 2, text is considered reflowable—that is, it changes as the text size changes. The book also changes as it is read on different devices, which may use different fonts, have a different size display screen, etc. The text will reorder itself as needed to just as most websites do on different browsers and screen sizes.

In EPUB 3, the layout can now be set to a fixed layout where a page will appear the same no matter what device it is on.

The first thing you need to do is set up a viewport in each XHTML file. An entry needs to be added to the <head> section as shown:

```
<meta content="width=1893, height=2689" name="viewport"/>
```

For the specific XHTML file, the display coordinates are now (0, 0) in the top-left corner and (1893, 2689) in the lower-right corner. The viewport setting does not change the resolution of your display; it only renumbers the existing values. If an image is displayed on the screen that has dimensions of 1893 ×2689 (in pixels), the image fills the whole screen instead of going out of the display area. The width and height values can be set larger or smaller than the actual display size.

NOTE

If each viewport will be a different size, such as in a comic book–style EPUB, then the dimensions can be set into the XHTML file. If an application such as Pixresizer is used to change all image sizes to the same size, then the viewport can be set in the CSS.

If the CSS is used to set the viewport, then each XHTML file needs to be linked to the CSS and an entry needs to be added as follows:

```
@viewport {
        width:1893px;
        height:2689px; }
```

All XHTML files attached to the CSS style sheet will be set to the same viewport size. Table 8-2 shows other properties available for the CSS viewport.

Property	Value	Description
min-width	auto, device-width, *absolute, percentage*	Minimum width of display
max-width	auto, device-width, *absolute, percentage*	Maximum width of display
min-height	auto, device-height, *absolute, percentage*	Minimum height of display
max-height	auto, device-height, *absolute, percentage*	Maximum height of display
width	auto, device-width, *absolute, percentage*	Width of display
height	auto, device-height, *absolute, percentage*	Height of display
min-zoom	auto, *number, percentage*	Minimum zoom factor to magnify viewport
max-zoom	auto, *number, percentage*	Maximum zoom factor to magnify viewport
zoom	auto, *number, percentage*	Zoom factor to magnify viewport
orientation	auto, *portrait, landscape*	Display orientation

Table 8-2 CSS @viewport Properties

Property	Value	Description
layout	prepaginated, reflowable	EPUB is displayed page by page or it flows according to device settings.
orientation	landscape, portrait, auto	Orientation is set to landscape or portrait. Auto can be either.
spread	none, landscape, portrait, both, auto	Orientation of two pages when device is in set mode. None is not allowed, both can be in either portrait or landscape, and auto is for no set behavior.

Table 8-3 Rendition: Properties

If needed, some settings can be done in CSS as well as in the XHTML file in case the reading system supports only one method.

In the OPF, an XML namespace needs to be added to the <package>:

```
prefix="rendition:http://www.idpf.org/vocab/rendition/#"
```

The namespace allows the use of rendition: with various properties to manipulate the viewport, as shown in Table 8-3.

These settings are located in the OPF in the <metadata> section as shown:

```
<meta property="rendition:layout">pre-paginated</meta>
<meta property="rendition:orientation">portrait</meta>
<meta property="rendition:spread">none</meta>
```

In the example, the pages are prepaginated, or set as whole pages. This is especially useful for EPUBs dealing mainly with images or items that must fit on a single page.

The page orientation is set to portrait, so the pages are in a portrait orientation. The spread is set to none, which should prevent two pages from being displayed at once. The none setting may not work on all devices.

Another setting is the page spread, shown in Table 8-4.

Property	Description
page-spread-left	Displayed on left side
page-spread-right	Displayed on right side
page-spread-center	Displayed alone

Table 8-4 Page-Spread Settings

The page-spread properties allow for a page to be specifically a left or right page when two pages are displayed at once. Page-spread-center should make a page appear alone (that is, it may not be centered) in a two-page display. Some devices may not manage this property properly.

The settings are placed in the OPF spine as follows:

```
<itemref idref="cover" properties="page-spread-center" />
<itemref idref="Page_01.xhtml" properties="page-spread-left" />
<itemref idref="Page_02.xhtml" properties="page-spread-right" />
<itemref idref="Page_03.xhtml" properties="page-spread-left" />
<itemref idref="Page_04.xhtml" properties="page-spread-right" />
```

NOTE

If a page must be displayed alone, set it as the same side as the image before and after it, such that all three are page-spread-left.

For an example file, see c08-02.epub, which is a full-screen comic book.

Embedding Audio and Video

Audio and video files can be embedded into the EPUB just as fonts can be embedded. The files can then be played at specific points, with or without reader intervention.

Audio Files

Audio files are specified by the EPUB 3 standard to be an MP3 or MP4 (AAC LC).

NOTE

Converting files to MP4 using Advanced Audio Codec with Low Complexity (AAC LC) will be covered in the section on SMIL.

A listing of media types is shown in Table 8-5, including the audio and video formats. The table is not an exhaustive list and will be changed as the EPUB 3 standard is changed and enhanced.

To embed an audio file using Sigil, right-click the Audio Folder and select Add Existing Files. Choose the audio files you need to add to your EPUB and select Open. The file is now embedded in the EPUB and must be set up in the XHTML file to be played.

NOTE

When an MP4 audio file is used, it must be the Advanced Audio Codec with Low Complexity (AAC LC).

Media Type	Description
image/gif	GIF image
image/jpeg	JPEG, JPG image
image/png	PNG image
image/svg+xml	SVG image
application/xhtml+xml	XHTML file
application/font-woff	WOFF font
application/vnd.ms-opentype	OTF font
application/x-shockwave-flash	Flash video
application/smil+xml	Media overlay
audio/mpeg	MP3, M4A audio
audio/mp4	MP4 audio (AAC LC)
audio/ogg	OGG audio
audio/webm	WEBM audio
audio/wav	WAV audio
video/mp4	MP4 video
video/mpeg	MPEG-1 video
video/ogg	OGG video
video/quicktime	QuickTime video
video/x-ms-wmv	Windows Media video
video/x-flv	Flash video
video/webm	WEBM video
text/css	CSS
text/javascript	JavaScript

Table 8-5 Media Types

Property	Value	Description
class	*value*	Uses CSS on the control
id	*string*	Specifies the ID of the control to link to the CSS
controls	controls	Shows controls
autoplay	autoplay	Starts playing without intervention
autobuffer	autobuffer	Loads audio file even when not autoplayed
loop	loop	Continuously plays
src	*filename*	The audio file to be played

Table 8-6 <audio> Attributes

To set up an audio file within the XHTML file, you use the <audio> tag as shown in Table 8-6.

To play an example audio file named sample.mp3 with visible controls, no autoplay, no autobuffer, and no looping, use the following code:

```
<audio class="audio1" src="../Audio/Sample.mp3" controls="controls">
This device does not support audio playback.
</audio>
```

The example shows the class set to audio1, and an entry in CSS can be used to change its visual effects, as shown in Figure 8-2.

```
.audio1 {
      border-style: solid;
      border-width: 2px;
      background-color: light-gray; }
```

NOTE

The id attribute can be used and the CSS entry would start with #id_name.
For example, if the id="song1", then the CSS entry would start with #song1.

Notice the untagged line, "This device does not support audio playback." Naturally, the line is displayed if the device does not support audio playback, but it can be changed

Figure 8-2 Audio control

as needed. The line should be included when using audio tags in case the file is loaded on a device that either does not support audio or does not support a particular format. In this case, the audio may have multiple fallbacks to assure an included format is supported. Instead of placing the "src" in the <audio> tag, <source> tags are used.

```
<audio class="audio1" controls="controls">
      <source src="../Audio/Sample.mp3" type="audio/mpeg"></source>
      <source src="../Audio/Sample.mp4" type="audio/mp4"></source>
      <source src="../Audio/Sample.ogg" type="audio/ogg"></source>
      This device does not support Audio playback.
</audio>
```

In this example, the device will first try to play the MP3 file, then the MP4 file, and finally the OGG file. If none of the three are supported, then the message is displayed.

Autoplay, autobuffer, and loop are used similar to "controls." The attribute is placed within the tag followed by an equal sign and the attribute again in quotes, as shown:

```
autoplay="autoplay"
autobuffer="autobuffer"
loop="loop"
```

NOTE

Do not place invisible audio controls in an EPUB that is set to autoplay and loop since this may annoy the reader.

NOTE

The <audio> tag can be set up in SIGIL, but cannot be played from within SIGIL.

Video Files

For video files, the IDPF does not specify which formats should be supported. Most of the video formats are device dependent, so you may want to check the formats supported by the device for which you are making EPUB files.

NOTE

If you want to support a wide range of devices and reading systems, stick with MP4.

Look back at Table 8-5 for the various media types for video files.

Embedding video files is the same as embedding an audio file, except in Sigil, the video file will be saved to the Video folder.

To play an example video file named sample.mp4 with visible controls, no autoplay, no autobuffer, and no looping, use the following code:

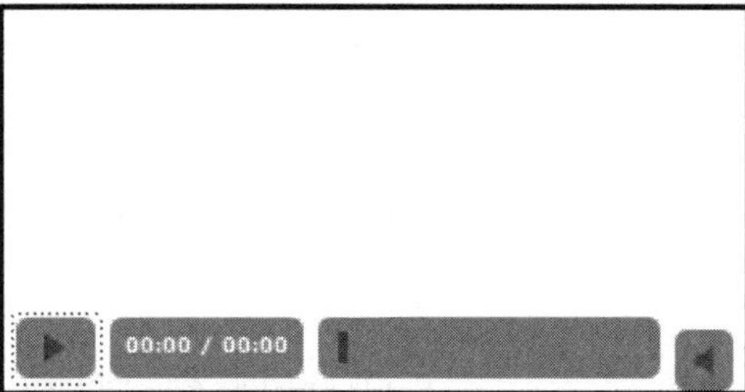

Figure 8-3 Video control

```
<video class="video1" src="../Video/Sample.mp4" controls="controls">
This device does not support video playback.
</video>
```

The example shows the class set to video1, and an entry in CSS can be used to change its visual effects, as shown in Figure 8-3.

```
.video1 {
      border-style: solid;
      border-width: 2px;
      background-color: light-gray; }
```

NOTE

The id attribute can be used, and the CSS entry would start with #id_name. For example, if the id="clip1", then the CSS entry would start with #clip1.

To set up a video file within the XHTML file, you use the <video> tag as shown in Table 8-7.

Most of the attributes are the same as with the <audio> tag, except for height, width, and poster. Height and width are self-explanatory since they have been used in many other XHTML tags discussed in Chapter 2. Poster is a URL ("../Images/") to an image (see Figure 8-4), which is shown when the video is stopped so the box is not empty. The following code demonstrates:

NOTE

Be sure the video window matches the ratio of the poster and the video dimensions so the two fit properly within the video window. If needed, use Pixresizer or a similar application to change the poster dimensions to match the video resolution.

```
<video class="video1" controls="controls" src="../Video/Sample.mp4"
poster="../Images/Curtain.jpg" height="315px" width="412px">
      This device does not support video playback.
</video>
```

Property	Value	Description
class	*value*	Uses CSS on the control
id	*string*	Specifies the ID of the control to link to the CSS
controls	controls	Shows controls
autoplay	autoplay	Starts playing without intervention
autobuffer	autobuffer	Loads audio file even when not autoplayed
loop	loop	Continuously plays
src	*filename*	Audio file to be played
height	*length*	Height of video window
width	*length*	Width of video window
poster	*url*	Image to display when video is not playing

Table 8-7 <video> Attributes

Fallback video files are created the same way as the <audio> fallbacks.

For <audio> and <video> samples, see c08-03.epub.

NOTE

The <video> tag can be set up in Sigil, but cannot be viewed from within Sigil.

Figure 8-4 Poster image

Synchronized Multimedia Integration Language

Synchronized Multimedia Integration Language (SMIL—pronounced "SMILE") is used to synchronize audio with text so the EPUB can read to you. It can be useful in teaching people to read because the words, sentences, and paragraphs can be highlighted as the text is being read.

NOTE

The process of setting up an EPUB with SMIL can be challenging. As with other things in this book, it takes practice.

The best way to start is with Sigil. Like with all EPUB 3 files, start by creating everything you can with Sigil and create the EPUB 2 part of the file. By creating the XHTML, CSS, images, and fonts and embedding the audio and video, you will have completed the majority of the work. You can also validate everything in Sigil to make sure your code is up to the standards. Of course, you may receive errors about audio and video not being referenced, but you can ignore this since you'll add the code later.

After the initial EPUB is set up, you need to create the audio files that will be used with the narration. A great program for this is Audacity from http://audacity.sourceforge.net/download/. Once installed, you'll need to add two libraries: LAME MP3 encoding library and the FFmpeg import/export library found at http://audacity.sourceforge.net/download/plugins. Once these are installed and you have a microphone, you are ready to go.

Creating Narrative Files Without a Microphone

If you do not have a microphone, you can use the program Balabolka to create audio files. Balabolka reads text files (as well as HTML and EPUB) using computer voices and can create an audio (MP3) file of what is read. If needed, you can buy add-on voices from various companies to work with Balabolka (SAPI4 or SAPI5).

Once an audio file is made, you'll need to listen to it and follow along with the text to be sure the word pronunciation is correct. If not, you can change the text within Balabolka so it sounds correct. Re-create the audio file and use it as a narration file. The next step is to label the sections as needed (discussed later in this chapter).

Audacity can do quite a bit with audio, but you really only need the basic functions. Once the program is started, there is a control bar, shown in Figure 8-5, which controls the basic recording and playback.

Figure 8-5 Audacity recording controls

Select record (the circle) and start your narration. Press stop (the square) when done. It is best to always save the project so you can go back and manipulate things if needed. Figure 8-6 shows an example of a narration in Audacity. Once your narration is completed to your satisfaction, the timing needs to be determined.

To select areas of the audio file, use the selector tool as shown in Figure 8-7. The top tool is the selector tool, and the bottom is the magnify tool. The magnify tool allows you to enlarge the wave forms, which does not affect your audio, to be able to select parts easier. Use the play button (the triangle) to play the selection and make sure you selected only the part you need. When the selection is done, press CTRL-B to label it and give it a name that

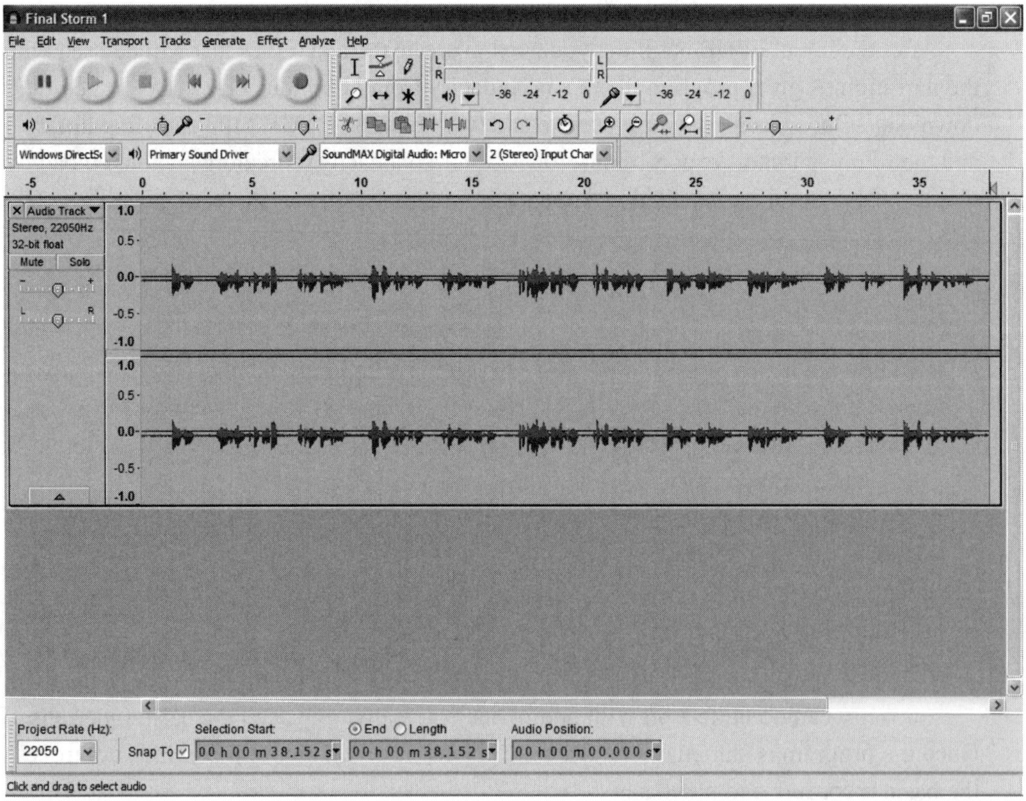

Figure 8-6 Audacity narration

Figure 8-7 Audacity selector and magnify tools

enables you to know what it is. Once all of the sections are labeled, as shown in Figure 8-8, you can start the next step.

Select Files and then Export Labels. Select where you want the file saved and give it a name. A sample output is shown in Figure 8-9.

Export the audio file to MP4 or M4a formats and save it. In your EPUB file, you need to place all audio files in the Audio folder (or whatever folder name you want). Open the EPUB in your compression program to set up the SMIL files.

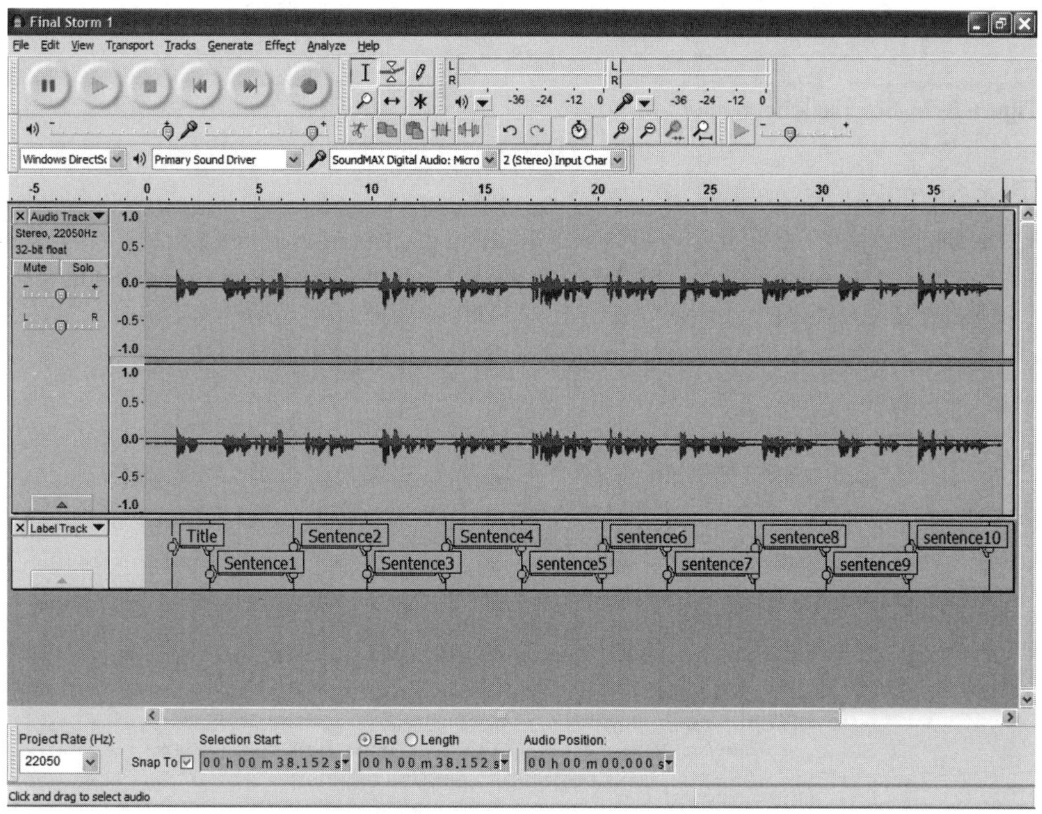

Figure 8-8 Labeled Audacity file

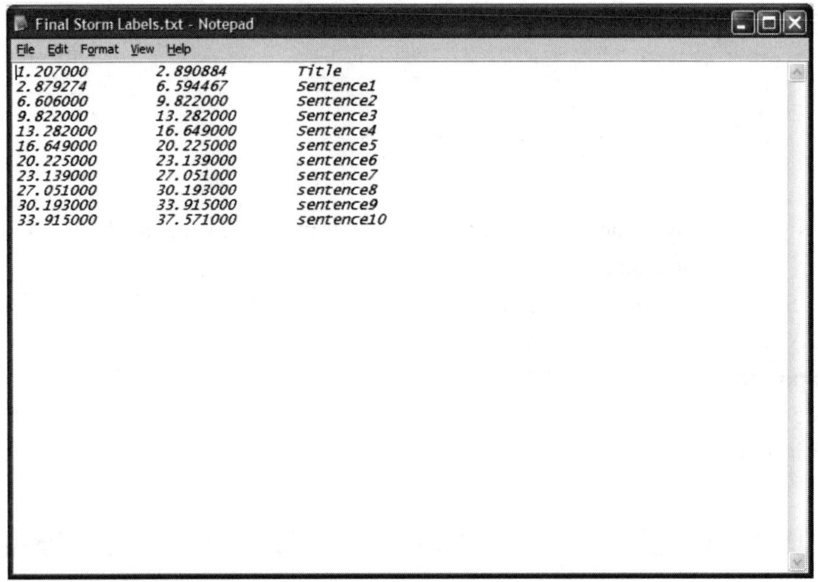

Figure 8-9 Sample label output

SMIL File

A sample SMIL file is shown in Figure 8-10 using the data from Figure 8-9.

The SMIL file is an XML file that lists the XHTML file to which the audio file is connected as shown:

```
<smil xmlns=http://www.w3.org/ns/SMIL xmlns:epub=http://www.idpf.org/2007/ops version="3.0">
    <body>
            <par id="title1">
                  <text src="Text/Final-Storm.xhtml#title"/>
                  <audio src="../Audio/Final-Storm.m4a" clipBegin="1.207s" clipEnd="2.880s"/>
            </par>
            <par id="sentence01">
                  <text src="Text/Final-Storm.xhtml#sentence01"/>
                  <audio src="../Audio/Final-Storm.m4a" clipBegin="2.880s" clipEnd="6.594s"/>
            </par>
            <par id="sentence02">
                  <text src="Text/Final-Storm.xhtml#sentence02"/>
                  <audio src="../Audio/Final-Storm.m4a" clipBegin="6.606s" clipEnd="9.822s"/>
            </par>
            <par id="sentence03">
                  <text src="Text/Final-Storm.xhtml#sentence03"/>
                  <audio src="../Audio/Final-Storm.m4a" clipBegin="9.822s" clipEnd="13.282s"/>
            </par>
            <par id="sentence04">
                  <text src="Text/Final-Storm.xhtml#sentence04"/>
                  <audio src="../Audio/Final-Storm.m4a" clipBegin="13.282s" clipEnd="16.649s"/>
            </par>
            <par id="sentence05">
                  <text src="Text/Final-Storm.xhtml#sentence05"/>
```

```
            <audio src="../Audio/Final-Storm.m4a" clipBegin="16.649s" clipEnd="20.225s"/>
        </par>
        <par id="sentence06">
            <text src="Text/Final-Storm.xhtml#sentence06"/>
            <audio src="../Audio/Final-Storm.m4a" clipBegin="20.255s" clipEnd="23.139s"/>
        </par>
        <par id="sentence07">
            <text src="Text/Final-Storm.xhtml#sentence07"/>
            <audio src="../Audio/Final-Storm.m4a" clipBegin="23.139s" clipEnd="27.051s"/>
        </par>
        <par id="sentence08">
            <text src="Text/Final-Storm.xhtml#sentence08"/>
            <audio src="../Audio/Final-Storm.m4a" clipBegin="27.051s" clipEnd="30.193s"/>
        </par>
        <par id="sentence09">
            <text src="Text/Final-Storm.xhtml#sentence09"/>
            <audio src="../Audio/Final-Storm.m4a" clipBegin="30.193s" clipEnd="33.195s"/>
        </par>
        <par id="sentence10">
            <text src="Text/Final-Storm.xhtml#sentence10"/>
            <audio src="../Audio/Final-Storm.m4a" clipBegin="33.195s" clipEnd="37.571s"/>
        </par>
    </body>
</smil>
```

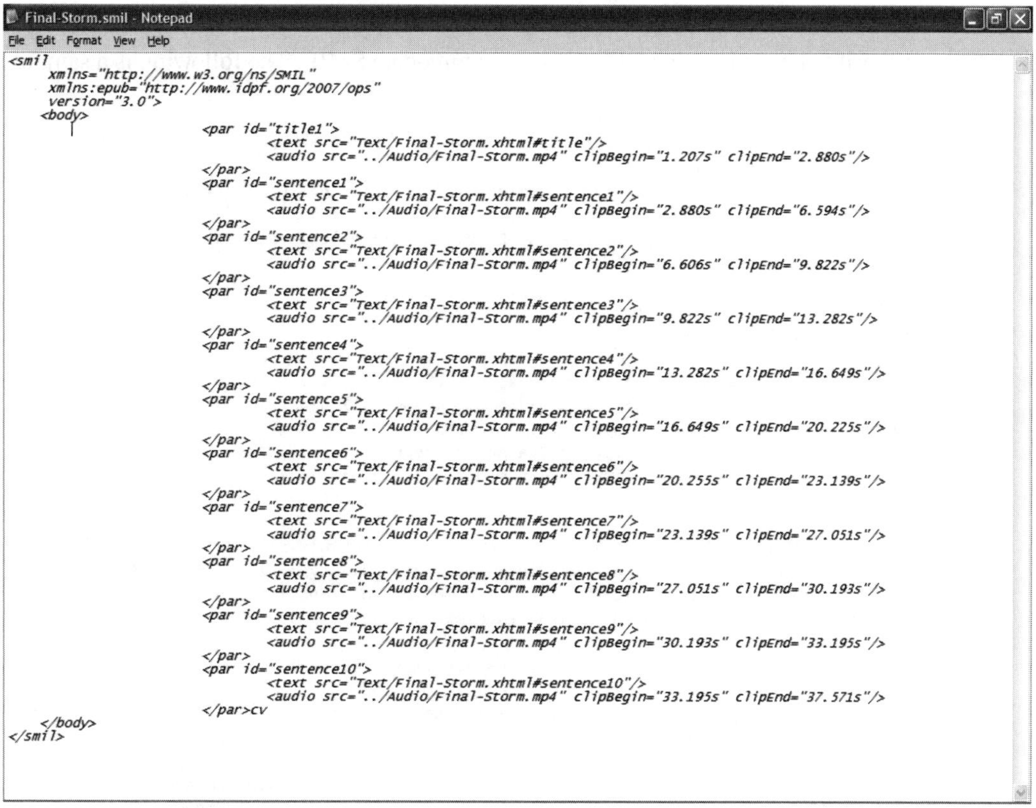

```
Final-Storm.smil - Notepad
File Edit Format View Help
<smil
    xmlns="http://www.w3.org/ns/SMIL"
    xmlns:epub="http://www.idpf.org/2007/ops"
    version="3.0">
    <body>
            <par id="title1">
                <text src="Text/Final-Storm.xhtml#title"/>
                <audio src="../Audio/Final-Storm.mp4" clipBegin="1.207s" clipEnd="2.880s"/>
            </par>
            <par id="sentence1">
                <text src="Text/Final-Storm.xhtml#sentence1"/>
                <audio src="../Audio/Final-Storm.mp4" clipBegin="2.880s" clipEnd="6.594s"/>
            </par>
            <par id="sentence2">
                <text src="Text/Final-Storm.xhtml#sentence2"/>
                <audio src="../Audio/Final-Storm.mp4" clipBegin="6.606s" clipEnd="9.822s"/>
            </par>
            <par id="sentence3">
                <text src="Text/Final-Storm.xhtml#sentence3"/>
                <audio src="../Audio/Final-Storm.mp4" clipBegin="9.822s" clipEnd="13.282s"/>
            </par>
            <par id="sentence4">
                <text src="Text/Final-Storm.xhtml#sentence4"/>
                <audio src="../Audio/Final-Storm.mp4" clipBegin="13.282s" clipEnd="16.649s"/>
            </par>
            <par id="sentence5">
                <text src="Text/Final-Storm.xhtml#sentence5"/>
                <audio src="../Audio/Final-Storm.mp4" clipBegin="16.649s" clipEnd="20.225s"/>
            </par>
            <par id="sentence6">
                <text src="Text/Final-Storm.xhtml#sentence6"/>
                <audio src="../Audio/Final-Storm.mp4" clipBegin="20.255s" clipEnd="23.139s"/>
            </par>
            <par id="sentence7">
                <text src="Text/Final-Storm.xhtml#sentence7"/>
                <audio src="../Audio/Final-Storm.mp4" clipBegin="23.139s" clipEnd="27.051s"/>
            </par>
            <par id="sentence8">
                <text src="Text/Final-Storm.xhtml#sentence8"/>
                <audio src="../Audio/Final-Storm.mp4" clipBegin="27.051s" clipEnd="30.193s"/>
            </par>
            <par id="sentence9">
                <text src="Text/Final-Storm.xhtml#sentence9"/>
                <audio src="../Audio/Final-Storm.mp4" clipBegin="30.193s" clipEnd="33.195s"/>
            </par>
            <par id="sentence10">
                <text src="Text/Final-Storm.xhtml#sentence10"/>
                <audio src="../Audio/Final-Storm.mp4" clipBegin="33.195s" clipEnd="37.571s"/>
            </par>cv
    </body>
</smil>
```

Figure 8-10 Sample SMIL File

The XHTML file is located in the Text folder and named final-storm.xhtml. The first section we are looking at has an ID of title. The text at title coincides with the audio file final-storm.mp4 between the sections at 1.207 seconds (clipBegin) and 2.880 seconds (clipEnd).

The <audio> tag shows the 'src' file (notice it uses the '..' while the <text> tag does not). If clipBegin is not specified, the default is the beginning (0.000 seconds), and if clipEnd is missing, the default is the end of the audio file.

The section is within a <par> tag. The <par> tag is for parallel, and a <seq> tag does exist, for sequence. The <seq> tags do not need to be used if the <par> tags are used, and vice versa, but the <seq> tags are not used for narration. Each XHTML file and audio file should be placed into separate SMIL files, as shown in the sample EPUB file c08-04.epub.

NOTE

Only use the <par> tags. If the <par> tags are replaced with <seq> tags, the narration will not work.

OPF File

Changes need to be made to the OPF file to accommodate SMIL. The following is a sample:

```
<?xml version="1.0" encoding="utf-8"?>
<package xmlns="http://www.idpf.org/2007/opf" unique-identifier="BookId" version="3.0"
prefix="rendition:http://www.idpf.org/vocab/rendition/#">
  <metadata xmlns:dc="http://purl.org/dc/elements/1.1/" xmlns:opf="http://www.idpf.org/2007/
opf">
    <dc:identifier id="BookId" opf:scheme="UUID">urn:uuid:87b6ec11-af61-4af1-afde-
d86b45fb61a0</dc:identifier>
    <dc:title>C08-04</dc:title>
    <dc:creator opf:role="aut">Cassandra Ann Johnson</dc:creator>
    <dc:language>en</dc:language>
    <meta property="media:duration" refines="#path_overlay">10.574s</meta>
    <meta property="media:duration" refines="#final_overlay">37.571s</meta>
    <meta property="media:duration" refines="#glad_overlay">23.034s</meta>
    <meta property="media:duration">0:01:11.179</meta>
    <meta property="media:narrator">Cassandra Ann Johnson</meta>
    <meta property="media:active-class">-epub-media-overlay-active</meta>
  </metadata>
  <manifest>
    <item href="toc.ncx" id="ncx" media-type="application/x-dtbncx+xml" />
    <item href="Images/Cassandra.jpg" id="Cassandra.jpg" media-type="image/jpeg" />
    <item href="Text/Title.xhtml" id="Title.xhtml" media-type="application/xhtml+xml" />
    <item href="Text/Path-of-Fate.xhtml" id="Path-of-Fate.xhtml" media-overlay="path_overlay"
media-type="application/xhtml+xml" />
    <item href="Text/Final-Storm.xhtml" id="Final-Storm.xhtml" media-overlay="final_overlay"
media-type="application/xhtml+xml" />
    <item href="Text/A-Glad-Heart.xhtml" id="A-Glad-Heart.xhtml" media-overlay="glad_overlay"
media-type="application/xhtml+xml" />
    <item href="Styles/Style.css" id="Style.css" media-type="text/css" />
    <item href="Audio/Path-of-Fate.mp4" id="path_media" media-type="audio/mp4" />
    <item href="Audio/Final-Storm.m4a" id="final_media" media-type="audio/mpeg" />
```

```
    <item href="Audio/A-Glad-Heart.mp3" id="glad_media" media-type="audio/mpeg" />
    <item href="smil/Path-of-Fate.smil" id="path_overlay" media-type="application/smil+xml" />
    <item href="smil/Final-Storm.smil" id="final_overlay" media-type="application/smil+xml" />
    <item href="smil/A-Glad-Heart.smil" id="glad_overlay" media-type="application/smil+xml" />
  </manifest>
  <spine toc="ncx">
    <itemref idref="Title.xhtml" />
    <itemref idref="Path-of-Fate.xhtml" />
    <itemref idref="Final-Storm.xhtml" />
    <itemref idref="A-Glad-Heart.xhtml" />
  </spine>
</package>
```

Notice there is no <DOCTYPE> entry, which Sigil tends to place in the XHTML file (the DOCTYPE should not be used in EPUB 3 files).

One main point to notice is the media duration, as shown:

```
<meta property="media:duration" refines="#path_overlay">10.574s</meta>
<meta property="media:duration" refines="#final_overlay">37.571s</meta>
<meta property="media:duration" refines="#glad_overlay">23.034s</meta>
<meta property="media:duration">0:01:11.179</meta>
<meta property="media:narrator">Cassandra Ann Johnson</meta>
<meta property="media:active-class">-epub-media-overlay-active</meta>
```

The first line defines the duration of the audio file portion being used for the overlay associated with the path_overlay file. The second is for the final_overlay file, and the third is the glad_overlay file. The fourth line is the overall duration of all the overlays added together. The fifth line is the name of the narrator. The information is metadata that may or may not be used by the reading system. The final line is the name CSS uses to "highlight" the XHTML file for the appropriate times during the audio playback. The CSS portion is the main reason for the time synchronization (see the sample file c08-04 .epub for synchronization examples).

The time synch can be for whole paragraphs, sentences, or words. The timing can be as granular as you want to make it, as shown in the sample c08-04.epub.

Another main area for SMIL is the OPF <manifest> section, specifically these two lines:

```
<item href="Text/Path-of-Fate.xhtml" id="Path-of-Fate.xhtml" media-
overlay="path_overlay" media-type="application/xhtml+xml" />
<item href="smil/Path-of-Fate.smil" id="path_overlay" media-
type="application/smil+xml" />
```

The <item> for the XHTML entry has an attribute media-overlay, which has a value that matches the ID of the SMIL file. The SMIL file has an ID that is used in the XHTML media-overlay to which it is connected. The ID is also used in the <metadata> media:duration line.

XHTML Files

An example of an XHTML is shown here:

```
<?xml version="1.0" encoding="UTF-8" ?>
<html xmlns="http://www.w3.org/1999/xhtml" xmlns:epub="http://www.idpf
.org/2007/ops" xml:lang="en">
<head>
      <title>Final Storm</title>
      <link href="../Styles/Style.css" rel="stylesheet" type="text/css"/>
</head>
<body>
      <h1 id="title">Final Storm</h1>
      <p><br/></p>
      <p id="sentence01">Shudders and chills dispense through my thoughts</p>
      <p id="sentence02">Passing winds thunder heavy haunts.</p>
      <p id="sentence03">Stormy clouds hover and decay</p>
      <p id="sentence04">Suspense weaves into the next day.</p>
      <p id="sentence05">The weeping willow allows little shelter to me.</p>
      <p id="sentence06">As I collapse now on bended knee.</p>
      <p id="sentence07">Thoughts swimming with fear of all lost</p>
      <p id="sentence08">No deed now done could spare the cost.</p>
      <p id="sentence09">Time is finished, spent with care.</p>
      <p id="sentence10">Failure lights the sky with a sinister stare.</p>
</body>
</html>
```

Nothing too important here, except the id of each section should coincide with the #name used in the SMIL file. Notice the id can be from a header, paragraph, span, or other tags.

NOTE

Make sure that all id values are unique within an XHTML file, or SMIL will not work. Also make sure that each SMIL entry has an associated id (the id is case-sensitive).

CSS File

The final section is the CSS to which the XHTML file is linked. Only one entry needs to be set to manage the highlighting done to the XHTML text displayed, as shown:

```
.-epub-media-overlay-active {
    background-color: #abc; }
```

Instead of changing the background color, any CSS settings may be used, such as borders, outlines, colors, bold, underline, etc.

The name used comes from the OPF <metadata> section as follows:

```
<meta property="media:active-class">-epub-media-overlay-active</meta>
```

NOTE

The -epub-media-overlay-active name can be changed to any valid CSS name, but needs to be the same in the CSS style sheet.

Putting It All Together

Now SMIL may seem a bit jumbled, but let's try to put this together. First look at Figure 8-11, and then we'll cover each section of code.

In the OPF, the XHTML is connected to the SMIL file as shown:

```
    <item href="Text/Path-of-Fate.xhtml" id="Path-of-Fate.xhtml" media-overlay="path_overlay"
media-type="application/xhtml+xml" />
    <item href="Text/Final-Storm.xhtml" id="Final-Storm.xhtml" media-overlay="final_overlay"
media-type="application/xhtml+xml" />
    <item href="Text/A-Glad-Heart.xhtml" id="A-Glad-Heart.xhtml" media-overlay="glad_overlay"
media-type="application/xhtml+xml" />
    <item href="smil/Path-of-Fate.smil" id="path_overlay" media-type="application/smil+xml" />
    <item href="smil/Final-Storm.smil" id="final_overlay" media-type="application/smil+xml" />
    <item href="smil/A-Glad-Heart.smil" id="glad_overlay" media-type="application/smil+xml" />
```

The duration of each audio file is set, as well as all of them together:

```
<meta property="media:duration" refines="#path_overlay">10.574s</meta>
<meta property="media:duration" refines="#final_overlay">37.571s</meta>
<meta property="media:duration" refines="#glad_overlay">23.034s</meta>
<meta property="media:duration">0:01:11.179</meta>
```

The name of the narrator is specified:

```
<meta property="media:narrator">Cassandra Ann Johnson</meta>
```

Finally, the CSS class name is specified for the highlighting:

```
<meta property="media:active-class">-epub-media-overlay-active</meta>
```

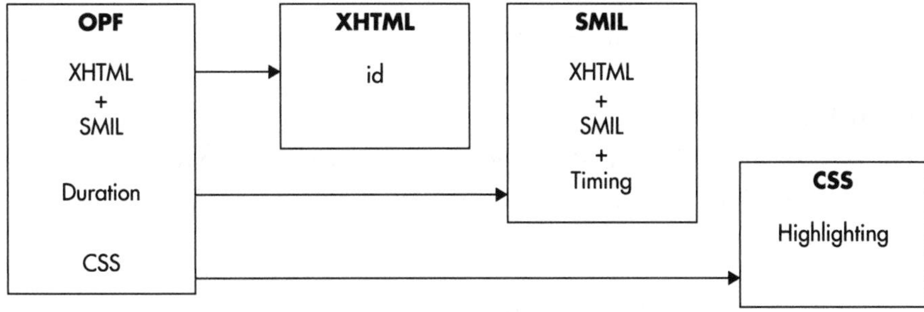

Figure 8-11 The big picture (SMIL)

Next, the XHTML has every line to be highlighted specified by a unique id as shown:

```
<h1 id="title">Final Storm</h1>
<p><br/></p>
<p id="sentence01">Shudders and chills dispense through my thoughts</p>
<p id="sentence02">Passing winds thunder heavy haunts.</p>
<p id="sentence03">Stormy clouds hover and decay</p>
<p id="sentence04">Suspense weaves into the next day.</p>
<p id="sentence05">The weeping willow allows little shelter to me.</p>
<p id="sentence06">As I collapse now on bended knee.</p>
<p id="sentence07">Thoughts swimming with fear of all lost</p>
<p id="sentence08">No deed now done could spare the cost.</p>
<p id="sentence09">Time is finished, spent with care.</p>
<p id="sentence10">Failure lights the sky with a sinister stare.</p>
```

The third area of SMIL is the actual SMIL file, which connects an XHTML file (and an id) with an audio file and the timing. Listed are two sections:

```
<par id="title1">
<text src="Text/Final-Storm.xhtml#title"/>
      <audio src="../Audio/Final-Storm.m4a" clipBegin="1.207s" clipEnd="2.880s"/>
</par>
<par id="sentence01">
      <text src="Text/Final-Storm.xhtml#sentence01"/>
      <audio src="../Audio/Final-Storm.m4a" clipBegin="2.880s" clipEnd="6.594s"/>
</par>
```

The XHTML file is listed with the id as highlighted. The next line lists the audio file connected with the XHTML file and its specified start and stop times for the clip.

Finally, there is the CSS entry to match the listing in the OPF. The entry can be manipulated with any CSS style to highlight the specified text being narrated, as shown:

```
.-epub-media-overlay-active { background-color: #abc; }
```

NOTE

Do not forget the period in front of the style name in the CSS file.

SMIL Problems

With many files involved in the SMIL setup, many things can go wrong. Look over the previous section "Putting It All Together," and compare it to your file sections. If you still have problems, consider the following:

- Make sure your audio file actually plays audio.
- Check all of the filenames in the OPF and SMIL (EPUB 3 is case-sensitive).

- Check that the id names in the XHTML file match the names in the SMIL file.
- Make sure the XHTML and SMIL files are connected in the OPF.
- Check that the CSS style name matches the one in the OPF.
- Be sure the XHTML files are linked to the CSS file.

Text to Speech

At the time of the writing of this book, text to speech (TTS) has not been supported. Hopefully, it will be supported within an EPUB 3 device or reading system in the near future.

According to the IDPF standard, the basic setup is similar to SMIL. The difference is that the <audio> tags are removed from the SMIL files along with the duration settings in the OPF (leave the <meta property="media:active-class">-epub-media-overlay-active</meta> line for CSS interaction). Of course, the audio files in the OPF will not be needed since the reading system will supply the narration audio.

NOTE

When the TTS is implemented, this book can be revised to include the appropriate information, as it may be different from what has been suggested.

Flash Animation

EPUB 3 can support Flash (.swf) files for animation. The first step is to create the Flash file. Free programs such as Clipyard (www.goldshell.com/clipyard) for Windows or QFlash (http://sourceforge.net/projects/qflash/) can be used to create Flash files.

The Flash file is embedded into the Misc folder, or whichever folder you want, just as you embed fonts, images, sound, and audio files.

Once the Flash file is in the EPUB, the OPF needs to be checked to verify that the media-type is correctly set to application/x-shockwave-flash.

To place the file into the XHTML file, the <object> and <param> tag are used, as was covered in Chapter 2.

```
<p>
<object data="../Misc/clouds.swf" type="application/x-shockwave-flash"
width="550px">
<param name="movie" value="../Misc/clouds.swf"/>
<param name="loop" value="true"/>
<param name="play" value="true"/>
</object>
</p>
```

The <object> tag lists the source file in the data attribute. The type is listed again with the type attribute. The width attribute gives the value of the width of the window in which the Flash file is viewed.

NOTE

For most items like this and the <video> tag, either width or height can be used and the other dropped. The one dropped should be similar to auto and will keep the aspect ratio of the original window size.

The <param> tag is used to show that the file is a movie, set to loop continuously and play automatically.

Chapter 9

JavaScript

JavaScript is an important part of EPUB 3. It helps add more functionality to your EPUB files. With the ability to program functionality into the EPUB, your imagination and skill are the only limits. Like most things, it is important to practice. JavaScript is no exception.

I need to make something clear about this chapter before we begin. Books on JavaScript can be quite large, so this chapter is not an exhaustive overview of JavaScript. The contents are a basic primer to get you started so you can understand some basics of JavaScript code when you see it in an EPUB. So, let's get started.

Getting Ready

You need two basic things to get ready to practice JavaScript. You need to download Notepad++ from www.notepad-plus-plus.org (Notepad++ will need some add-ons). For Linux systems, you could use Gedit or Geany. Also, you will need a web browser program (Google Chrome and Chromium have good support for CSS and JavaScript).

NOTE

Be aware that at the writing of this book, Sigil does not support JavaScript. It should be added in the future. You may check Sigil to see if it has been added before using Notepad++.

Notepad++ is an incredibly powerful text editor. It lets you specify a file type, such as HTML, JavaScript, etc., so you can work on a particular file. Of course, you can create simple text files as well.

Download and install Notepad++ and then open it. Once opened, go to Plugins on the menu and select Plugin Manager and then Show Plugin Manager. Now a window should appear showing a list of available plug-ins that can be added to Notepad++.

The list is in alphabetical order, so go down the list and select ImgTag, NewFileBrowser, Tidy2, and XBrackets Lite. Once all of these are checked, click the Install button. After the plug-ins have been installed, Notepad++ should ask to restart itself. Select Yes, and the program should restart. When Notepad++ starts up, select Plugins | NewFile&Browser | Settings. Make sure that the option for New File 1 is set to HTML. The second should be set to JS for JavaScript; then click Save.

The XBrackets Lite plug-in allows for the autocompletion of ending brackets when you type the beginning bracket. If you find this useful, you should go into the settings for it and enable it. Tidy2 is an HTML plug-in that cleans up the HTML code so it is easier to read. Again, you can use it if you need it.

Once you have made all of the appropriate settings, go to Plugins | NewFile&Browser and then select Create New File 1. You should see something similar to Figure 9-1.

The code that appears is a basic HTML file with a section ready for JavaScript. You can use the basic template or load in an existing XHTML file from your EPUB. A good way to get a file from your EPUB is to open the file with the View Content method (for Windows) as described in Chapter 1. Once the EPUB is opened in a compression utility, drag an XHTML file to a folder and then load it in Notepad++.

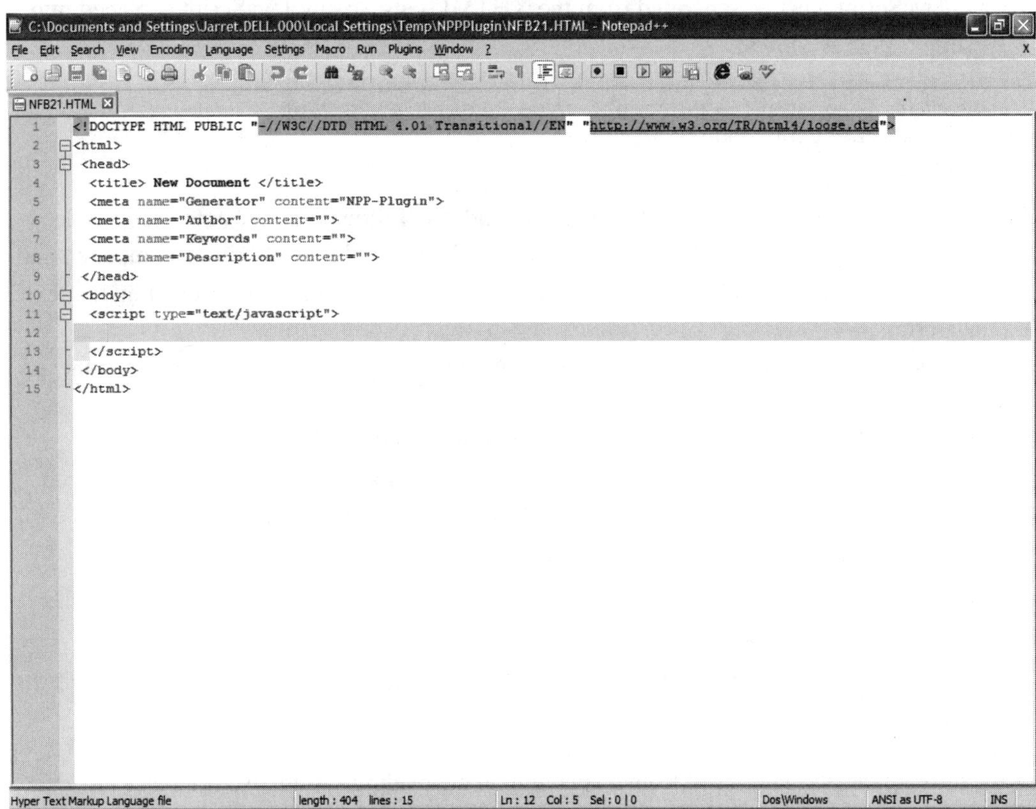

Figure 9-1 Empty Notepad++ HTML file

Setting Up a Spot for JavaScript

Keep in mind that JavaScript is not Java. Java and JavaScript are two completely different computer languages.

JavaScript can be embedded, or placed, into an XHTML file. It also can be placed into an EPUB, although this feature is only supported by EPUB 3 devices.

NOTE

EPUB 3 devices are not required to support JavaScript. If a reading system supports EPUB 3, be aware it may not support JavaScript.

JavaScript must be separated from the XHTML tags, so any JavaScript is placed into <script> tags as shown:

```
<script language="javascript" type="text/javascript">
     Javascript code
</script>
```

The first tag starts the scripting section, and it is followed by the JavaScript code. Once the code is finished, the end tag is used to show that the JavaScript is completed and the XHTML code should resume. The MIME type is also given with the opening tag text/javascript.

The last line is the closing </script> tag. All JavaScript code is placed between these two tags.

If a reading system does not support scripting, then the tags will be ignored. The problem is that the code between the tags is not ignored and will not display the desired result shown in Figure 9-2, taken from the following code included in c09-01.epub (available at www.mhprofessional.com/EPUB):

```
<body>
  <script type="text/javascript">
    document.write("Hello.  How are you?");
  </script>
 </body>
```

To prevent the JavaScript from displaying on the reading system, we can place the code in a comment section. HTML supports comments, which are ignored and not displayed.

// document.write("Hello. How are you?"); //

Figure 9-2 JavaScript output on nonsupporting device

The characters used to denote a comment in HTML are not the same in JavaScript. The comment characters are <!-- to start the comment and --> to end it. A comment can cover multiple lines, so you need to place the beginning comment after the <script> tag and the end comment before the </script> tag as shown:

```
<script language="javascript" type="text/javascript"><!--
      Javascript code
--></script>
```

So, if this is done in the previous example, the output would be a blank screen on a nonsupporting JavaScript device. You can test this with c09-02.epub.

Be aware that on some EPUB 3 devices, commenting out the JavaScript makes it inaccessible. It is advised *not* to add the comment marks in these cases.

With XHTML files, you need to do the same commenting, but use the following code:

```
<script language="javascript" type="text/javascript"><![CDATA[
      Javascript code
//]]><script>
```

NOTE

Commenting out the JavaScript code in a file with an XHTML extension will sometimes cause it to be inaccessible. To make it work, rename the extension to HTML. See sample file c09-03.epub.

To add comments in JavaScript, use // at the beginning of the line to comment that single line.

The sample file c09-02.epub also includes the tags <noscript> and </noscript>. These tags are used by systems that do not support scripting. As long as the <script> code is commented out and some XHTML tags are placed in the <noscript> elements, then you should get some type of message. For example, in the c09-02.epub file, the following was added after the </script>:

```
<noscript>
<p>This feature is not supported on your device.</p>
</noscript>
```

On a non-JavaScript device, only a message "This feature is not supported on your device." should be displayed.

JavaScript Programming

You have had a little taste of JavaScript, but there is quite a bit more to cover. Remember to practice everything you learn.

Variables

You may be thinking, "No, not algebra!" Don't worry—it's not quite the same. In any programming language, you need a placeholder to represent values. A variable holds on to values so you can use them when needed and make changes when required.

A variable is a name given to the placeholder. A variable name can begin with _, $, a number, or a letter. Keep in mind that JavaScript is a case-sensitive language. That is, the variable A is different from a and Value1 is different from value1. Be consistent when capitalizing any letters within a variable.

Variables are declared using the var command. For example, if you wanted to declare a variable named x and set it equal 5, the declaration would be:

```
var x=5;
```

NOTE

All declarations and statements need to end with a semicolon.

Be aware that a variable needs to be declared only once. An error occurs if a variable is declared more than once with var.

You could just as easily declare the variable x to be used but not assign it an initial value, as shown:

```
var x;
```

Multiple declarations can be done at once. For example, if we wanted to set x to 5, y to 9.5, and z to –23, we would do the following:

```
var x=5, y=9.5, z=-23;
```

There are two types of variables: global and local. These are discussed later in this chapter.

Variables can hold different types of data. Each type of variable then has a different data type.

Numbers

Numbers are an easy one. The variable represents some type of number. Whole numbers and even decimals can be represented with a numeric variable. Three examples follow:

```
var x=5, y=9.5, z=-23;
```

Strings

Strings are variables containing letters. The values are enclosed in quotes, as follows:

```
var name = "Cassandra";
```

As we noted earlier, multiple variables can be defined on one line:

```
var name1 = "Cassandra", name2 = "Eilly", name3 = "Alyse";
```

Numbers can also be placed in a string, but then it must be converted to a number to allow addition functions to be performed on it (other math functions such as subtraction, multiplication, etc., will convert the values automatically):

```
var num1 = "987";
```

With strings, there is some distinction between the single quote (') and double quote ("). Let's look at the following:

```
var string1 = "He said, 'Sit down,' before he laughed.";
```

The string is fine and will work. The problem occurs when you want to include the double quotes instead, such as:

```
var string1 = "He said, "Sit down," before he laughed.";
```

You see that now there are more than two double quotes, and it appears as if there were two strings with characters between them. The line will not work and will cause an error. So, to fix this problem, we use an escape code as shown in Table 9-1.

Escape Code	Output Value
\<	Less-than symbol
\>	Greater-than symbol
\;	Semicolon
\"	Double quote
\'	Single quote
\\	Backslash

Table 9-1 Escape Codes

So, now to fix the previous line, we would use:

```
var string1 = "He said, \"Sit down,\" before he laughed.";
```

In an EPUB, since everything is in XHTML, we can also use those codes. For instance, instead of using \n for a new line, we can use <br />:

```
var string1 = "He said, \"Sit down,\" before he laughed. <br />";
var string2 = "We ate, we laughed and then went home.";
document.write(string1+string2);
```

In this case, the two lines would not be printed as one line, but two.

What Is document.write?

With a reading system, whether a device or an app, there is a place for the text to be displayed. The display area is treated as your "document" and you can perform tasks in this area. Whatever is enclosed in the parentheses will be written to the display unless the statement is an error. In the case of "document.write(string1+string2);" we are writing the contents of string1 followed by string2.

If using an XHTML file, use the command XHTMLDoc.Write( ) instead.

Document.Write and XHTMLDoc.Write do not work very well on EPUB reading systems. There are other ways to display text to the screen from JavaScript, which will be covered later in this chapter.

Boolean

Boolean variables have two values: true or false. A Boolean variable can be set up as follows:

```
var var1=false;
var var2=true;
```

Boolean values are useful when dealing with conditional statements, which will be discussed later in this chapter.

Null

If a variable is defined without giving a value, the value is "undefined," as in the following code:

```
var x;
document.write(x);
```

The output would say "undefined." The reason the value was given as undefined is because it wasn't defined or set. If you want a variable to not be undefined but not give it a value, you can set it to null. The null value is the same as nothing.

If you see the following code, are the two variables the same?

```
var x=null;
var y;
```

They are the same. If you print out the contents of x and y, x is null and y is undefined. If you test them as being equal, JavaScript says they are the same. The reason they are the same is because both set to a value of nothing.

Math Operators

The math operators are mostly straightforward and easy to understand. Like math class in school, you have addition (+), subtraction (–), multiplication (*), division (/), and modulus (%). Modulus is the one term that most people haven't heard of—at least not by that name. Another, more familiar term that means the same thing is "remainder."

Look at the following code:

```
var num1=100;
var num2=25;
var num3=3;
var addNum=num1+num2;
var subNum=num1-num2;
var multNum=num1*num2;
var divNum=num1/num2;
var modNum1=num1%num2;
var modNum2=num1%num3;
```

The answers for these would be

- addNum = 125
- subNum = 75
- multNum = 2500
- divNum = 4
- modNum1 = 0
- modNum2 = 1

The first four are easy to understand. The answer for modNum1 is 0, which is the remainder of 100 divided by 25. For modNum2, the answer is 1 since 100 divided by 3 is 33 with a remainder of 1.

Two simple math operators that are useful are the operators to add or subtract 1 from a variable. To add 1, you name the variable and follow it with two plus (+) signs. Subtraction is done with two minus (–) signs. An example of each follows:

```
adding++;
subtraction--;
```

It is possible to also add strings. Look at the following:

```
var x="key";
var y="latch";
var z=x+y;
```

Can you guess what z would contain? The answer is "keylatch." It is possible to make z = y + x, which would make the contents of z equal to "latchkey."

Because you can add strings, the results are similar even when the strings are numbers. If the variables are strings of numbers and you use any math operator other than addition, the variables are converted to numbers and the result is given. The following shows an example:

```
var a="321";
var b="111";
var c=a+b;
var d=a-b;
```

The value of c is 321111 because the two strings are joined together. Variable d holds the value of 210. The multiplication, division, and modulus operators perform the actual math function.

NOTE

The exception to the rule about adding strings is when you place a string in a variable and then add one with ++. The variable will be converted to a number and 1 is added to it.

Assignment Operators

An assignment operator, as you saw in previous sections, is used to assign a value to a variable. The main assignment operator is the equal sign (=). For example, to assign the value of 5 to a variable named number1, you would use the following code:

```
number1=5;
```

NOTE

In most code examples, it is assumed the variable has been previously declared. In the previous example, the var number1; code has already been executed.

To assign a value from a math operator, we could do the following:

```
count=count+41;
```

Here we are taking the value of count and adding 41 to it and then placing the value back into count.

We could do the same thing with the following code:

```
count+=41;
```

The process can be done with the other math operators as shown:

```
count-=41;
count*=41;
count/=41;
count%=41;
```

Arrays

Arrays are a set of variables with the same name. Think of it as a stack of variable holders. Each holder is numbered to differentiate it from the others. It is important to remember that when numbering the holders, the first one is 0 and not 1.

For example, if we wanted to place five names in an array, we would do the following:

```
var names = new Array ("Devyn", "Logan", "Caleb", "Morgan", "Grant");
```

Notice we declare the variable as an Array and add in five names. There are five elements to the array, and they are numbered 0 to 4 (making a total count of five). To reference an individual element, you place the number of the element in brackets ([#]). For example, the fourth element, Morgan, would be names[3].

Be aware that arrays can hold numbers as well as strings.

Properties

Properties are the characteristics of an object. Objects are any data type that has properties and methods, both of which are covered later in the chapter.

Properties can describe an object—for now, this is an array. For example, we can use the length property to find how many elements are in an array. Properties are connected to the variable but separated by a period. To print out the length of the names variable, we would execute the following code:

```
document.write(names.length);
```

Methods

Methods allow some action to be done with the object to which it is connected. Similar to properties, methods are separated from the variable name by a period.

Methods usually manipulate the data within the variable or perform some task with the data. For example, the write method for document will write the specified variable or property to the document.

concat The method concat allows two arrays to be joined into one array. For instance, if we had the two following lists of names, we could join them into a third array:

```
var names1=new Array ("Devyn", "Logan", "Caleb");
var names2=new Array ("Eilly", "Alyse", "Morgan", "Grant");
var names3=names1.concat (names2);
```

The length of names3 would be given as 7, and its contents would be "Devyn", "Logan", "Caleb", "Eilly", "Alyse", "Morgan", "Grant".

The order of the concat statement determines the order. The order of each individual array is kept the same, but if the statement were names2.concat (names1), it would change the order of names3. The contents of names3 would be "Eilly", "Alyse", "Morgan", "Grant", "Devyn", "Logan", "Caleb".

join The join method is used to create a string from the array list. If we needed to print a list of every element in an array, we would have to print out each element one at a time. The join method joins each element, separating them with a comma by default, as shown:

```
var list1=names3.join();
```

The output of this statement would be:

```
Devyn,Logan,Caleb,Eilly,Alyse,Morgan,Grant
```

You may have noticed the parentheses after the join method. Parentheses are usually used to pass some type of information to the method. In this case, we can specify the character or characters to use to separate elements. In the following statement, we will separate the array elements with a comma and a space to make the output string look a little nicer, as shown:

```
var list1=names3.join(", ");
Devyn, Logan, Caleb, Eilly, Alyse, Morgan, Grant
```

sort Sort is a method that is self-explanatory. It sorts the elements in the array in alphabetical order. For example, if we used the previous array called names3, we could sort it and see the output as shown:

```
names3.sort();
Alyse, Caleb, Devyn, Eilly, Grant, Logan, Morgan
```

Notice that the sort occurs in place. What this means is that the sorted values are placed back into the original array of names3.

Sorts are done on the elements as if they were strings. Even if the elements were numeric, they would be converted to strings before being sorted. Because of this conversion, the number 4 would alphabetically occur after 15.

reverse The reverse method is used to reverse the order of the elements in the array. The first element is now the last, while the last is now the first. If you needed an array to be in descending order, it would be easiest to sort it alphabetically and then perform a reverse on it. If we did a reverse on names3 after it had been sorted, the results would be:

```
Morgan, Logan, Grant, Eilly, Devyn, Caleb, Alyse
```

Multidimensional Arrays

So far we have discussed one-dimensional arrays, which can be thought of as a stack of holders. With multidimensional arrays, we are talking about multiple stacks of holders.

Let's assume we have two holders in three stacks as shown in Figure 9-3. The array would be initialized as shown:

```
var set1=new Array [[5,3,7],[6,9,1]];
```

The first set is (5,3,7) and is referenced by the element 0. The second set is (6,9,10) and is referenced by element number 1.

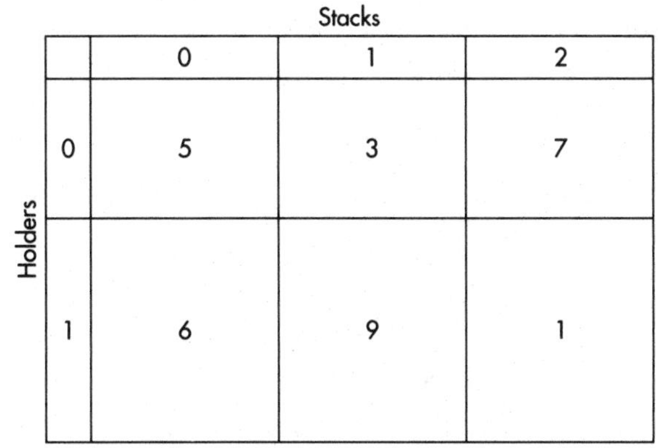

Stacks

Holders	0	1	2
0	5	3	7
1	6	9	1

Figure 9-3 Multidimensional arrays

To access the third element, the number 7, it would be done as set1[0][2]. Individually within the first set, the number 7 is the third element, so it is numbered as 2. The specific values are as follows:

```
set1[0][0]  // is '5'
set1[0][1]  // is '3'
set1[0][2]  // is '7'
set1[1][0]  // is '6'
set1[1][1]  // is '9'
set1[1][2]  // is '1'
```

Associative Arrays

Arrays are usually accessed by using the element numbers. But what about an array that has a dozen or more elements? It can become difficult to keep track of what data is in which element. Instead of numbering the elements, we can name them. For instance, look at the following code:

```
var user=new Array();
user["firstname"]= "Cassandra";
user["height"]="58";
user["weight"]="95";
```

This list could continue on quite a while. If an element needed to be referenced, it would be done the same way. If we were to output a sentence with the name, height and weight, it would look like this:

```
document.write("The person is " + user["firstname"]+" and their height
is "+user["height"]+" inches tall with a weight of " + user["weight"]
+ " pounds.");
```

The output is:

```
The person is Cassandra and their height is 58 inches tall with a
weight of 95 pounds.
```

Functions

Functions are sections of reusable code that can be run as many times as needed. Functions can be very helpful when using forms.

What About Forms?

Forms are useful in XHTML to create an input box and get some type of user input. An example would be to ask for a name. Buttons can also be added to select when the information has been entered.

The form is part of XHTML code and is not placed in the <script> section. Let's look at the following code:

```
<form>
Your Name: <input type="text" />
<input type="button" value="Done" onclick="validate()" />
</form>
```

After the form is started, Your Name: is printed followed by a box for input, which allows for text to be typed into it. The next line has a button that is labeled Done. Once the button is clicked, a function called validate is processed. In most cases, these functions will process the data within the input box to verify the contents. We'll cover other form styles later in this chapter.

So if we use a form to ask for a name, we can call a function to perform a task on the input data. In most cases, a <script> tag is placed in the <head> section of the XHTML file. Within this section is where functions are placed. Functions can also be placed within the <body>, but sometimes it is easier to keep the code simpler by moving the functions out of the main script sections within the <body>.

Let's make a simple function to check the name typed in the form. First you start with the word "function" followed by the function name—in this case, printdata. Anytime a function is made or referenced, it must be followed by parentheses. The function statement is ended with an open curly bracket ({), or brace, to show the beginning of a section of code that belongs to the function. Once we have included all the code for the function, we end it with the closing brace (}). So far we have:

```
function printdata() {
}
```

Now, to print out the data in the input box, we must be able to access the form. The forms are treated like arrays. The first form in a document is forms[0]. In the previous example of a

Your Name: Done

Figure 9-4 Sample form

form, there were two elements: the input box and a button as shown in Figure 9-4. The input box is elements[0] and the button is elements[1].

Since the form is located on the display, it is accessed as part of the document. To access the data in the box, the code would be document.forms[0].elements[0].value. We can write out the data as shown in the following code:

```
function printdata() {
      document.write(document.forms[0].elements[0].value);}
```

Similar to associative arrays, objects can be given names and accessed with those as shown:

```
<form name="thisform">
Your Name: <input type="text" name="inputbox" />
<input type="button" value="Done" name="donebutton"
onclick="printdata()" />
</form>
```

The function would look like:

```
function printdata() {
    document.write(document.forms["thisform"].elements["inputbox"].value);}
```

You're probably still wondering about the parentheses. The parentheses are used to pass parameters to a function. For instance, if we were writing JavaScript code and occasionally we needed to know what value a specific variable contained, we could do it with a function. An example is shown:

```
function showdata(data) {
      alert(data);}
```

Within the coding would be a line such as:

```
showdata(count);
```

This would pass control to the showdata function, passing the variable count to the parameter data. Inside the function, the alert would be performed with the count variable.

What Is the Alert?

Instead of printing information to the screen, you can have a box pop up with information in it. The data placed in the parentheses can be variables or literals. The alert box will appear with the specified data printed in the box and include an OK button. Once you click the OK button, the box disappears.

This is a quick and easy way to display data without cluttering your display and messing it up if you are trying to produce a specific layout.

An example of an alert box is shown in the following illustration from the code:

```
alert("x = " + x);
```

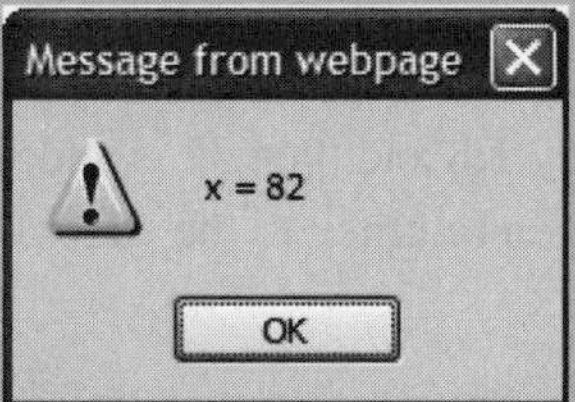

Keep in mind that is useful from a coding standpoint. You should use this when you need to check variables from the interface you use to check your JavaScript code. Alerts do not work on some EPUB reading systems. The document.write also will not work correctly on some EPUB reading systems.

NOTE

Similar to the comment lines used in HTML and XHTML file extensions, document.write works in files with the HTML extension and not XHTML. The files can be written in the same manner—just rename the file extension.

You may wonder why I have even covered these details. Some of your code should be tested before you place it into an EPUB. You can test your code in Notepad++ and then copy the code to Sigil, making sure the comment marks are in place. Once you know it all works, then you import the EPUB into Readium. Readium is a good tester for EPUB 3 files.

Multiple parameters can be passed. Any function can have zero to infinite parameters. For example, you could create a function with three parameters as shown:

```
showdata(count1, count2, count3);
```

Of course, this function would be called in the same way as a function with one parameter. If a parameter is not needed, it can be left blank. For example, to call the previous function with a value for count1 and count3, the code would be:

```
showdata(x,,y);
```

Return

Some functions may not simply perform tasks on data, but are used to perform calculations and return data that represents the calculations. For instance, to create a function to convert Celsius to Fahrenheit, you would use the following code:

```
function convertToF(Celsius) {
      var temp = (Celsius * 1.8) + 32;
      return temp;}
```

The parameter is passed to the function as Celsius. The variable is then used in the equation; it is multiplied by 1.8 and then 32 is added to the result. The value is placed into the variable temp that is then returned to the statement that called the function. The calling statement is:

```
var C = convertToF(45);
```

You can see that the function's result is placed in the variable called C. The variable C now can be used with an alert or a document.write. The value held in C is 113.

Global and Local Variables

Variables can be used in a program as a whole or specifically in functions, depending on where they are created. If a variable is declared, or defined, within a function's braces, it only exists within those braces. In this case, the variable is a local variable. It only exists locally within the function itself.

If the variable is declared outside a function, it can be used anywhere, even within the function. These variables are global variables since they can be accessed throughout the program. Take the following example:

```
var global = 56;
var local = 1;
function someFunction() {
      var local = 7;
      document.write("Global: " + global + "<br />");
      document.write("Local: " + local + "<br />");
}
someFunction();
```

```
document.write("Global: " + global + "<br />");
document.write("Local: "+ local);
```

The output would be:

```
Global: 56
Local: 7
Global: 56
Local: 1
```

The first two lines (Global: 56 and Local: 7) are from within the function. Inside the function, the global variable should still be set as 56. The local variable was set to a value of 7. Outside the function, the global variable is still 56. The local variable outside the function is set to 1 as shown in the last two output lines.

Objects

Objects are data types that you can create yourself, as well as properties and methods for those objects. Let's make an example object and look at it in detail:

```
function book (title, isbn, author, year) {
      this.title=title;
      this.isbn=isbn;
      this.author=author;
      this.year=year; }
```

We now have an object called book, which has four holders. The object has four properties: title, isbn, author, and year. Since the name of "this" is used, it is replaced with the value attached to it, as shown:

```
var epub=new book ("EPUB from the Ground Up", "0071830529", "Jarret W.
Buse", "2013");
```

Now the object is created and we have an object with four properties: epub.title, epub .isbn, epub.author, and epub.year. These can be accessed and changed as needed throughout a program.

We can create multiple objects with different names, such as adding one to the object we previously created:

```
var nada=new book ("Nada the Lily", "1481041444", "Henry Rider
Haggard", "1892");
```

Now we can access the two together in JavaScript:

```
document.write (epub.title + " makes reference to " + nada.title);
```

Objects can also be created in the following manner:

```
epub={title: "EPUB from the Ground Up", isbn: "0071830529", author:
"Jarret W. Buse", year: "2013"};
nada={title: "Nada the Lily", isbn: "1481041444", author: "Henry Rider
Haggard", year: "1892"};
```

Methods

Methods can be created for objects that perform some task on the object's data. For instance, if we wanted to compare the age of the books by the publishing date, we would use the following code:

```
var date1=new Date();
var year=date1.getFullYear();
alert("The book 'Nada the Lily' is " +(year - nada.year) +" years
old.");
```

With all the code put together, the alert is shown in Figure 9-5.

Methods can be made to perform many different tasks on the object for which it has been created.

Conditions

Conditions are statements that are used to test something. The test can compare the data in a variable to another variable or a specific value. There are three types of conditional statements: the if statement, if-else statement, and the switch statement.

if statement

The if statement compares one or more values to another value. Depending on the result, certain tasks are then performed. For instance, the value in the variable count can be tested to see if it is less than 5 as shown:

```
if (count < 5){
}
```

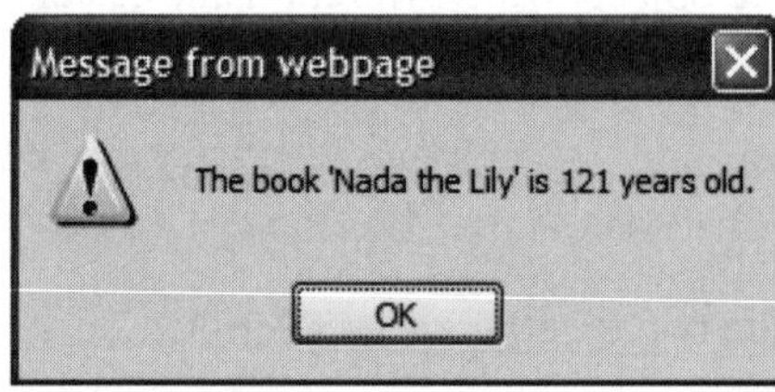

Figure 9-5 Alert from object

If the value of count is less than 5, the code within the braces is executed. If the value of count is greater than or equals 5, the code in the braces is skipped. The code in the braces can be one or more lines as needed, based on the condition.

NOTE

The comparison section must be in parentheses. If the comparison is not in parentheses the if statement is skipped or generates an error.

Instead of comparing count to a number, we can compare it to another variable as shown:

```
if (count < counter){
}
```

Literals can also be used to test for a certain value:

```
if (name == "Morgan"){
}
```

Initially, you may be wondering about the double equal signs (==). If one equal sign is used, we are assigning a value to a variable. Two equal signs are for comparison or to test if they are the same. Table 9-2 shows a list of comparison operators.

Operator	Description	Example
==	Compare equality	count==2
<=	Less than equal to	count<=2
>=	Greater than equal to	count>=2
>	Greater than	count>2
<	Less than	count<2
!=	Not equal	count!=2
!==	Not equal values or types	count!==counter
===	Equal values and types	count===counter

Table 9-2 Conditional Operator Types

The last two lines in Table 9-2 may seem a bit confusing. Values can be equal, in a sense, even when the two variable types are different. For example, if we set one variable to 2 and another to "2", they would be different types as shown:

- var counter=2; //type is numeric
- var count="2"; //type is string

If we use the === operator, the value would be false when comparing the two. The first is a numeric variable, and the second is a string variable since it is in quotes.

If we compared counter to count using the double equal signs (==), the result would be true. Why? When two variables are compared and one is numeric, the other is converted to numeric before they are compared. So the following statement would run the code in the braces:

```
var counter=2; //Numeric
var count="2"; //String
if (count==counter) {
}
```

It is possible to place one if statement within another. This is called nesting. Say, for instance, we wanted to check if the value of count is between 5 and 10. We would use the following code:

```
var count=7;
if (count>5) {
      if (count<10) {
            alert("The number is between 5 and 10");
      }
}
```

In this example, count is set to 7. The first if statement checks to see if count is greater than 5. Since the statement is true, the code in the braces is executed. The next line tests that count is less than 10. The condition is also true and causes the code in the braces to run, which creates an alert. If either if statement were false, the alert would not have been excuted.

Statements can become difficult if they are nested too deeply. To help ease this problem, we can create one if statement using special operators, as shown in Table 9-3.

As shown in the previous example, we are testing that the value in count is greater than 5 *and* less than 10. The code would look like this:

```
var count=7;
if ((count>5) && (count<10)) {
      alert("Between 5 and 10");
}
```

Operator	Description
&&	AND operator
||	OR operator
!	NOT operator

Table 9-3 Logical Operator Types

Now the count value can be tested on one line to see if it is between 5 and 10. Notice that the condition sets are each enclosed in parentheses while they both are enclosed in one as well. The conditions must always be within parentheses even if there are ten or more items being tested on one line.

AND Using the AND operator tests that both conditions are true on either side of the &&. If someone asks for a pen and paper, you give them both a pen and paper. The AND requires that both sides be true. If either side of the AND is false, then the whole statement is false. If you give someone a pen and no paper, it cannot be what they needed: a pen and paper.

OR The OR operator tests to see if either statement is true. If one or both statements on either side of the OR (||) are true, then the whole statement is true. An OR statement can only be false if both statements are false.

NOTE

The | key is above the ENTER key on the keyboard and under the BACKSPACE key.

If someone asks for a pen or paper, you can give them a pen, paper, or a pen and paper. Each of these would be true for the statement given. The only way it could be false is to give them a pencil or some other type of writing instrument or material to write on.

NOT The NOT operator is used to change a true statement to a false one and a false one to a true one. For example, if someone does *not* want a pen or paper, they do not want pen, paper, or pen and paper. Basically, figure out what value the comparison would be and change the answer to the other one, true to false and false to true.

```
var count=2;
if (!(count>5) || !(count<10)) {
      alert("Not between 5 and 10");
}
```

The statement is true since count is *not* greater than 5 OR count is *not* less than 10. Count is set to 2, and the first condition is true, while the second condition is false. The condition is now true since the AND was changed to an OR. In most cases, changing an AND to a NOT also requires it be an OR.

if-else statement

The if statement allows code to be executed if the condition is true. What if code should be executed when the statement is true as well as when it is false? That is where the if-else statement is needed. The code looks like this:

```
if (condition1) {
      execute code when condition is true;
} else {
      execute code when condition is false;
}
```

Now we can perform different tasks when the condition is true or false. For example, if we sold books, giving a discount of 10 percent for those who bought more than ten books, but only 5 percent for all others, the code would be:

```
if (bookcount>10) {
      discount=10;
 } else {
      discount=5;
}
```

Switch

A switch is a set of possible conditions. An example is shown:

```
var counter=1;
switch (counter) {
      case 1:
            alert("1");
            break;
      case 2:
            alert("2");
            break;
      case 3:
            alert("3");
            break;
      default:
            alert("A number greater than 3");
}
```

In this example, we are testing the value of counter, which is initially set to 1. When the switch condition is checked, we are looking at the value of counter. The first section is where it is equal to 1. In this case, it is true, so the alert statement is performed, followed by the break statement. The break statement causes control to exit the switch; otherwise, each statement would be checked. The default statement is executed whenever the other values are not performed. If you did not break out after a true statement, then the default section would be performed as well. The default section does not need a break since it is the last section anyway. One could be used, but it is not necessary. If, for any reason, the switch value could be something other than the values listed, use a default section.

Loops

Loops are used to perform a set of code over and over for a specified number of times. There are three types of loops, and any can be used, based on personal preference.

For Loop

The for loop is used to run code a specific number of times. A counter allows you to specify a starting count and an ending count. If needed, you can break out of the for loop when certain conditions are met. The counter also allows you to specify a counting increment for each loop. The syntax is as follows:

```
for (start; test condition; increment) { code to run }
```

To add the numbers 1 to 10, for example, use the following code:

```
var sum=0;
for (var x=1; x<=10; x++) {
      sum += x;}
alert ("The sum of the numbers 1 to 10 is " + sum);
```

The value of sum is 55 when done. The loop starts with x = 1 and continues while x <= 10. When x = 11, the test condition fails and the for loop ends. During each loop, the value of sum, which starts at 0, is incremented by the value of x (sum += x). At the end of each loop, x is incremented by 1 (x++).

Any number of lines of code can be placed between the braces. When a certain condition is reached, you can use a break statement to exit the for loop. There is also a continue statement that skips the current for loop iteration and begins the next, such as:

```
Var sum=0;
for (var x=1; x<=10; x++) {
      if (x%2==0) {
```

```
            continue; }
        sum += x;}
alert ("The sum of the odd numbers 1 to 10 is " + sum);
```

The answer is 25. The added if statement checks whether the value of x is divisible by 2. If x divided by 2 has no remainder (x%2==0), then the iteration is skipped and the sum is not incremented. Only the odd values are incremented into sum.

While Loop

The while loop specifies a condition and processes the loop over and over until the test condition is returned as false. For example:

```
var sum=0;
var count=1;
while (count<=10) {
        sum += count;
        count++; }
alert ("The sum of the numbers 1 to 10 are " + sum);
```

The difference between the while loop and the for loop is that you must initialize and increment the counter.

By using the while loop, the condition is tested before the loop is run. If the condition tests false, then the loop is not executed.

Do While Loop

The do while loop is similar to the while loop, except that the loop is executed once before the condition is tested, as shown:

```
var sum=0;
var count=1;
do {
        sum += count;
        count++;
}while (count<=10);
alert ("The sum of the numbers 1 to 10 are " + sum);
```

Here the test condition is not examined until the loop has completed one time. If the value of count were set to 11 at the beginning, the loop would execute once.

Events

When certain things happen in an EPUB, then certain code can be run. The things that occur are events. Various events can be used, which are listed in Table 9-4.

Event	Description	Placement
onload	When document is done loading	<body>
onunload	When the document is unloaded or removed	<body>
onclick	When the element has been clicked or tapped	element
ondblclick	When the element has been double-clicked or double-tapped	element
onsubmit	When a form is submitted	<form>
onreset	When a form is reset	<form>
onchange	When a text box loses focus and the text has changed	<input>

Table 9-4 Events

For instance, consider a form with an input text field and a button on a page as shown:

```
<form action="Page2.xhtml" method="get" onsubmit="return validate()">
      <input type="text" value="" name="txtname" />
      <input type="submit" value="Start" />
</form>
```

Let's look at this line by line. The first line shows it is a form. The action specifies what page is loaded when the form is submitted. The (action=) method determines how data is sent to the referred page. The get method sends the data appended to the URL. The post method sends the data in the header. When the form is submitted, the validate() function is run, and the value returned from it is returned to the submission. The form is submitted if the onsubmit returns a true value.

The second line generates a text box (type="text") with an initial value of null (value=""). When the data is sent in the URL, it will be sent with the name txtname—for example, ?txtname=Grant in the URL since it uses the get method.

The third line is a button, labeled Start, that is used to submit the data to the action page.

Another example involves the onload event, which is placed in the <body> tag as shown:

```
<body onload="fillIn()">
```

When this page is loaded, the function fillIn() is executed. The function can help place JavaScript data within the displayed page. This is covered next in the "Example Functions" section. Also, check the sample file c09-04.epub.

Example Functions

There are many useful features in JavaScript that can assist you in EPUB. One involves passing data from one page to another and the ability to retrieve the data for use. A second is the ability to print data from JavaScript to the display to be included into the EPUB.

Passing Data

To pass data from one file to another when it is loaded is tricky. The first method demonstrates some commands in JavaScript, but the second method that will be discussed is often easier.

First Method We previously covered the get method used in forms. This method provides a means to place form data in the URL. What can be done with the data in the URL? We can retrieve the data and allow it to be passed from one page to another. An example is given in c09-04.epub of a personalized book. On the first page, the reader enters their name. The information is passed on to the next page and then the next. The name is substituted in place of the character's name in the book. This is a short example, but it shows a lot of different techniques.

NOTE

Keep in mind that this example is just demonstrating JavaScript code. The method does work, but on EPUB devices, the data would be lost when a reader goes back a page.

Now to get the form data from the URL. JavaScript has a special built-in function called window.location.search. The command retrieves the data, called a query string, and places it in a variable as shown:

```
var holder = window.location.search;
```

Once the string is retrieved, we can manipulate the data to get the information we need. We can use something similar to the following:

```
function splitParameters() {
      var pquerystr;
      var array1=new Array;
var wquerystr=window.location.search;
      if (wquerystr.indexOf("?") >= 0) {
            pquerystr = wquerystr.substring(para.indexOf("?")+1,
wquerystr.length);
      } else {
            pquerystr = wquerystr; }
      array1=pquerystr.split("&");
      return array1;
}
```

To use the function, we create an array and then execute the function as shown:

```
var listOfData = new Array;
listOfData = splitParameters();
```

The function first creates a variable (pquerystr) and an array (array1). Then, the variable pquerystr (part of query string) is created and the query string is retrieved and placed into wquerystr (whole query string).

The wquerystr is checked for the value of a question mark, which should be the first character (wquerystr.substring("?")). If the question mark is found, then the section of the wquerystr where the question mark is located is moved one over to the right (past the "?"). The rest of the string is taken and placed into pquerystr. If the question mark doesn't exist, then all of the query string is placed into pquerystr.

The next line (array1=pquerystr.split("&");) is used to look through the pquerystr and find the "&" that are used to separate the data values. Once split, the values are placed into array1 and returned back to the calling statement, where the contents of array1 are placed into listOfData.

To retrieve the needed values out of the array, we can use the following function:

```
function searchParam(array1,searchstr) {
      var found = " ";
      for (i=0;i<array1.length;i++) {
            if (array1[i].indexOf(searchstr)>=0) {
                 found=array1[i].substring(array1[i].
indexOf("=")+1,array1[i]
                 .length);
                 break; }
      }
      return found; }
```

In this function, we pass the array from the previous function (listOfData) and the search string we are looking for in the query string. For example:

```
var readerName=searchParam(listOfData, "txtname")
```

Here we're looking through the array listOfData and looking for the query data of txtname. The data connected to the text box named txtname, if found, will be placed into the variable readerName.

The variable found is created and a for loop is performed starting at 0 and iterating through the number of elements in the array (array1.length). The array is checked one element at a time to find the searchstr. Once found, it retrieves the information after the equal sign and places the data in found. A break is used to exit the loop, and the value in found is returned and placed into readerName.

Second Method The second method used to pass data is similar to cookies. To set up this ability, you need to use the following code:

```
function startStorage() {
      var storage = window.sessionStorage;
      storage.setItem("txtname", "");
      storage.setItem("place", "");
}
```

The code can be placed on the form load event to start the storage of data and initialize the data elements. The elements can be set up as blank and when the data is received, it can replace the existing stored data.

For instance, if we retrieve a value for txtname, we can place it in storage as shown:

```
var value = document.forms[0].txtname.value;
storage.setItem("txtname", value);
```

Now that the data is stored, it can be retrieved from any page within the EPUB by using the following command:

```
storage.getItem("txtname")
```

Be aware that when using the setItem or getItem method, there are two parameters for setItem and one for getItem. The two for setItem are the key and its value. The key is the name used to keep it separate from the other elements. With getItem, the key is the only parameter and is used to retrieve the specific element.

See the sample file c09-05.epub for an example of using the storage method to pass data between pages.

Printing Data to the Screen

You should have seen this procedure in the sample files c09-05 and c09-06. Here is an example and the details:

```
var uname2 = storage.getItem("txtname");
document.getElementById("name").innerHTML = uname2;
```

In this case, the data is retrieved from storage and placed into the variable called uname2. The second line finds in the document an element with an ID of "name." Inside this element (innerHTML) with a matching ID, the contents of the variable uname2 are placed.

The HTML code for the placement would appear as:

```
<p>Hello, <span id="name"> </span>.  How are you?</p>
```

As long as the variable uname2 contains some data, the data will be placed into the <span> element.

One line must exist with innerHTML for each insertion ID. If you have an innerHTML line that points to a nonexistent ID, errors will occur. Since most reading devices do not show an error but try to continue, other insertions may not occur.

External JavaScript Code

Instead of placing all of the JavaScript code into the XHTML file, you can create an external file of your most-used functions. Once the file is created, you add it to the Misc directory in Sigil and add a link to it as shown:

```
<script type="text/javascript" src="..\Misc\validate.JS">
```

Other functions and code can be placed after the line before the end script (</script>) tag. With the external files imported in with this command, it works just as if the functions were located in the XHTML file.

Index

Symbols

Numbers

A

B

C

D

E

F

G

H

I

J

K

L

M

N

O

P

Q

R

S

T

U